TRUTH
FOR
ALL
TIME

# Grace— amazing grace

## Unpacking the reality of God's incredible love

A NEW AND REVISED
EDITION WITH STUDY
QUESTIONS FOR GROUP
DISCUSSION

**Brian H Edwards**

DayOne

© Day One Publications 2011
First printed 2003
Second edition 2011
Reprinted 2016

ISBN 978–1–84625–336–2

British Library Cataloguing in Publication Data available

Published by Day One Publications
Ryelands Road, Leominster, HR6 8NZ
☎ 01568 613 740   Fax 01568 611 473
email—sales@dayone.co.uk
web site—www.dayone.co.uk
☎ Toll Free 888 329 6630 (North America)

Cover design by Wayne McMaster
Printed by T J International

*The doctrines of divine grace are like honey to the soul. Brian Edwards takes the bottle of grace off the top shelf of theology and puts it down low for all to reach. He opens it up and pours the honey of grace lavishly over the warm bread of our lives until it fills every crack and crevice. Doctrinal concepts like justification and incarnation come to life—and are applied to life—while remaining true to the biblical teachings of the Reformation. From God's eternal plan to our daily struggles with pain and prayer, this book sweetens the soul to the praise of the glory of God's grace. Taste it, and by grace your eyes will be brightened.*

**Dr Joel R. Beeke, President, Puritan Reformed Theological Seminary, Grand Rapids, Michigan**

*As Brian Edwards tells us, 'Grace encompasses all the great truths of Christianity, for without grace they would have no meaning.' He then guides us on a delightful tour that takes us from God's common grace for all mankind to the ultimate grace of heaven for God's people. I have never read anything better on the subject than this superb and sure-footed treatment.*

**Dr John Blanchard, evangelist, author and Christian apologist**

*Grace is the heart of Christianity. It makes the gospel unique and puts the 'good' in good news. As stewards of God's grace, it is essential for the church to teach this doctrine and for believers to practice it. No one explains it better than Brian Edwards. This new edition with small group discussion starters will cause readers to pause, investigate, question, reflect, discuss, embrace, wonder at and rejoice in God's grace. It is a perfect discipling tool for one-to-one mentoring, couples or family devotions, small group study and adult Sunday school classes. I cannot wait for our congregation to benefit from its publication.*

**Dr Reggie Weems, Pastor, Heritage Baptist Church, Johnson City TN, USA**

# Commendations

*Humbling but empowering, scriptural yet startling – on first reading this vital book, I instantly found myself quoting its opening pages. I defy anyone to start and not want to continue! It's not just the delightfully-turned phrase but the sharply-contemporary challenge; not just the eloquent beginning, but classic Edwards sustained throughout. And not just for quoting, but for taking it in and making it work. How we view God's grace prompts and informs our attitudes to everything else.*

**Christopher Idle, Pastor, preacher and hymnwriter**

*John Newton swam deeper and deeper in the ocean of God's Grace in the decades of discipleship which followed his dramatic conversion to Christ. Brian Edwards has captured something of how the richness of Grace pervaded the life and ministry, the struggles and joys of this great man of God. I commend this book and its Study Guide which will especially help individuals or Small Groups apply the great truths of grace to discipleship today.*

**Trevor Archer, Director of Training, The Fellowship of Independent Evangelical Churches**

Dedicated to Rosie for her love, encouragement
and strong prayerful support

# Contents

# Amazing Grace

'The immeasurable riches of his grace in kindness towards us in Christ Jesus'
Ephesians 2:7

G race is the most beautiful word in our language and the supreme description of God.

Grace is the creator of faith. It is uncreated and eternal, for wherever God is, there is grace. Grace is not simply what God does, it is what God is. Grace is the ultimate expression of God and the most attractive of all his perfections. It cocoons the gospel as the heavens envelop planet earth; it sustains trust as air sustains life; it is the controller of hope as the mind is to action; it is the energy of evangelism as the heart is to the body. Grace is perfect, all-embracing and costly, because grace is expressed ultimately in Jesus Christ who is, in himself, the fullness of grace. Christ came from the Father 'full of grace and truth' and from his grace 'we have all received grace upon grace'. Grace is the twin of truth, and both are expressed supremely in Christ.

Though grace is everywhere, it is seen by only a few, embraced by even fewer, and understood fully by none. Grace is often a mystery, a puzzle. It is present above the mindless destruction and passionate hatred of men; it is there in our shattered plans, frustrated expectations, and broken hearts; and it is to be found even in the dull grind of our daily routine. Can grace really be present here on earth always and everywhere? Yes, because the absence of grace is hell.

Grace is greater than the words salvation, justification, sanctification or glorification; it is far greater than peace or joy, forgiveness or reconciliation. Grace encompasses all the great truths of Christianity, for without grace they would have no meaning. Grace conceives every hope offered to the human race, and gives birth to all the benefits of the Christian faith. Grace is not love, it conceives love; it is not mercy, it gives birth to mercy. Grace is both love and mercy in action.

Without grace, God would not be known, and without God, grace would have no meaning. God is always all that he is; but we can never know all that he is, and we cannot see anything that he is for long. But there is one glory of God's character that is always visible—and that is grace. Grace is the universal evidence of God all around us; it is also the unseen hand on the helm of world affairs. Few have eyes to see it, but grace does not have to be seen to be believed and it does not have to be believed to be seen. Grace is enjoyed even when men curse it, but it is celebrated best when they embrace it. When men choose to ignore God's love or rebel against his word, the fact that he withholds his judgement is due to grace; when he allows bad men to prosper and good men to suffer that too is grace.

Simply to define the word grace as God's undeserved mercy towards a sinner is to probe its meaning as deeply as a pond skater penetrates the water. Grace is not merely God's attitude towards undeserving rebels, it is ultimately and above all *God giving himself* to us and for us—as the Man on a cross.

## Grace in the Old Testament

When the apostle Paul wrote of: 'The immeasurable riches of his grace in kindness toward us in Christ Jesus', he wrote as a Jew and therefore possessed a full understanding of the history of the word 'grace'. There were two words in Paul's Hebrew Old Testament that approached the idea of grace. One was the word *ḥesed*, which was a two-way word. On the one hand it could refer to God's resolute love towards us: 'The *steadfast love* of the LORD never ceases; his mercies never come to an end; they are new every morning; great is your faithfulness' (Lamentations 3:22–23). Whilst on the other hand it could refer to our loyal love to each other or to God himself: 'I [God] desire *steadfast love* and not sacrifice' (Hosea 6:6).

When Grace is used of the relationship between men and women it clearly refers to acts of free kindness where no obligation was at stake. God's loyalty to his covenant with his chosen people is on the basis that it was a covenant born out of his own undeserved love alone. For this reason, the word most commonly used in the New Testament to translate *hesed* is the word 'mercy'. In the Old Testament, the noun of this word *hesed* is used thirty-two times—twenty-five in the Psalms alone—and it refers to the 'holy ones' or 'saints' who have received the mercy of God. Mercy is the child of grace.

The other Old Testament Hebrew word that approaches the idea of grace is the word *hanan*. It meant 'favour', and was always a one-way response from a superior to an inferior. This word could be used of our relationship to each other, but it was never used of our response to God. The first use of it in the Bible is found when we are told that, 'Noah found *favour* in the eyes of the Lord' (Genesis 6:8). David used it as a verb: 'Turn to me and *be gracious* to me' (Psalm 25:16), and again, '*Be gracious* to me O LORD, for I am in distress' (Psalm 31:9). Of the fifty-six occasions where it is used as a verb in the Old Testament, forty-one refer to God's way of behaving. As a noun it is a common word for the favour of a superior person, but as an adjective, all thirteen occasions found in the Old Testament refer to God.

God used both *hanan* and *hesed* to describe his own matchless character to Moses: 'And the LORD passed before him and proclaimed, "The LORD, the LORD, a God merciful and *gracious*, slow to anger, and abounding in *steadfast love* and faithfulness, keeping *steadfast love* for thousands, forgiving iniquity and transgression and sin"' (Exodus 34:6–7). This was a description never forgotten, and again and again God's people drew comfort from it (see for example: Numbers 14:18–19; Nehemiah 9:17; Psalm 85:10–11; 103:8; 145:8; Joel 2:13; Jonah 4:2). Both *ḥanan* and *ḥesed* are found in David's great psalm of sorrow: 'Have *mercy* upon me, O God, according to your *steadfast love*' (Psalm 51:1). David clearly understood mercy to be the result of God's steadfast love. Mercy is always the child of grace.

To appreciate the depth of this grace we must understand the character of God. He is majestically powerful, magnificently holy, inconceivably wise and fearfully just. And that is exactly where the problem of the human race lies. In the light of this awesome and supreme God we are helpless and hopeless; or as Paul describes our condition: 'Having no hope and without God in the world' (Ephesians 2:12).

Grace was revealed when God planned good for this fallen world; but he did not design this good immediately after the human race fell into sin—he designed it long before then. Though it came to birth when God first responded to Adam after the Fall, it was conceived in eternity. Whenever God speaks and whatever he says is evidence of his grace; whenever God acts and whatever he does, that too is always grace. Whether God warns or promises, condemns or acquits, it is grace. The first record of grace after the Fall is found in the words: 'The LORD God called to the man and said to him, "Where are you?"' (Genesis 3:9). God did not have to call—he knew exactly where Adam was; and Adam did not want God to call—he was in hiding. That voice was God's undeserved initiative—that is grace. He spoke to a rebel. God judged Adam's sin but provided at once for his restoration—and that is all grace.

The law of God in the Old Testament, for all its rigorous demands and severe punishments, was an expression of God's grace; this is precisely why Paul concludes that the law is 'holy, righteous and good' (Romans 7:12). Paul's reasoning is that through the law we recognise sin as 'sinful beyond measure' (v 13), and only when we acknowledge the reality of sin will we be ready to receive the grace of forgiveness and reconciliation. We should always think of 'the grace *of* law'; because law is grace.

John MacRae was brought up on the far west coast of the Scottish Highlands at the end of the eighteenth century. As a shepherd in the wild mountains, MacRae was careless about his soul until God's grace broke into his heart. When she heard of his conversion, an old lady in his area commented, 'If John MacRae has become a new man, surely the latter day glory is not far off!' MacRae became a preacher in 1830 and for more than forty years he preached powerfully across the Western Isles and Highlands of Scotland. Shortly before his death he wrote a letter to his daughter Jane, and in it he included his view of grace: 'What a meaning there is in that word "grace" for such as I am. It contains everything necessary for the salvation of the sinner, leaping over mountains of aggravated rebellion, infinite in its absolute freeness. What I need is to realise this in its power and glory.' We need the same realisation.

## Grace and the Gospels

The word 'grace' (*charis* in the Greek) never appears in the Gospels of Matthew or Mark, though its meaning is constantly in view. Luke, a close companion of Paul for many years, only uses the word to describe Mary's relationship with God, 'you have found *favour*' (1:30) and our Lord's with his heavenly Father, 'Jesus increased … in *favour* with God and man' (2:40, 52; the word 'gracious' is used in 4:22). However, stories illustrating grace abound. The parables of the wedding garment, the prodigal son, and the invitation to the marriage feast are each illustrations of the true meaning of grace. But such parables as the rich man and Lazarus or the unmerciful servant are no less illustrations of grace. All the parables of Christ illustrate grace and all his works and words are beautiful pictures of grace. We do not deserve that God should communicate with us at all; the fact that he spoke so generously through his Son is nothing other than grace.

John in his Gospel develops the word and conspicuously introduces us to grace in a phrase that has produced a field-day for commentators.

John 1:14–17 reads, 'The Word became flesh and dwelt among us, and we have seen his glory, glory as of the only Son from the Father, full of grace and truth … And from his fullness we have all received, grace upon grace. For the law was given through Moses; grace and truth came through Jesus Christ.'

The little word here translated *upon* in the phrase 'grace *upon* grace', when it is used as a comparison or contrast as it is here, carries the idea of something that comes as a replacement. In other words, whilst we had grace and truth before Christ—through the law and priesthood given by Moses—it is through Jesus Christ himself that we receive the *fullness* of both grace and truth (v 14). Grace in the Old Testament has been exchanged—replaced—for the fullness of grace in Christ. That is the meaning of 'grace upon grace'. Truth and grace both came through Moses, but both have found their fullest expression in Jesus Christ.

John 1:14–17 is the only place where the Apostle John uses the word *charis* in his Gospel—just four times in four verses—but it is a brilliant introduction to the word and a fitting preface to the way Paul employs it. Dr Donald Guthrie rightly observed that, 'The mission of Jesus was a supreme revelation of the God of grace.'

## Grace for Paul and his colleagues

In the New Testament, the good news of Jesus Christ is called, 'The word of his grace' (Acts 14:3) and 'The gospel of the grace of God' (Acts 20:24). For his part, Paul summarises the whole of the gospel in four words, 'By grace … through faith' (Ephesians 2:8).

For the apostle Paul, grace was his favourite word—and with very good reason. The achievements of Paul were colossal. His dramatic conversion and then his firm loyalty to the gospel under pressure must have been an incredible encouragement to the first Christian communities. Added to this he was the man who spearheaded the first unevangelized fields mission and planted churches right across Asia Minor and into Greece. His planned vision to encircle the Roman Empire with gospel churches, which appears to be woven into Romans 15, remains a challenge for us even today. His deliberate and efficient action to organise the young churches into vital training centres is still our model for evangelism. From these centres Christians would go out to evangelise the world. And of course it is Paul who by the power and influence of the Holy Spirit has given us so many of those valuable teaching letters in our Bible.

But Paul had not always been a Christian, even though he had always been very religious. He himself tells us that as a well educated Pharisee he was proud whilst pretending to be humble, a lawbreaker whilst teaching the law to others, and a blasphemer whilst claiming to serve the true God. In addition, he was a persecutor and destroyer of the church whilst believing that he belonged to the only true church; he was also an ignorant and violent man, whilst he thought he possessed the wisdom of God.

Then one day, shortly after the death and resurrection of Jesus Christ, this proud and zealous Jew was dramatically converted by the one he so bitterly hated. His life was radically changed; and in the light of this it is not surprising that Paul loved to tell his story. He does this twice in Acts when he is on trial, and there are frequent references in his letters to the revolution of his life after that encounter on the road to Damascus. Paul looked for a word that would adequately sum-up what God had done for him.

In five striking phrases Paul revealed the progression of his thinking when he looked at himself in the light of what he once was. Somewhere around the year AD 57 Paul wrote 1 Corinthians from Ephesus and in this letter he claimed, 'I am the least of the apostles' (1 Corinthians 15:9). A little later to the same church he confessed, 'I am nothing' (2 Corinthians 12:11). Five years later whilst under house arrest in Rome he declared, 'I am the very least of all the saints' (Ephesians 3:8), and in the same year, but now writing from a Roman prison cell, he admitted, 'I am the foremost (of sinners)' (1 Timothy 1:15). Finally, two years later in AD 64—the year of the great fire in Rome possibly started by the Emperor

Nero to create a brown-field site for urban redevelopment—Paul wrote, 'I am not ashamed' (2 Timothy 1:12).

What do these five 'I am' phrases of Paul have in common? We may conclude that they are each Paul's personal put-down, because twice he says, 'I am the least', once he claims, 'I am nothing', and once: 'I am the worst'. But then he writes, 'I am not ashamed', which is hardly self-deprecating. So the common denominator cannot be a belittling of himself.

The key that is common to these five phrases is contained in a word that appears close by in the context of each of them. In 1 Corinthians 15:10 Paul wrote, 'by the *grace* of God I am what I am'; in 2 Corinthians 12:9 he reflects on God's promise: 'My *grace* is sufficient'; in Ephesians 3:8, he declared, 'this *grace* was given (to me) to preach to the Gentiles'; in 1 Timothy 1:14, Paul added that 'the *grace* of our Lord overflowed for me'; and finally in 2 Timothy 1:9, he concluded that he had been saved not because of works, 'but because of (God's) own purpose and *grace*'. In other words, whenever Paul confessed his own great sin and failure or his hope for his ultimate security, it is always firmly in the context of this magnificent word 'grace'.

Paul came to love that word, and as a noun he used it almost one hundred times in his correspondence—twenty times alone in his letter to the Christians at Rome and eleven times to the Ephesians. In every sense he would have been lost without it. He begins and closes each of his letters with a salutation including the word grace: Romans 1:7, 'Grace and peace to you', and he signs off in Romans 16:20, 'The grace of our Lord Jesus Christ be with you.' Similarly in 1 Corinthians 1:3, 'Grace to you and peace', and finally in 16:23, 'The grace of the Lord Jesus be with you'. Yet again in 2 Corinthians 1:2, 'Grace to you and peace' and he concludes with the well-used, 'The grace of our Lord Jesus Christ and the love of God and the fellowship of the Holy Spirit be with you all' (13:14). Paul follows the same pattern in his epistles to the Galatians, Ephesians, Colossians and Thessalonians.

Writing to Timothy, Paul varies the greeting only slightly by adding a third word, 'Grace, mercy and peace' (1 Timothy 1:2 and 2 Timothy 1:2). Titus in Crete, missed out on the mercy, but not on grace (Titus 1:4). Both these young pastors were left with a message to pass on to their churches, because the last phrase in each letter is plural and means—as he spelt out to Titus—'Grace be with you *all*' (Titus 3:15). There are no greetings at all in Hebrews and the word 'grace' does not appear until 2:9. However, from there on we have some rich uses of the word in Hebrews, and the writer closes with: 'Grace be with all of you' (13:25).

Even Peter picked up on this greeting and included it in his two letters, 'Grace and peace be multiplied to you' (1 Peter 1:2 and 2 Peter 1:2). He then weaves grace into his conclusions in 1 Peter 5:12 and 2 Peter 3:18. The fact that John, who used it sparingly in his Gospel, also includes 'Grace, mercy and peace' as his greeting in 2 John 3, and begins and ends his letters to the churches with grace (Revelation 1:4 and 22:21), implies either that this had become a standard greeting in the early church or else John had been reading a lot of Paul! Jude is an odd man out by greeting his readers with, 'Mercy, peace and love' (Jude 2); but even he does not overlook the word 'grace' altogether (v 4). James nearly skips grace completely but squeezes it into just one part of his letter in 4:6 where he borrows from Proverbs 3:34 and paraphrases with 'God opposes the proud but gives grace to the humble.'

## New words for old

Today, we may greet our friends with the meaningless, 'Hi!' In the first century a common greeting was the Greek word *chairo*, meaning 'joy'; but for thousands of years the Hebrew greeting among the Jews had been *shalom*, 'peace'. The Greek equivalent of the Hebrew word for peace was *eirene*—from which we get our word 'irenic' (peaceable). Paul changed the Greek salutation to *charis* ('grace') and combined it with the Jewish greeting to make up his own: 'Grace and peace' (*charis kai eirene*).

*Charis* was a well-used word in the first century, and generally it referred to the favour shown by a superior to an inferior, the deserving to the undeserving. In the Acts of the Apostles the early church found 'favour with all the people' (Acts 2:47), and the Roman Governors, Felix and Festus, showed favour to the Jews (Acts 24:27 and 25:3,9). The word was also used of the response of the one who received this favour, so that 'thanks to the gods' (*charis tois theois*) was a common expression. In fact, Paul used it in this way himself in Romans 6:17 'Thanks be to God …', and in 1 Timothy 1:12 'I thank … Christ Jesus our Lord …' and 2 Timothy 1:3 'I thank God whom I serve …' In each place the word 'thank' translates the word *charis*.

Paul was a master of language, and one of his great pleasures was to give old words new meanings. There were so many facts about the Christian faith that were unfamiliar to converted pagans—and even to converted Jews—that rather than coin a brand new word, Paul often preferred to take an old one and give it new value. With the word *charis* he takes it out of the commonplace and clothes it with a wonderful new meaning. From the condescending, patronising favour of a superior, Paul turns *charis* into the most expressive word in our Christian language. So much did Paul love this word that often he could not leave it to stand on its own but felt that he must adorn it with adjectives or adverbs. He writes of 'much more grace', 'abundant grace', 'superabundant grace', 'abounding grace', 'reigning grace', 'exceeding grace', 'exceeding abundant grace', 'glorious grace', 'sufficient grace' and even, 'incomparable riches of grace'.

For Paul, grace was the only way to explain his salvation, it was the key to all his benefits in the Christian life, it was the single-word summary of his message to the world and the only guarantee that the One who had found him would never lose him. God's choice of his people is 'of grace', we are justified freely 'by grace' and saved 'by grace', we have access to God 'through grace' and all spiritual gifts come to us 'according to grace'.

Paul seems to have made a conscious decision to commandeer this word grace in order to express God's response to us. He never once soils it by using it to describe our response to God. On only two occasions in his letters Paul allows himself the use of the word *charis* to describe our relationship to each other. In 2 Corinthians 8:6–7 he writes of the 'act of grace' when he refers to the church's giving, and in Colossians 4:6 he urges that our speech should always be 'gracious'—although even these have a clear God-ward dimension. Beyond this, the word belongs to God. If every other word was denied him, grace is the one Paul would retain to explain the very heart of his gospel. If you asked him how sinners could be rescued from themselves, from Satan and from hell, he would reply simply, 'By grace'; and if you enquired on what ground this could be, he would respond, 'Jesus Christ and him crucified'.

For Saul of Tarsus there was nothing more wonderfully reassuring than to receive grace, and there was nothing more dreadful than to come close to it and then to 'fall away from grace'. The most glorious experience known to Paul was to be embraced by grace—and the most terrifying possibility was to reject it.

John Newton was born in 1725 in Wapping, one mile down river from the Tower of London, and he died eighty-two years later barely one mile away in the City. His life in-between is well summed up by his own epitaph written on a plain marble slab that can be found in the parish church of St Mary Woolnoth in the City of London. Part of it reads:

John Newton
once an infidel and libertine
a servant of slaves in Africa
was
by the rich mercy of our Lord and Saviour
Jesus Christ
preserved, restored, pardoned
and appointed to preach the faith
he had long laboured to destroy.

Abandoning his mother's Christian faith, the young Newton became an arrogant unbeliever. Having rejected God and his conscience, he lived as he pleased. A blaspheming, drunken, promiscuous sailor filled up his teenage years until, herded onto a warship and pressed into His Majesty's service at the age of nineteen, he refined his anti-Christ philosophy and dragged others with him. Eventually Newton turned up in West Africa as a slave trader and sunk so low that he became the pity and scorn of slaves himself.

In March 1748 John Newton was on his way back to England when a violent storm smashed into the little ship *Greyhound* and for weeks the crew nursed their shattered boat across the Atlantic, expecting a choking grave with every shift of wind. In his terror Newton called out to God for help and his prayer was heard. After days of remorseless battering by the ocean and his conscience, John yielded to the claims of Christ, believed the promises of God's word, and received his first hope of forgiveness. Somewhere on board the broken ship Newton found a little book of sermons, and one in particular he read over and over again, it was based on the words of John the Baptist recorded in John 1:29, 'Behold the Lamb of God which taketh away the sin of the world'. This Easter sermon was entitled, 'The merits of Christ's passion', and in it he read these words: 'We can think and talk of Christ dying for our sins and yet live in them. We can hear of his being accused and condemned and yet not condemn nor so much as accuse ourselves for our sin. We can read over the whole history of our Saviour's passion with dry eyes, and be no more troubled at it than if we had been in no way concerned in it.'

As the shivering, starving sailor read those words he found salvation in Christ. Just four weeks after the terrifying storm that almost sank Newton's hope of salvation, the broken *Greyhound* struggled into Lough Swilly, one of the northernmost points of Ireland. The date was 8 April 1748, which in that year was Good Friday—a neat coincidence for the man who had been reading an Easter sermon. Less than two hours after they had anchored in the comparative shelter of the bay, a gale blew at sea with such a force that the ship would certainly have been broken to pieces had it still been beyond the Lough.

John, who was born in the rough waterfront village of Wapping and whose formal education amounted to just two years at an inferior school, found in Christ alone the grace of God. And Saul, who grew up as a graduate in the university city of Tarsus close to the wild frontier of the Roman Empire, had long before found exactly the same. These two men, seventeen hundred years apart, had both experienced the meaning of grace, and each had begun an adventure in which their life would explore and enjoy the incredible wealth of amazing grace. For this reason, since John of Wapping and Saul of Tarsus have so much in common, we will return in this book to the life of John to illustrate the teaching of Paul. Years later John Newton turned his experience into what has become one of the most popular hymns of the Christian church. It was written for his congregation at Olney in Buckinghamshire to sing on New Year's morning 1773 and was based upon the text for his sermon from 1 Chronicles 17:16–17.

AMAZING GRACE—HOW SWEET THE SOUND –
that saved a wretch like me!
I once was lost, but now am found;
was blind, but now I see.

2. God's grace first taught my heart to fear,
his grace my fears relieved;
how precious did that grace appear
the hour I first believed!

3. Through many dangers, toils and snares
I have already come;
his grace has brought me safe this far
and grace will lead me home.

# Chapter 1

**4.** The Lord has promised good to me,
his word my hope secures;
my shield and great reward is he
as long as life endures.

**5.** And when this mortal life is past
and earthly days shall cease,
I shall possess with Christ at last
eternal joy and peace.

**6.** The earth will soon dissolve like snow,
the sun no longer shine;
but God, who called me here below,
will be for ever mine.

John Newton 1725–1807
Verses 1–5 © in this version Jubilate Hymns.
This text has been altered by *Praise!*
*Praise!* No. 772

## FOR GROUP DISCUSSION

**1.** Can you think of another life that well illustrates the word 'grace'?

**2.** Turn to Numbers 14:18–19; Nehemiah 9:17; Psalm 51:1; 85:10–11; 103:8; 145:8; Joel 2:13; Jonah 4:2 and consider where in the history of Israel they were reminded of God's grace.

**3.** Why do you think the Hebrew word *ḥanan* 'favour' was never used in the Old Testament of our response to God?

**4.** Where does grace begin in the story of this world, and where does it end?

**5.** Check out the five 'I am' phrases of Paul, and find where the word grace appears.

# Universal grace

'He himself gives to all mankind life and breath and everything' Acts 17:25

It is not only the Christian who can declare with the psalmist, 'God does not deal with us according to our sins, nor repay us according to our iniquities' (Psalm 103:10), the whole world should be singing that song. The God of supreme order, perfect beauty, unbridled wisdom and unlimited power, has not dealt with our fragile, ugly and rebellious world as it deserves. Even since the Fall of the human race into sin, the whole universe—and our planet earth in particular—is filled with the evidence of God's grace, his undeserved love in action. This is often referred to as 'common grace' but 'universal grace' is a better term. We might even call it 'prodigal grace', or 'lavish grace', because it is scattered so liberally across the globe. Universal grace does not mean that all receive the same, but that all receive some. God's grace is more abundant and more obvious to some than others, but none is overlooked altogether.

When the seraphim in the temple called out: 'Holy, holy, holy is the LORD of hosts; the whole earth is full of his glory' (Isaiah 6:3), from their vantage point they must have enjoyed a large understanding of the universal grace of God. Paul summarised it in his sermon to the people at Athens: 'He himself gives to all mankind life and breath and everything' (Acts 17:25). Our Lord, as always, reduced the same great theology to a plain and simple statement: 'He is kind to the ungrateful and the evil' (Luke 6:35). What is this universal grace?

## The gift of spiritual life is universal grace

The Apostle John described Christ as the true light coming into the world but then added that this is the light which 'enlightens everyone' (John 1:9). The creation story expresses it like this 'So God created man in his own image, in the image of God he created him; male and female he created them' (Genesis 1:27). This meant that many of the great attributes—or characteristics—of God are reflected in the human race, such as: wisdom, understanding, appreciation of beauty, compassion—and a sense of eternity.

The preacher in the book of Ecclesiastes tells us that God 'put eternity into man's heart' (3:11). This is why we have never found a people, anywhere in the world, who do not worship. Their worship may be primitive as they honour the moon, the anaconda or grandma; it may even be evil as they offer cruel sacrifices, scourge their own bodies or bitterly persecute all who are not of their religion. But all over the world, people have a sense of God, an awareness of accountability, a belief in life beyond here. Somehow we all know that there is something more. Even in our hard-nosed scientific age of apparent unbelief, the world's bestsellers and blockbuster movies all reflect this. The Narnia stories of C S Lewis, the Middle Earth saga of J R R Tolkein, the magical Harry Potter world of J K Rowling, and even books and films like *The Final Odyssey* and *Star Wars* all speak of more beyond.

At the Fall into sin by Adam and Eve, God might have sucked the soul out of mankind, he might have withdrawn that gift of 'light'; the light of knowing that there is more beyond. He might have left us all not merely to be atheists—believing that there is no God—but without even the evidence that there is a being called God whom we may choose not to believe in.

No one is born an atheist. This enlightenment of which John speaks in his Gospel is the knowledge that there is a God, and that in this world there is much more than meets the eye—there is more beyond. Religion is part of being essentially human. It is groping darkly after God, longing to find him, somehow, somewhere; religion is a hand reaching out from the shadows into the unknown. At Athens Paul declared that God's universal grace is what caused the Athenians to seek God: '... so that men would seek him and perhaps reach out for him and find him, though he is not far from each one of us.' (Acts 17:27–28). Atheism is sub-human, it is humanity aping the ape—trying to live like the animals, as if there is no God. But he is not using his superior intelligence to draw the obvious conclusion from the evidence around him. When the jungle tribesman rejects his brain he turns his god into wood, but when the college professor rejects his God he turns his brain into wood.

In her book *Leading Little Ones to God*, Marian Schoolland has a beautiful way of explaining this part of universal grace to a small child: 'Some people say there is no God. They do not pray at all. But deep down in their hearts there is that little voice that says, "Yes, there is a God"'. It is this same voice that sends a shiver of uncertainly when death is close: perhaps, after all, there is more beyond. The evidence of spiritual life in the human race is part of the universal grace of God.

## Our active conscience is universal grace

In the Old Testament God gave his law to Israel so that they might be distinguished from all the nations around them and might become the envy of those nations (Deuteronomy 4:5–8). His law was good and it was meant for good. It was intended to increase their joy; and this is why the psalmist could often reflect on how much he loved and found pleasure in the law of the Lord: 'I find my delight in your commandments, which I love. I will lift up my hands towards your commandments which I love, and I will meditate on your statutes' (Psalm 119:47–48). The law is a tyrant only to the lawbreaker.

But not everyone has access to God's law, so a significant part of the image of God in all men and women is 'conscience'. This is our awareness that there is right and wrong, good and evil, kindness and wickedness. It is what the eighteenth century German philosopher Immanuel Kant called: the 'categorical imperative'; he saw it as mankind's sense of 'ought'.

Paul describes the significance of conscience in Romans 2:14–15, 'When (those) who do not have the law, by nature do what the law requires, they are a law to themselves, even though they do not have the law. They show that the work of the law is written on their hearts, while their conscience also bears witness, and their conflicting thoughts accuse or even excuse them.' Here, precisely, is the conflict of conscience. This is what is often referred to as 'the natural law'—the sense of right and wrong that everyone possesses. Rats and rabbits do not have a conscience but the human race does. Mark Twain got close to the truth: 'The human race is the only animal that can blush, and the only one that needs to.'

Even the ancient Greeks referred to this natural law; they called it *nomos agraphos* ('law unwritten'). It was, they believed, the only basis for universal standards of right and wrong. Paul's argument is that when their conscience guides them correctly and they obey it, then, unknowingly, they are obeying the moral law of God. This means that even those who have never heard the gospel of Jesus Christ and have no knowledge of the law of God, can still do actions that are good. It is this conscience that makes many people sensitive to the needs of others and leads to the compassion of famine relief and global disaster aid. It is conscience that keeps our fallen world from falling apart.

Conscience is also that part of the human life that is aware of God and of eternity—and our accountability to God *in* eternity. However, our conscience has become so perverted and spoiled by sin that most people turn truth into a lie and worship anything other than God himself. The very thing that marks us out from the animal kingdom has now become spoiled. In Paul's vivid expression in 1 Timothy 4:2, he claims that our 'consciences are seared'. The Greek word for 'seared' gives us our word 'cauterise', and in Paul's day it referred to the branding of a slave with a hot iron. The conscience of everyone is naturally branded with the beliefs and standards of the society around and not by the law of God.

Some years ago, after preaching at a summer holiday camp, the campers presented me with a beautiful clock that goes backwards. That clock is still in perfect working order and tells the time accurately—but according to a very warped sense of timekeeping. At least it was more consistent than a clock our church once had that not only ran backwards, but was inconsistently slow as well; no amount of careful calculation could ever arrive at the correct time from that useless item.

Everyone has a conscience, and everyone's conscience is in working order; the tragedy is that our conscience too often works to a different rule than God's law. As time passes and we are more and more influenced by the standards of society, like our church clock our conscience becomes less and less reliable. Sadly it often works in reverse—and this is why some can carry out the most horrendous acts of cruelty and terror and convince themselves that what they are doing is right. Occasionally, after a particularly vile murder or act of brutality, the media refer to those responsible as 'animals'. Sadly they are not; if they were, they could not be held responsible for their actions. But it is a perversion of human nature when instead of admiring the beauty of a lion we mimic its behaviour. It is the universal grace of conscience that makes cruel human behaviour so appalling.

### The beauty and design of creation is universal grace

When God completed creation he saw everything that he had made 'and behold, it was very good' (Genesis 1:31). That does not mean that it was the best he could do, it means that it was the best that could ever be done. God does not botch, and he cannot do anything that is less than the most perfect it could ever be. There is beauty even in this fallen world; so much of creation still reflects the Creator. In Romans 1:20 Paul claims, 'Since the creation of the world God's invisible qualities—his eternal power and divine nature—have been clearly seen, being understood from what has been made, so that men are without excuse.'

The power of the snow-capped mountain, the awesome majesty of a vast echoing canyon, the complex design of the laced wings of a butterfly, the mystery of the migration of birds, and the beauty of a field carpeted with flowers all reflect a God who delights in exquisite beauty and intricate design. The very words, 'power, awesome majesty, designer, mystery, beauty' are descriptions of God himself. The thing created will always tell us something about the creator.

It is irrational to attribute to blind evolution that which rightly belongs to the wisdom of God. The psalmist wisely mocked: 'The fool says in his heart, "There is no God"' (Psalm 14:1). But even such a fool can enjoy God's creation, admire his wisdom, marvel at his design, revel in the kaleidoscope of his colours and shades, glory in the infinite variety of sights and tastes, smells and touch, and stand transfixed before his starry galaxies in the heavens. If the stars came out only once a year the whole world would stay up all night to enjoy the spectacle and it would be the same with the exquisite cacophony of birdsong in the dawn chorus. When the atheist simply exclaims, 'Wow!' he betrays the poverty of his wooden mind and soul. Instead of 'Wow!' he should worship.

This is all God's universal grace. After the Fall, God could have left us with a world that knew only darkness and pain, the gloom of unrelieved evil, the foul smell, cruel sights and bitter taste of the worst that rebel sinners are capable of. A fallen world could have been colour blind, tasteless and tone deaf. Instead, God has limited his judgement and poured out the grace of his rich variety of beauty and order on an undeserving world. After the devastation of the universal Flood in the time of Noah the whole earth could have been left as one vast rain forest, or arid wilderness or biting snowscape; instead, we have a diversity of ice and desert, mountain and plain, jungle and scrub, savannah and grassland, wide oceans and rippling streams.

Creation enshrines awe-inspiring design. If the moon were ten percent nearer the earth than it is, daily huge tides would sweep even the mountains bare. The stars change their position just slightly each night, but every 365 days 6 hours 9 minutes and 9.6 seconds they are back where they started. If the myriad of stars and planets did not move in this perfect harmony then our mariners and explorers could never have navigated around the world. Even our atomic clocks were originally set by the stars—what is known as sidereal time—and our most sophisticated global positioning devices depend ultimately upon this perfect order in creation. God has even given us a wise pattern of day and night to regulate our work and rest; and wherever we live in the world, in one full year we will have the same amount of daylight and darkness as everyone else. There is a perfectly ordered symmetry about the universe.

In God's response to suffering Job, God surveyed his control of the natural world from the planets to the earth, from the stars to the sea, from the mountains to the mines, from the animals that act wisely to those that act stupidly, from the powerful to the weak, from the seasons to the sunshine and the storms, and above the poetry of this passage stands the opening text, 'Where were you when I laid the foundation of the earth?' (Job 38:4).

The dolphin has a remarkable ability to streamline the flow of water over its body virtually to eliminate drag. Submarine engineers discovered that the secret was not in a perfectly smooth skin as we might imagine, but a skin with small indentations that keyed-in the boundary layer of air that it pulled down from the surface, thus holding it close to the body and reducing drag. The engineers copied this, making very small indentations to roughen the surface of the submarine hull. A more obvious example of the same principle is the dimpled golf ball.

As a result of the work of Sir James Lighthill, scientists have begun to understand the 'clap and fling principle' of the wings of butterflies and moths. They clap their wings at the top and as the wings spread out they cause two vortices of air which increases the lift. This is why insects can fly using wings that, according to our best calculations, should not be able to lift them off the ground. Yet still scientists cannot tell how the bumble bee flies since its body weight and apparent wing size and structure imply that it could never take off, let alone manoeuvre delicately around the flowers in our garden. On both sides of the Atlantic scientists are at work in this area with the hope of increasing the flight efficiency of our clumsy, cumbersome, mechanical aeroplanes. In a similar way, the hummingbird—with a heart beat of 20 per second, a wing beat of 200 per second and the ability to fly forward, backward or hover—makes a cross between a modern supersonic fighter, a jump jet and a helicopter look positively prehistoric.

When the human race uses its God-given intelligence it will never cease to learn from the God-given creation. That is universal grace. We should be unashamed to declare with the psalmist: 'You have multiplied, O Lord my God, your wondrous deeds and your thoughts toward us; none can compare with you! I will proclaim and tell of them, yet they are more than can be told' (Psalm 40:5). The inevitable conclusion, as the Old Testament prophet sees it, is that no one 'taught him knowledge or showed him the way of understanding.' Paul agreed that God's wisdom and knowledge are both unsearchable and inscrutable (Romans 11:33). If we do not learn this much from the design of creation then we are fools of the first order.

## The kindness of God's provision is universal grace

In his kindness to the 'ungrateful and evil' God allows them to enjoy the warmth of the sun, the gently refreshing rain, the cooling breeze, the abundance of his harvest and the pleasure of his colours, sounds, tastes and smells. As our Lord himself simply expressed it: 'He makes his sun rise on the evil and on the good, and sends rain on the just and on the unjust' (Matthew 5:45).

Abundance it most certainly is. There is more than sufficient food and water on this earth to fill every hungry mouth and satisfy every thirsty child. And though the world could survive on a basketful of different fruits and vegetables, God has given us truck loads of variety instead. We could enjoy the pleasure of a handful of diverse species of colourful birds and fish and interesting animals, or a few dozen scented flowers, pretty shrubs and magnificent trees. But instead, God created an almost inexhaustible variety of species—an estimated 9,000 different sorts of birds, 20,000 of trees, 200,000 of flowers, and well over 300,000 of beetles!

The psalmist claimed, 'The LORD is good to all, and his mercy is over all that he has made' and as a consequence, all his created works should give thanks to him (Psalm 145:9–10). The whole world is dependent upon God for food and it is by his provision of the cycle of life and growth and the seasons of the year that he 'satisfies the desire of every living thing' (vs 5–16). Millions may not recognise this—and because of the selfishness of a fallen human race millions are denied the benefit of it—but it will be part of the sentence of final judgement to be made aware of what has been staring us in the face for a whole lifetime. We have no excuse for not having wide eyes for God's open hand—'everything created by God is good' (1 Timothy 4:4).

But what of the searing heat of the desert, the lashing tropical storm and the freezing Arctic ice flow?' Those are reminders that all is not well with the world because sin has spoiled a perfect creation. It is even grace when things are abnormally out of step with an ordered world. We may well question whether God would really create a cruel burning desert or a howling Arctic waste and then call it 'very good'? The truth is that he didn't. These are the harsh legacies of sin which God has left to show that all is not well. Everything that is not as it should be is a reminder not only that everything is not as it was, but that everything is not as it ultimately will be.

And when the unexpected happens—when mountains spit fire, the earth cracks open or snow falls in July, this too is a reminder that even in the midst of the beauty and order, creation is still captive to the burden of decay and death (Romans 8:19–22). When the very beauty that reflects God turns ugly, that too is universal grace. It is a legacy of the Fall through which God reminds us that whilst sin deserves judgement like this, he so often holds back his hand and pours out grace instead.

Just when the world is thoughtlessly enjoying the universal grace of a God who has provided generously more than all we need, something, somewhere goes wrong—disastrously wrong. That is a warning. And that too is grace. Unfortunately people don't listen; suffering in the world only makes them, as the writer Somerset Maugham claimed, 'petty and vindictive'. However, when a criminal ignores the warnings of the law, the activity of the courts and the evidence of the prison system, who is at fault?

## The unseen providence of God is universal grace

Asaph the psalmist was in a fix. Exactly what his problem was he doesn't tell us, but it kept him awake at night and made him feel that God had forgotten him. His response was not simply to despair, but to spend some of his time recollecting the goodness of God to his people in the past. His mind went back to the time when God brought the Israelites out of Egypt and safely across the Red Sea on dry land. What impressed him about this story, and the subsequent way that God led them through the wilderness, was that God himself was not seen. This is how he graphically describes it: 'Your way was through the sea, your path through the great waters; yet your footprints were unseen' (Psalm 77:19). Asaph should not have been surprised since that is true for the whole world, all of the time.

God does not often advertise himself when he gives away his benefits for free. Although he is at work constantly in this world, more often than not we do not see how. Christians frequently thank God for unseen safety in the course of a day. In the Old Testament David did the same: 'You know when I sit down and when I rise up ... You search out my path and my lying down and are acquainted with all my ways ... You hem me in, behind and before, and lay your hand upon me' (Psalm 139:2–5). But whilst that is a specific understanding and encouragement for those who are on the side of God, the reality is also true for everyone in this world. God is not so limited that he knows all about his own people but little or nothing about anyone else.

If the kings and rulers of the nations are in the hand of God (Ezra 6:22), why them alone? No one is beyond the control of God, and for that matter, no one is beyond the protective care of God when he chooses. The unbeliever has no right to claim such care, but he may nonetheless receive it. The 'lucky escape', 'great good fortune' and 'sheer coincidence' that is arrogantly boasted of by so many, is always the hand of God—though rarely is it seen as such. What else could the psalmist mean when he declared that God's steadfast love extends to the heavens, his faithfulness to the clouds and that, 'man and beast you save' (Psalm 36:6)?

## Imagination and appreciation are universal grace

By comparison with the creativity, aesthetic pleasure and inventive genius of the human race, animals are soulless, mindless and colourless. I was puzzled that we can be considered close relatives to the chimpanzee when I watched the enthusiasm of the scientist who had discovered one such primate using a stick to dig ants out of a hole in a tree. With all the millions of years he has supposedly had to perfect his art I would have expected him to have advanced at least as far as a hand drill!

I know that animals are intriguingly adaptable: the Arbour bird builds a series of attractive nests for his mate to choose from, and the Weaver bird can plait an incredible dome of reeds at the end of a slim branch—but they have all about reached their limit. Man's resourcefulness and creativity is stunning by comparison. A survey of bird song in Britain unsurprisingly put the Blackbird at the top of the poll; beautiful it certainly is—though there are better—however, his repertoire is seriously limited. The Indian Myna and its relative the European

Starling, are versatile mimics in the world of birds, but few of us would wish to spend an evening listening to the twittering of starlings at our local concert hall.

By contrast, the creative art of the human race in colour, music and sculpture—and our ability to appreciate and enjoy such inspired design—is part of our uniqueness that marks us off from the animal world. It is all part of God's universal grace in the reflection of his image and likeness in us. We have little evidence that the goat, living high up on a breathtakingly beautiful mountain range, or the eagle soaring into a shimmering valley, or the bullock grazing in the lush pasture of a peaceful English village, have any appreciation of the awesome beauty or tranquil calm around them other than its purpose in providing their next meal. One good reason why God created Eve as a 'compatible' companion to Adam was that not one of the animals around him was capable of sharing in Adam's awe and wonder at the beauty of God's perfect creation.

Beyond all this, it is God's universal grace that has given the human race a mind to explore, discover and invent. The discovery of the atom, invention of the silicon chip and our understanding of the human DNA and gene system are just a few of many areas of knowledge that are of immense value to the human race. Sadly, because our conscience is seared by sin, we have abused so much that God has given us, and everything good we find a bad use for. But we cannot blame the Creator for our misappropriation of his grace.

## The church in the world is universal grace

When Jesus told his disciples that they were salt and light in this world (Matthew 5:13–16), he set before the church a marker that in its two thousand year history the professing Christian church has often lost sight of. We cannot excuse some of the terrible acts committed by the so-called church. Although Christianity is entitled to define itself by the life and teaching of its leader, it must also be judged by the quality of life and influence of its followers. The Crusades, the Inquisition, the traffic in human slaves, and some of the negative legacy of colonialism, have no support from the teaching of either Christ or his disciples.

However, a Christianity that follows the teaching and example of Christ has always been a powerful force for good in this world. It is the Bible that taught justice, the value of life, freedom and compassion; and it is Protestant Christianity in particular that has recognised this and applied it most vigorously. Because of its two thousand year history, Christianity is bound to be vulnerable. There are renegades in every walk of life. Everybody knows the Judas who lives or works next door, but he was the only one of twelve—that's eight percent failure. The inconsistencies in Christian history are anomalies rather than normalities. It is Christians who so often remind the world of integrity and loyalty at work, who demonstrate the value of love and purity in marriage, who reach out in warmth and compassion to those in fear and anxiety, and who provide for the poor and suffering in the world.

When atheistic humanism ransacks history in order to discredit the Christian faith, we are entitled to ask what is the legacy of atheism to the modern world? The regimes inspired by a belief that there is no God—of which there have been and still are many—have an impressive record of genocide and torture over their short one hundred year history. How many atheistic missions are scattered in the hard places of the world caring with famine relief, or opening schools, hospitals, dispensaries and leprosariums? How many agricultural projects, literacy programmes, and self-help schemes have been initiated by Humanism? Where is the army of young atheists dedicating their lives in tough parts of the world to humanitarian care? And where are the hundreds of missions, inspired by a belief in no God, that are involved in such care? Christians in the United Kingdom alone give in excess of two billion pounds each year to support their caring work. We may ask what the comparable figure for atheistic humanism is.

Across the world today, those who take the Bible as their instruction manual are influencing society by their honesty, hard work, compassion and purity. At the age of five, Ban Mau was sent by his parents to train as a Buddhist priest. The harsh treatment he received caused him to run away several times, but he was always taken back to the temple. By the age of thirteen he escaped and joined a band of guerrillas attacking the Burmese government; later he enlisted in a mercenary group fighting the communists in Thailand. Finally, wounded by a land mine, he left the army and earned his living by making illegal liquor. Ban Mau began to observe a group of Christians in his village: they lived good lives and worked hard and honestly. They also carried a book that taught about love and compassion to those in need. Eventually he heard the Christian message and decided to follow Christ. Right now, Ban Mau is involved in Bible translation and evangelism. Who benefits a society most: a guerrilla, drug dealer and a purveyor of illegal liquor—or a Bible translator?

Stories like this can be multiplied literally tens of thousands of times. Christians are the most peaceful, law-abiding, honest and hard working citizens in society. Our Lord expected the lives of his disciples to count in society and their good works would cause others to 'give glory to your Father who is in heaven' (Matthew 5:16). It was this expectation of Christ that his church should be salt and light in the world that led Paul to emphasise the importance of the reputation Christians should have in the world. The Corinthians were to be 'letters of recommendation ... known and read by all' (2 Corinthians 3:1–2); the Thessalonian Christians were encouraged to 'live properly before outsiders' (1 Thessalonians 4:12); and Timothy was reminded that a Christian leader 'must be well thought of by outsiders' (1 Timothy 3:7). Peter was equally adamant that if Christians are to suffer, it must be because of what they believe and not how they live (1 Peter 4:12–16). This is part of God's universal grace to a rebellious world.

## The long patience of God is universal grace

God's universal grace is always intended to lead to the knowledge of himself. He allows sin and evil to remind us that all is not well. Even growing old is grace if we view it as reinforcing our short, uncertain life and preparing us for eternity. The German philosopher, Friedrich Nietzsche dismissed suffering as 'senseless'. Somerset Maugham claimed that it makes character 'petty and vindictive'. Oscar Wilde called it a 'revelation'. But C S Lewis was wiser than all when he declared suffering to be 'a roadblock on the way to hell'.

Sadly, the universal grace of God passes over so many; they learn nothing from it. Even when God shows himself to be upright, kind and wise, they go on doing evil. Through the prophet Jeremiah, God identified those who take this grace for granted and attribute it to their own wisdom, power, wealth or their good luck: 'Let not the wise man boast in his wisdom, let not the mighty man boast in his might, let not the rich man boast in his riches, but let him who boasts boast in this, that he understands and knows me, that I am the Lord who practices steadfast love, justice and righteousness in the earth. For in these things I delight' (Jeremiah 9:23–24).

As years pass into centuries and centuries into millennia God is waiting patiently, not willing that any should perish, but that all should come to repentance and faith in Jesus Christ. Despots brutally ill-treat their citizens but God does not immediately take action; the widow and orphan cry for justice and still God remains silent; the cynic blasphemes God and mocks his Creator, and he does the same day after day as if God is not listening; a man steals and kills on Sunday but God does not pay out on Monday; the humanist publishes his arrogant philosophy but the print shop does not burn down. Does all this point to a disinterested or powerless God? God is waiting, allowing more time for repentance. It is universal grace.

Universal grace points only in one direction—towards the God that

Peter calls 'The God of all grace' (1 Peter 5:10). Paul pleaded with the congregation at Rome in case some were strangers to the grace of God: 'Do you presume upon the riches of his kindness and forbearance and patience, not knowing that God's kindness is meant to lead you to repentance?' Those who presume on God's patience to continue in their unbelief, simply stack up more judgement that will inevitably fall—sooner or later. God is rich in his kindness, forbearance and patience. The more time we have, then the more we can discover of his wisdom, power and love. The more we ignore it, then the more judgement grows.

All grace is ultimately in Jesus Christ. There is no true grace anywhere that does not come from and is not defined by, the person of Jesus Christ who is the radiance of the glory of God and the exact character of the reality of God himself (Hebrews 1:3). Grace is a person and not a cold, lifeless theology. It is seen above all in the cross of Christ where the anger of God and the love of God met; and where love conquered wrath. Grace belongs exclusively to God.

FOR ALL THE GLORIES OF THE EARTH AND SKY,
for night's soft voice, and morning's silent haze,
for trees that whisper, and for winds that sigh,
we give you praise.

2. For summer sunshine and for cooling showers,
for stars that light the heavens' darkening maze,
for dewdrops sparkling on the newborn flowers,
our hearts would praise.

3. For lightning's flash, and thunder's echoing roar,
for seas that beat upon their endless ways,
for wild waves' anthem on a rock-bound shore,
we offer praise.

**4.** For mighty mountains and eternal snows,
enduring changeless through the changing days,
for moonlit valleys and for sunset glows,
accept our praise.

**5.** Yet for Christ's great redeeming work of love,
our souls their highest hymn of thanks would raise,
for free salvation streaming from above,
we render praise.

**6.** For all the matchless wonders of your grace
seen in that cross on which we humbly gaze,
for peace and pardon to a fallen race,
your name we praise.

Mrs G Golden
Copyright control
*Praise!* 205

## FOR GROUP DISCUSSION

**1.** 'No one is born an atheist'. What is the evidence for this and what are its implications?
**2.** From Psalm 19 how would you explain universal grace?
**3.** How should we respond to the accusation that 'nature red in tooth and claw' illustrates a world either without God or out of God's control?
**4.** What evidence is there of Christians as salt and light in our contemporary society?
**5.** Can you defend the claim that 'Grace belongs exclusively to God.'?

# Sovereign grace

'Oh, the depth of the riches and wisdom and knowledge of God! How unsearchable are his judgements and how inscrutable his ways!' Romans 11:33

If God is willing to prevent evil, but is not able to
Then He is not omnipotent.

If He is able, but not willing
Then He is malevolent

If He is both able and willing
Then whence cometh evil?

If He is neither able nor willing
Then why call Him God?

So goes the Epicurean riddle that was adopted by the philosopher David Hume in the eighteenth century. It is compelling and challenging.

Tuesday 11 September 2001 was one of the many dates in history on which the world changed course. At precisely 8.45am the Boeing 767 of American Airlines flight 11 was pitilessly flown into the North Tower of the World Trade Centre in New York by al-Qaeda terrorists. Eighteen minutes later a second 767, this time United Airlines flight 175, crashed into the South Tower. The carnage and destruction that followed in New York City, together with American Airlines flight 77 that plunged into the Pentagon almost one and a half hours later, is now all part of the dark side of history. Thousands died in the fireball that engulfed and destroyed the 110 storey, quarter mile high towers. In London the *Daily Mail* front page headlines the following morning read simply: 'Apocalypse—NY Sept.11th 2001'.

As the sickening newscasts flashed across the world, many thought that they were watching a horror movie: the result of a scriptwriter's imagination and a brilliantly surreal set arranged by a Spielberg-type director. Soon we would realize that it was all a vivid film or a bad dream—but it wasn't. It could not really happen—but it did. No one could do such a callously evil thing—but they could. The world, we were told, would never be the same again. Perhaps. But the persistent question was: What kind of world will it look like in the future? Will it really be any different from the past? Would our world democracies led by our political leaders simply 'sort it'? Would we rely upon the intelligence services and Western hardware to 'settle the score'? Would we trust in a political, economic or military response—and that alone? Or, above all else that we may have to do, would we cry to the God of peace for help and ask for his wisdom? Would we look and listen for his voice in all this? In short, would God be brought into the situation for better reasons than simply to throw him out of it?

Whether human cruelty or a natural disaster, Christians, like everyone else, have to answer some painfully hard questions. Where is God in all this? Is there a purpose? How should I pray? What for? Who for? Can I still believe in a God of grace and love? Should I keep quiet about God and just hope that people don't ask me questions? Or is there something courageously positive that the Christian can say to a grieving and sceptical world?

Every year of every century throughout human history has seen cruelty—often on a scale that dwarfs the New York inferno—that most people find hard to believe. Millions died in the Nazi death camps, and millions more in that regime's carnage across Europe. The atheism of the

Communist era eclipsed even the Nazis' grand achievement, and across war-torn Africa millions more die in horrific cruelty. Has grace worn thin among the sunken mass graves and the stench of rotting corpses? Has the Christian nothing to say in the blackened ghost town where once children laughed and played on their way to school? Must the Christian remain silent?

Christians do not glibly pretend to have all the answers, but they need to reaffirm boldly and without hesitation some of the great certainties of the Christian faith. Can there be such a thing as grace when the worst that men can imagine is planned and executed so incredibly successfully? Here are four simple but vital statements of Christian conviction:

### First, nothing happens anywhere or at anytime without God's knowledge beforehand

There are no surprises with God. He is never waiting for a BBC or CNN news bulletin to keep him informed. He knows everything that happens, everywhere—not at the time but before the time.

Through the prophet Jeremiah, God revealed something of himself: '"Am I a God at hand", declares the LORD, "and not a God afar off? Can a man hide himself in secret places so that I cannot see him?" declares the LORD. "Do I not fill heaven and earth?" declares the LORD' (23:23–24). The Old Testament psalmist takes us further and personalizes it: 'O LORD you have searched me and known me! You know when I sit down and when I rise up; you discern my thoughts from afar. You search out my path and my lying down and are acquainted with all my ways. Even before a word is on my tongue, behold, O LORD, you know it altogether' (Psalm 139:1–4). The same theme follows into the New Testament: 'No creature is hidden from his sight, but all are naked and exposed to the eyes of him to whom we must give account' (Hebrews 4:13). All thoughts and words are open to God and nothing is planned or carried out in secrecy from him.

## Second, God plans all events in this universe

The issue gets tight at this point, but we cannot avoid it unless we make God as helpless in the foreknowledge of events as we are. It is not just that he knows what will happen, but he determines everything that will happen. God does not simply see what is coming and then decide whether he will stop it from happening or else let it happen. He will sometimes allow evil people to carry out their plans as part of his greater plans. God never surrenders control, but he often withdraws his hand of protection.

The most outstanding example of this is found in the crucifixion of Jesus. Preaching on the day of Pentecost shortly after the death of Christ, Peter declared, 'This Jesus, delivered up according to the definite plan and foreknowledge of God, you crucified and killed by the hands of lawless men' (Acts 2:23). The vicious death of Christ as the result of an illegal court, trumped-up charges, and endorsed by a weak governor, is a matter of history. But Peter is aware that even this evil action was the 'definite plan' that lay behind the 'foreknowledge of God'. Behind the evil plans of men are the good plans of God—always—though this may not be obvious at the time.

This dual understanding of evil is found frequently in the Bible. Commenting on the Egyptian Pharaoh who cruelly treated the Israelite slaves, God says, 'For this very purpose I have raised you up, that I might show my power in you, and that my name might be proclaimed in all the earth' (Romans 9:17); doubtless it did not appear to the Israelites that God was in control, as they groaned under the whip of their Egyptian slave drivers.

Eight hundred years later Sennacherib of Assyria devastated the land of Judah, marched his terrifying army to the walls of Jerusalem and mocked Hezekiah and his God. In reply, God scorned Sennacherib for his arrogance of behaving as if his successes over the nations and his threats to Jerusalem were all his own doing: 'Have you not heard that I determined it long ago? I planned from days of old what now I bring to pass, that you should turn fortified cities into heaps of ruins … But I know your sitting down and your going out and coming in, and your raging against me. Because you have raged against me and your complacency has come into my ears, I will put my hook in your nose and my bit in your mouth, and I will turn you back on the way by which you came' (2 Kings 19:25, 27–28). That night Sennacherib saw his entire army decimated under the walls of Jerusalem, and some time after his return to his capital Nineveh he was assassinated (vs 35–37).

Similarly it may not have appeared to the eyes of Jews in exile in the time of Daniel that God was in control when King Cyrus of Persia came to power; the fact that God referred to him as 'my shepherd, (who) shall fulfil all my purpose' (Isaiah 44:28) was perhaps little comfort to the Jew who struggled to survive in the pagan environment of his Persian exile. But it was true. These three rulers—Pharaoh, Sennacherib and Cyrus— who were separated by one thousand years and as many miles and who reigned as undisputed despots over empires which were gained and held by the brutal and unforgiving power of the sword, each served God's purpose in the next stage of Israel's story.

Can it be that terrorists capable of callous evil are not merely in the hand of God but are somehow fulfilling his purposes? Yes, it must be. Or else God is as much a helpless victim of evil men as we are. God is not the author of evil or the perpetrator of wickedness, but he plans the violence and cruelty of evil men for his own purposes. Nothing is beyond his control. And there is nothing that does not fit into his sovereign plans. Nothing is senseless with God.

This is equally true of our personal circumstances, and wisely the Bible reminds us: 'In the day of prosperity be joyful, and in the day of adversity consider: God has made the one as well as the other' (Ecclesiastes 7:14). The Bible never backs away from acknowledging that God has a purpose in everything that he allows to happen in this world: 'The LORD has made everything for its purpose. Even the wicked for the day of trouble'

(Proverbs 16:4). This does not make God complicit in evil, but it does make him in control of it. Even the cast of a dice is under his command (Proverbs 16:33).

### Third, God is therefore in total control of all events in the world

In the story of the deep suffering of Job, he lost almost everything—his family, property, friends, reputation, health and even the love of his wife—yet in the light of his own misery and in his despair and agony, he was not afraid to reaffirm that the unseen God is in control of the detail of the whole universe from the moment of creation even to the mystery of his own experience. Job concluded, 'He is wise in heart and mighty in strength—who has hardened himself against him and succeeded? ... Who can turn him back? Who will say to him, "What are you doing?"' (Job 9:4,12). The pagan king, Nebuchadnezzar was compelled to admit to the sovereign power of God who 'does according to his will among the hosts of heaven and among the inhabitants of the earth; and none can stay his hand or say to him. "What have you done?"' (Daniel 4:35). Certainly Paul was aware of Job's triumph when he penned Romans 11:33–36. That is all sovereign grace.

Jesus claimed that not even a sparrow falls to the ground without the knowledge of God and, in an even more striking picture, that even the hairs on our head are numbered (Matthew 10:29–30). It is beyond belief that God should be taken by surprise by the actions of cruel terrorists or that he was not the silent listener at all their secret preparations. After terrible atrocities, world leaders will spend hours of intense discussion with senior advisers planning how they can regain the initiative and establish control. New strategies are called for and new precautions are set in place; new departments are set up and new orders go out across the world. But it is not so with God. Not for one millisecond does he ever lose total control. There is never any crisis management with God.

After a particularly heart-rending disaster in which many school children were engulfed in the choking mud of a landslide, a clergyman registered his response on the radio by claiming, 'This must be one of those occasions when the Almighty made a mistake'. Such an anaemic theology sent a shiver down my spine. His was a pathetically weak and unreliable deity who was a miserable and forlorn victim of the world he had created but apparently was now incapable of controlling. I would rather worship a God who is in total control and takes ultimate responsibility for all that happens in this world—and then face the issue of whether this makes him the willing spectator of evil—rather than believe in a God who is little more than a cringing sugar daddy in the face of natural disasters.

### Fourth, God is wise, purposeful and just in all his plans

Nowhere is this more simply expressed than in Romans 11:33, 'Oh, the depth of the riches and wisdom and knowledge of God! How unsearchable are his judgements and how inscrutable his ways!' The visible tragedies that God allows and the unknown tragedies that he prevents; the evil that the devil unleashes and the righteousness that is overturned; the good that God gives and the good that he withholds—all these are wise, purposeful and fair.

God's wisdom is too profound for us to understand and his plans are too deep for us to fathom. This is not a retreat into blind faith but the affirmation of trust in the God who is in charge. The alternative to God in total control is not God out of control, but no God at all. He cannot be God if he is not always in command. If for one moment the satanic evil of wicked men gains the upper hand and places God on the defensive then he is no longer God, and the devil rules.

God is always God. Nothing happens without his knowledge beforehand and everything happens as part of his plan. All events are totally under his control, and all his plans are wise, purposeful and just. How then must we respond to both personal tragedies and national atrocities if we believe in such a God? Our fall-back is always sovereign grace.

## We respond with confidence

If we abandon God when disaster strikes, then all hope is gone. We are left with unrestrained evil and blind chance pitted against polite morality and good intentions. The Christian declares God is still in control:

when volcanoes spit fire over a town

when mighty rivers deluge helpless villages

when the earth splits open and cities collapse

when the sun scorches the earth

when hurricanes devastate crops

when armies massacre civilians

when callous terrorists destroy whole communities

when death takes my friends and loved ones

when school kids murder their classmates

when a baby dies in its cot

when my dearest friend dies horribly

when disease wracks my own body

when those I trusted betray me

when my best plans collapse in a chaotic heap

We cannot always explain what is happening or immediately find the purpose in it. But we know who has the explanation and confidently we can pray for him to comfort those who mourn, to heal minds and bodies, and to defeat evil men across the world. Joseph was sold into slavery by his brothers who then lied to their father about his disappearance. Falsely accused of attempted rape in the household of his slave-master he barely escaped with his life and was thrown into prison—his reputation and any hope of release destroyed. It appeared that God had forsaken him. God either did not know of Joseph's desperate condition, or if he knew he did not care—or if he cared then the circumstances were beyond his control. Just how Joseph viewed these events at the time we are not told, though there is enough evidence in the story to save us from guessing, because years later when the whole situation had turned around, he could remind his brothers of their intention years before and conclude, 'You meant evil against me, but God meant it for good' (Genesis 50:20). That is sovereign grace.

## We respond with compassion

We see so much pain in our world and our human response mechanism copes by shutting down our anguish; we become desensitized to suffering. Terrible things are happening around us all the time and then suddenly it hits our soft, protected, democratic freedom. We have been blind and silent to so much suffering in the world, but then it is our turn and we want the whole world to feel for us and with us.

All over the world Christians are brutalised by cruel religious and non-religious groups and governments; churches are destroyed, congregations massacred, women and girls are raped and men are tortured. Every day of the year, far more people die either through deliberate genocide or from preventable hunger and thirst than were killed on September 11, but do we really care? Even Christians have lost the ability to cry over the condition of the widow and orphan. When it is far from our shores it is often far from our minds and terrible things can be done, even by our own armies, without so much as a whisper of objection. But compassion raises a voice of dissent and demands justice. Compassion is the very heart of God and the life of Christ (Matthew 9:36).

## We respond with constraint

Coincidentally, on Sunday 9 September 2001 I preached a sermon on Christian anger. It was in a series I had been following on the life of Samuel and the lessons for leadership that we can learn from this outstanding man. My text was from 1 Samuel 15:11, 'And Samuel was angry, and he cried to the LORD all night.' I commented that the sentence revealed an aspect of Samuel's character that is essential for any leader; a leader must at times be angry, because this reveals that he is a man who cares deeply—about God, and about God's law, about righteousness and justice, and about people. A man who is never angry has no convictions. Moses was angry in the valley of the golden calf (Exodus 32:19); Jonathan was angry at the way his father disgraced David, his own best friend (1 Samuel 20:34).

Righteous anger is a reflection of God himself; over thirty times in the Old Testament we read of the 'anger of the LORD' and there are almost one hundred more references to his anger and wrath. I reminded my congregation of the anger of Christ in the synagogue at Capernaum: 'He looked round at them with anger, grieved at their hardness of heart' (Mark 3:5). I distinguished between righteous anger (Ephesians 4:26) and the anger that is accompanied by bitterness, wrath, clamour, slander and malice (Ephesians 4:31).

Two days later the terrorists struck! We felt sick and distracted—and angry. We watched some in Palestine dancing and celebrating such inhuman carnage—and we became angrier still. We listened to the response of many around us: bomb all Muslims, blast Afghanistan, Iraq and anyone else who sympathised; turn away all asylum seekers, throw all Palestinians out of Israel. But blind and irrational reaction like this is not for the Christian. Those who believe in a God who is in control will pause to reflect and search for a purpose. Our concern is not for revenge but for justice; evil must be justly and righteously opposed. Beyond this, our concern must be to learn what God may be teaching us. The Christian who believes God has plans will pause to find a purpose.

## Finding a purpose

If God is in charge and always has a plan, can we ever discover his purpose? Paul reminded us: 'How unsearchable are his judgements and how inscrutable his ways!' His wisdom is deep—far beyond our understanding—and that is how we would expect it to be. If we could understand all there is to know about God and his ways, he would cease to be God, since he would be small enough to fit into the rational mind of a human being. So, why do such things happen? Here are four responses.

## First, God's purpose reveals the contrast between the badness of evil and the righteousness of good

Whilst it is certain that there are renegades among all philosophies of life that bring discredit to their founders, the contrast between the best that Christianity has offered the world in its two thousand year history and the best that atheism and the world religions have offered is evident for everyone to see. The Ten Commandments and the teaching of Christ in the Gospels still have a greater influence upon many nations than they choose to admit. Terrorism today survives only because of the freedoms enjoyed in nations that believe in the value of life. What governments, whether secular or religious, offer the best models for justice, freedom of conscience, compassion and the value of life? The answer, without exception, is those that have a legacy of Christian teaching and values. This is not to pretend that there has ever been such a thing as a Christian nation. It is all too obvious that the laws of God and the example and teaching of Christ have been relentlessly rejected by generations in Britain; but it takes many years of ingratitude and unbelief to squander entirely a rich legacy of social conviction. For all our wilful erosion of our Christian moral base, nations with a 'Christian' history are in the forefront of the relief of world famine and poverty, justice and freedom.

When God allows wicked men to triumph he is compelling us to think. The contrast between the wickedness of evil and the righteousness of good is intended to jump us out of our comfortable moral coma—that self-contented stupor that smugly believes we are morally superior to others. We should be asking just why we consider some actions to be wrong and others to be right? What was so very evil about the actions of 11 September 11? Many across the world believe that the destruction of over three thousand lives was a just response to what they consider to be a greater evil. How do we judge whether they are right or wrong, good or evil? By allowing such things to happen, God is forcing us to face such questions, and he is warning us that when we allow his laws to drift and we abandon the restraints that he sets on us for our good, then we are heading in the direction of a miserable moral maze. If we fail to take this lesson to heart when wickedness wins, then we have learnt nothing from sovereign grace.

The real tragedy of our western civilization is that we have allowed our moral base to be eroded so that we no longer have a clear definition of sin. The humanistic existential philosophy that controls so much of our thinking allows for no absolutes and therefore nothing is certainly right or wrong; today we can even talk about 'contradictory truth'—what is right for me may be wrong for you and vice versa. Once we have abandoned the rules that God gave us—and the Ten Commandments are a straightforward starting point—we have little or no hope of ever regaining a clear view of how we judge good and evil. At best, righteousness is simply what the majority like, and at worst it is a matter of national defence.

If I go on living high when in reality my bank balance is empty, it is nothing other than grace that bounces my cheques and forecloses my account. Similarly, when a nation is running down its stock of morality, it is grace when God allows evil to triumph. He is bouncing our cheque and alerting us to our moral bankruptcy.

## Second, God's compels us to act against evil

We take sin so lightly: worldwide slavery, easy abortion, endemic adultery and fast divorce, blasphemous boasting of irreligion, exploitation of the poor, haughty defiance of the moral laws of God;

these are all evidence of our selfish unconcern. Every year millions are left to die of hunger and disease in our deserts and wastelands and no action is taken against the nations that allow and often cause it to happen. Governments of the world remain silent at the blatant abuse of human rights in so many countries, simply because it is not in the interests of their national economy to raise a fuss. Then, suddenly, a few thousand die in a New York terrorist outrage and we come alive to injustice; our moral outrage knows no bounds. But we will only unite to defend ourselves, we still have little care for the defenceless millions. When wickedness wins, it is God's red alert to evil.

Christ forbade his followers to fight for his cause. True Christianity may result in suffering, but only because wickedness goes to war against it. There is no such thing as a holy war, whether or not it is religiously dignified with the word crusade or jihad. All war is unholy and evil, and if a religion does not denounce the concept of a 'holy war' then it is undoubtedly guilty in the eyes of God and is a religion to be rejected. Some wars have been necessary in the defence of freedom and justice—though not as many as history would like us to believe—but that does not make them holy. Christianity claims that all war is one of the evil results of a wicked world. To speak of a holy war is as precise as speaking of a holy lie, a holy theft, a holy rape or a holy murder.

Our response to wickedness should never be one of merely settling scores. Revenge will simply smash an iron fist where it thinks it will hurt most. Justice, on the other hand, will join forces to defeat evil honourably. If the nations had a mind to, they could destroy international terrorism—but they do not have a mind to. A sovereign God gives us a chance; he shocks us into action; he alerts us to a danger that not even the strongest nation can defeat on its own. It is utter selfishness if a nation merely defends its own interests when, together, we could work for global freedom and justice. Is that an impossible dream in a fallen world? Perhaps, but Christians should know how to pray for the impossible. The triumph of evil would be seen as grace if only we allowed it to spur us into just and effective action against all wickedness.

### Third, God's purpose displays the compassion that exists in the human race

There is something unique in the response of decent men and women at times of national and international disaster. The tears of sympathy, the letters of condolence, the e-mails and phone calls, even the feeling of outrage. There is a sense of unity in suffering. Whether it is the tiny premature baby gasping for life in the neo-natal incubator, the despairing community huddled in their rags on high ground as the torrent washes their flimsy homes into the raging river, or the dust choked firemen digging desperately at Ground Zero. Communities around the world that care for life, feel pain at the horror of the way people suffer and die.

This is not 'Christianizing' society because of its sudden sympathy and willing charitable response. But what God is showing us is what the human race is capable of. There is love, compassion, protective care, and understanding among us that is unknown in the animal world. That is a positive illustration that we are not animals, but are created in the image and likeness of God.

If a slag tip slides and engulfs a rabbit warren, do those that escape turn and spend days, even weeks, digging to rescue the buried bunnies? I have seen a herd of impala and blue wildebeest stop running the moment an animal is brought down by a cheetah; but instead of turning to charge, which would inevitably have forced the hunter to flee for its life, they simply snorted their breathlessness and resumed their grazing in sight of the big cat enjoying his meal. I know there are some animals that will defend their young at the hazard of their own lives, but when the battle is over and the young is taken, it is all soon forgotten. A cow mourns for its calf for one night only.

Where does the exceptional sympathy of the human race come from? It is nothing less that a reflection of the image of God. We are unique in creation. The reason why at worst the human race can behave more hideously than anything in the animal kingdom and can be repugnantly and totally evil, is because at best we can be beautifully and supremely good. We know how to be loving, kind, and compassionate, and therefore we are all the more guilty when we fail to be that. When God allows wickedness to win he is alerting us to the best, as well as the worst, that we are capable of. That too is sovereign grace.

## Fourth, God's purpose blows a trumpet of warning and offers a message of hope

When the tower in Siloam collapsed and killed eighteen people, Jesus drew two applications from their death: first, they did not die because they were more sinful than anyone else, and second, their death was a warning that we all die for our sin (Luke 13:4–5). What Jesus was saying was that this disaster, tragic though it was, would prove beneficial only if those who were not destroyed by it would learn from it. It is a warning of a judgement to come—of the ultimate effects of sin unrestrained and unforgiven. Terrible things happen to a community, not necessarily because that community is more sinful than others, but as a reminder that such tragedies are the inevitable result of a fallen world, and they point to a greater and final disaster. When God stands back and lets evil have its way, he is warning of the dreadful consequences of sin.

In John's apocalyptic vision in the Bible there is a vivid and poetic reflection of much that we see in our modern world: 'I looked, and behold, there was a great earthquake, and the sun became black as sackcloth, the full moon became like blood, and the stars of the sky fell to the earth as the fig tree sheds its winter fruit when shaken by a gale. The sky vanished like a scroll that is being rolled up, and every mountain and island was removed from its place. Then the kings of the earth and the great ones and the generals and the rich and the powerful, and everyone, slave and free, hid themselves in the caves and among the rocks of the mountains, calling to the mountains and rocks, "Fall on us and hide us from the face of him who is seated on the throne, and from the wrath of the Lamb, for the great day of their wrath has come, and who can stand?"'(Revelation 6:12–14).

Whenever we see or hear of a reflection of this dramatic picture in a modern disaster or outrage, it is a reminder that there is worse to come; it is a trumpet call from God alerting us to the inevitable outcome of sin and evil. If we will not learn that all is not well with the world, what will we learn? And if it does not convince us that we are not in control of the world we often boastfully assume we have mastered, what will convince us?

Every great tragedy is God's interim trumpet call of warning that there is a final day coming—and then a great divide. C S Lewis in his book *The Problem of Pain* expressed this clearly: 'God whispers to us in our pleasures, speaks in our conscience, but shouts in our pains: it is his megaphone to rouse a deaf world.' The final trumpet call from heaven will be heard at the end of time when the dead will rise and Christ will return with his angels in power and glory: 'The trumpet will sound … and we shall be changed' (1 Corinthians 15:52; 1 Thessalonians 4:16).

However, the same trumpet that warns of the law and of judgement will be a different kind of music to those who are waiting for his coming. It is the herald of that eternal kingdom where no sin and evil exists, but only pure joy and peace in the presence of a holy, just and righteous God and with Jesus Christ our Friend and Saviour. The cross makes all things new. Repentance and forgiveness lead to the promise of heaven. Christ offers new people here and new hope there. Perhaps our Lord would say to us: 'Early on the morning of 11 September 2001, thousands had no idea that they would soon be rushed into eternity. Do you think they died because they were more sinful than most? No, but unless you repent, you also will perish.'

# Chapter 3

GOD IS OUR REFUGE AND OUR STRENGTH,
our ever-present aid,
and therefore though the earth should move,
we will not be afraid;
though hills are thrown into the sea,
though foaming waters roar,
and though the mighty earthquake moves
the mountains on the shore.

2. A river flows whose streams make glad
the city of our God,
the holy place in which the Lord
most High has his abode;
since God is in the midst of her,
unmoved her walls shall stand,
for God will help at break of day,
when trouble is at hand.

3. The nations rage, and kingdoms fall,
but when his voice is heard
all earthly power shall melt away
before his mighty word.
The LORD of hosts is on our side,
our safety to secure;
the God of Jacob is for us
a refuge strong and sure.

4. O come and see what mighty works
the hand of God has done;
come, see what desolation great
he brings beneath the sun.

To utmost ends of all the earth
he causes wars to cease;
the weapons of the strong destroyed,
he makes a lasting peace.

**5.** 'Be still and know that I am God,
set over all on high;
the humbled nations of the earth
my name shall magnify.'
The LORD of hosts is on our side,
our safety to secure;
the God of Jacob is for us
a refuge strong and sure.

The Psalter 1912, alt.
© in this version Praise Trust
*Praise!* 46A

## FOR GROUP DISCUSSION

**1.** Is there any part of the Epicurean riddle that you agree with?

**2.** Is there any difference between the claim that 'God plans to use the violence and cruelty of evil men for his own purposes' and the claim that 'God plans the violence and cruelty of evil men for his own purposes'?

**3.** How far do you agree with the 'four simple but vital statements of Christian conviction?'

**4.** Discuss how you would respond briefly and simply to the accusation: 'How can you believe in God with all the suffering in the world?'

**5.** In the face of a terrible tragedy in the life of your non-Christian friend could you use Romans 11:33, and if so, how?

# The grace of law

'The law is holy, and the commandment is holy and righteous and good'
Romans 7:12

Across the River Jordan, on the western side of the road towards
the setting sun in the land of the Canaanites, were two great hills
rising some fifteen hundred feet above the valley floor. The land
between provided a natural amphitheatre and it was there that the twelve
tribes of Israel were to assemble at the two hills called Ebal and Gerizim.
On Ebal they built a cairn of stones and wrote on it the words of the law
of God they had received forty years earlier at Sinai. Beside the cairn they
built a stone altar on which they offered sacrifices for the forgiveness of
their sin. Wherever there was law, there was the offer of forgiveness.
Both the law and forgiveness were grace.

The Levites on Mount Ebal would declare the judgements that would
come if Israel broke the law, and the Levites on Mount Gerizim would
declare the blessings that would follow obedience to the law
(Deuteronomy chapters 11, 27 and 28). This law revealed by God to
Moses covered every area of the life of Israel and was, 'no empty word for
you, but your very life' (Deuteronomy 32:47). God was insistent that all
who lived in Israel, including foreigners, women and children, should
hear, learn and obey the law of God.

In our English translation of Deuteronomy 28 there are fourteen verses
recounting the blessings (vs 1–14), but fifty-four that focus on the penalty
of disobedience (vs 15–68). Why this disparity? The greater the blessing,
the greater the penalty if it is lost. Everyone wants a life of happiness, but
few want to take seriously the conditions attached. This was true of

Israel three and half millennia ago, and it is true today. But grace gave the law and the warnings—and the promises attached.

## Conscience and the grace of law

Conscience is universal, as we saw in chapter one. However, although conscience can tell us that there *is* right and wrong, it can never reliably tell us *what* is right and wrong. This is why standards change from generation to generation, from society to society, and from culture to culture. It is also why men can commit depraved and cruel acts and not only convince themselves that they are right, but that they are even pleasing their god. This is because our conscience is spoilt by sin (1 Timothy 4:2).

This is why God gave the world a revelation of his laws. He began in the Old Testament, and the psalmist declares that God's word is a lamp and a light to guide him through life (Psalm 119:105). The principles of God's law revealed in the Old Testament cover every area of life. The law was given chiefly through Moses 3500 years ago and is found in the books of Exodus to Deuteronomy. For convenience we can divide the laws given by God into two parts, though it must be understood that the Jews themselves never made this distinction. First there was the moral law which covered all human relationships including marriage and sex, social and business relationships, leadership and judges, employers and employees, health and safety, hygiene and employment, property rights, the treatment of animals and even ecology. The Ten Commandments are a summary of this moral law. The second part of the law was the priestly ceremonial which included the detailed religious observances which was God's way of preparing his people for the coming of Christ. The ceremonial law taught people the seriousness of sin by the death of an animal sacrifice; it led them to repentance and then, through the offerings and sacrifices, assured them of forgiveness and reconciliation with God.

The reason why the Israelites made no distinction between the moral and ceremonial law was that there was a vital link between the two. For them the law was one undivided piece; to break the ceremonial law was every bit as bad as breaking the moral law. Uzzah bore the same penalty for touching the Ark of God (2 Samuel 6:3–7 cf. Numbers 7:6–9) as he would have for committing murder or adultery (Leviticus 20:12, 14). The moral law revealed how holy God is and how far short everyone falls. The priestly law revealed how holy God is and how completely anyone can be forgiven. This is the grace of law.

## The law and the Christian

In the history of the church, the law has been seen by Christians to have three uses: first to convict sinners of sin, second to keep the unruly in check, and third to guide Christians in the path of holiness—this last one is what is known as 'the third use of the law'. But above these three there are two more important uses. The law reveals to the world what a holy, wise and gracious God we worship (Deuteronomy 4:6–8), and it is also our tutor to guard us and lead us to Christ (Galatians 3:24). The Greek word *paidagogos* that Paul uses here in Galatians carried the meaning of tutor in the first century, because the 'child minder' was often the educator as well.

If the law has any value at all we must learn how best to use it. Paul pointed out that the law is holy, righteous, good and spiritual (Romans 7:12, 14), and he repeated this to Timothy: 'We know that the law is good' (1 Timothy 1:8). He reminded the Christians at Rome that everything written in the Old Testament is intended for us (Romans 15:4), and when he encouraged Timothy to teach the Christians at Ephesus that, 'All Scripture … is profitable for teaching, for reproof, for correction, and for training in righteousness, that the man of God may be competent, equipped for every good work' it was the whole Old Testament that was in the apostle's mind (2 Timothy 3:16–17).

For the Christian, the value of the law is not as a big stick with which to be beaten constantly, but as a friendly guide to pull him back into line when he is tempted to stray. It is no longer his enemy as it once was. This must be what Paul meant when in Romans 7:6 he claimed, 'Now we are released from the law, having died to that which held us captive, so that we serve not under the old written code but in the new life of the Spirit.' It is this spiritual interpretation of the law that the Christian is looking for. Far from dismissing the value and significance of the law, this enhances it; the Christian is able to employ the law in a way that few in the Old Testament could. It is what Paul meant when he encouraged the Galatians—a church severely tempted to return to a strict observance of the Old Testament rule of law—to 'walk by the Spirit' (Galatians 5:16, 25); this was his new 'rule' for them (6:16). This new spiritual life can be compared, not to the government official who is overwhelmed by the bureaucratic red tape of officialdom, but to the relationship between a husband and wife who have family rules that will be observed in loving regard for each other's benefit. The Old Testament law was not intended as a club to beat the nation with. Doubtless this would have been true of some, but we have seen how David loved the law with all his heart.

## The Spirit and the law

In the New Testament Paul left us examples of how the law should be wisely and properly used. The law has a value for vital moral choices that we are confronted with in our society. It will no longer be the dead letter of the law that the Christian slavishly adheres to, but the application of law spiritually understood. This is precisely what Jesus did in his Sermon on the Mount and what Paul constantly did in his letters to the young churches.

One illustration of Paul's use of the Old Testament is found when he encouraged the young churches to support financially those working in gospel ministry. Paul focused on Deuteronomy 25:4, 'You shall not muzzle an ox when it is treading out the grain.' His reasoning in

1 Corinthians 9:8–11 is that this passage in the Old Testament law is not only, or even primarily, about our concern for the welfare of animals, but it has a much wider and more spiritual application. This is a perfect example of a Christian application of Old Testament law. The whole New Testament ethic is an exposition of Old Testament law. When one writer criticises 'expositions of the Decalogue [that] move from crime to "deeper applications"', he may have forgotten that this is precisely what Paul is doing here and exactly what our Lord did in his Sermon on the Mount.

Admittedly there are parts of the law where we find it hard to understand exactly what their application is for us today, but when applied through the filter of the life and ministry of Christ and the apostles, the Old Testament law is full of instruction. Here are just a handful of examples among many.

Leviticus 11 lists all the animals that Israel could eat or must avoid eating; they were known as the 'clean' and 'unclean' animals. Within that record is the instruction that if a housewife discovered that a lizard had fallen into her kneading bowl, she must break the bowl and destroy any food that was left in it (vs 33–34). That may seem a harsh response when she could more easily have washed out the bowl. However, the severity of the law would soon help her to realise that it would be far more sensible never to leave food overnight in an uncovered bowl, and that it would be wiser for her to turn all unused kitchenware upside down. This is not trivial when you consider that in some countries millions die from dysentery simply because such basic rules of hygiene are neglected.

Deuteronomy 22 is an Old Testament chapter that deals with lost property, neighbourliness, transvestism, ecology, health and safety, agriculture and horticulture, marriage relationships, adultery, and rape. Is there nothing for the modern world to learn in a passage like this? In any discussion on the wise use of the earth's resources, is there nothing to learn from the simple check on egg-collecting found in Deuteronomy

22:6–7? If our Victorian forefathers had paid attention to the principles enshrined in Deuteronomy 22:8 then thousands of little children, who were operating unguarded machinery, would not have been so brutally maimed and killed. This is precisely why Jesus told the Pharisees that they should not neglect tithing but should look for the 'weightier matters of the law' (Matthew 23:23).

This does not place us under the burden of insignificant rules and regulations if we allow the Spirit to guide us in interpreting and applying the law. Legalism is the result of an obsession with legal details. When we demand total adherence to the minutiae of the law we have forgotten how our Lord intended us to use it. The good citizen always loves good laws; it is only the law-breaker who hates them. The psalmist Asaph could think of nothing more wonderful in this life as a preparation for the next, than the guidance of God in his word leading him to God himself: 'You guide me with your counsel, and afterwards you will receive me to glory. Whom have I in heaven but you? And there is nothing on earth that I desire besides you' (Psalm 73:24–25). The more I understand the whole law of God the more I will know the meaning of loving God and loving my neighbour. Explaining this to a young reader, John Newton claimed that the Christian who uses the law in this way 'acquires an habitual, spiritual taste of what is right or wrong.' That is precisely the purpose of the grace of law.

When we are learning to play the piano, one of the most important points is to look carefully where we place our fingers on the keyboard. Similarly we have to pay attention to the notes on the sheet music in front of us; we must observe carefully whether a note is above, on or below the line and whether the note is black or white and whether it has a tail or not– it all makes a lot of difference. At first this is painfully slow and tedious. We make many mistakes and the concentration is enormous. I compare this to the way the Israelites used the Old Testament law. It was detailed and laborious and often it must have proved tedious and irritating—but it was all vitally necessary. In the course of time and with practice, it is possible to play accurately by obeying every rule of music— but the result may still be flat, insensitive and dead; it is without life or soul. That is like the legalism of a wrong use of Old Testament law. However, the concert pianist no longer focuses on those basic rules—she uses them and they are still essential if she is to play well—but now she concentrates on bringing life and soul into her music. Far from ignoring or destroying the rules she learnt in grade one, she now wants to give them greater value. She applies them in such a way as to express thought and feeling in order to make the music come alive and touch the soul— and she does so with hardly any conscious awareness of those basic laws. But if she makes a mistake, or is ever tempted to defy the rules of music, they are always there to bring her back into line. That is just how the New Testament Christian applies the law.

## No more Law?

At the very time when the moral downgrade in western civilization is crying out for clear standards of right and wrong, many Christians have cut loose the Maker's instructions. Whatever the reason, so-called 'new covenant theology' that denies any value of the Old Testament law for the life of the Christian, is becoming increasingly popular.

There are few subjects where evangelicals present such a kaleidoscope of differing opinions than on the place of the law of God in the life of the Christian. They range from the Christian Reconstructionist who writes law books based on the Old Testament for the guidance of governments today, and for their expected post-millennial age, to the dispensationalist and new covenant theologians who believe that the law should have no influence over Christians whatever. Michael Eaton in *A Theology of Encouragement* assures us that the law has no claim whatsoever upon the Christian and although we can 'derive wisdom from it' we cannot apply it to the modern society or to the life of the Christian.

Whatever arguments are levelled against the value of the law of God, we must take into account such biblical statements as:

'Do we, then, overthrow the law by this faith? By no means! On the contrary, we uphold the law'                                                      (Romans 3:31)
'The law is holy, and the commandment is holy and righteous and good'
(Romans 7:12)
'Whatever was written in the former days was written for our instruction'
(Romans 15:4)
'Keeping God's commands is what counts'
(1 Corinthians 7:19 *New International Version*)
'But we know that the law is good, if one uses it lawfully'        (1 Timothy 1:8)
'All Scripture ... is profitable for teaching, for reproof, for correcting, and for training in righteousness'                                          (2 Timothy 3:16)

## For Israel alone?

The law was a mark of God's special relationship with Israel, but in return they were intended to be an example to the nations. Their possession and practice of the law was meant to say to the surrounding tribes: this is how holy the only true God is and how holy his people live, and therefore this is how God expects all nations to live. By revealing the law to Israel alone, God was not suggesting that the nations could please themselves, else why did he punish them for their immoral life-style? In fact, by what measure was it immoral if God's law was not their standard? In Deuteronomy 4:5–8 God underlined the evangelistic value of the law by reminding his people that they were to be a witness to the nations who, learning of the laws of Israel may conclude: 'What great nation ... has a god so near to it as the LORD our God ... And that has statutes and rules so righteous as all this law?'

Significantly, in Deuteronomy 31:12–13 God included even the foreigners living in Israel among those who must listen to and obey the law: 'Assemble the people, men, women, and little ones, and the sojourner within your towns, that they may hear and learn to fear the LORD your God, and be careful to do all the words of this law, and that their children, who have not known it, may hear and learn to fear the LORD your God, as long as you live in the land that you are going over the Jordan to possess.' We cannot suggest that the phrase 'as long as you live in the land' means that God was perfectly content for them to abandon his law if they moved away from Israel. Did God have one acceptable standard for Israel and another for the rest of the world?

Besides, if no one other than the Jews in the Old Testament were under an obligation to the law, in what sense did Christ die to redeem *us* from the curse of the law (Galatians 3:13)? How can Christ be said to have died to purchase our freedom from the consequences of breaking a law that we were not expected to keep?

## Jesus 'fulfilled the law'

The little word 'fulfil' in the Sermon on the Mount, is surrounded by three significant statements of our Lord. In Matthew 5:17 he claims, 'I have not come to abolish the Law or the Prophets', in the following verse he declares, 'until heaven and earth pass away, not an iota, not a dot, will pass from the Law until all is accomplished', and in verse 19 our Lord warns, 'Therefore whoever relaxes one of the least of these commandments and teaches others to do the same will be called least in the kingdom of heaven.' It is unwise to suggest that the phrase, 'these commandments' refers to the teaching of Christ that follows since the whole context is the enduring Old Testament law, and verse 19 is an application of verse 18; in other words he is saying, 'the law lasts, and if you break it you will be least'. Only in John 14:15,21 and 15:10 do we have a record of our Lord referring to his own teaching as 'commandments'; that word is normally reserved for the Old Testament Law (for example Matthew 19:17 and 22:40).

The same word 'fulfil' is found in the account of our Lord's baptism in Matthew 3:15 when he responded to John the Baptist: 'It is fitting for us to fulfil all righteousness.' By this he did not mean that he should do away with righteousness, but that he must do everything to discharge his obligation to it. Therefore the same word in Matthew 5 means to carry out and accomplish everything expected in the law. John Newton once wrote, 'It is an abuse both of law and gospel, to pretend that its accomplishment by Christ released believers from an obligation to it as a rule.'

By his words and his actions Jesus reinforced a proper understanding and application of the law of God. For example, in his condemnation of the legalism of the Scribes and Pharisees he drew attention to their precise tithing of herbs. Whilst jibing at their pernickety insistence upon the minute counting of 'mint and dill and cumin', he complained that they had neglected, 'the weightier matters of the law: justice and mercy and faithfulness', but significantly added, 'These you ought to have done, without neglecting the others'(Matthew 23:23). Their tithing was not wrong but they had placed insistence upon the letter of the law above a life of love. Christ came to enrich the law, not destroy it; and he did this best of all by his life—his was the most beautiful expression of the law in action that this world will ever see. Newton claimed that Christ is the 'transcript of the law'.

## Love is all we need?

At the finale for the Queen's Golden Jubilee pop concert in her garden at Buckingham Palace on 3 June 2002 the catchy phrase: 'All we need is love, love is all we need' was sung with great enthusiasm by millions around the world. This gospel according to the Beatles is taken up enthusiastically by many today—and Christians can fall into the same trap.

In Romans 13:8–10 Paul lists four commandments and concludes that all the others may be summed up in this way: 'You shall love your neighbour as yourself.' Similarly in Galatians 5:14 he claims that the entire law is summed up in a single command: 'Love your neighbour as yourself.' In the first of these two statements, Paul used one word that is translated by the words 'fulfilled' and 'fulfilling', and that word is the one used by our Lord at his baptism and in his Sermon on the Mount in Matthew 5:17. As we have seen, it implies fully carrying out rather than destroying. But the word translated 'summed up' in Romans 13:9 is interesting because it means what it says: to condense something into a summary. That is exactly what the law of love is—it is a summary of the whole law—not a replacement for it.

There can be no doubt about this conclusion because in Galatians 5:14 Paul is not making love a New Testament substitute for Old Testament law since his statement: 'You shall love your neighbour as yourself' is a quotation taken directly from Leviticus 19:18! Besides, by suggesting that the commandments can be summed up in this one rule that we should love our neighbour as ourselves, Paul cannot mean that *all* commandments without exception are summed up in this way—at least the first three of the Ten Commandments relate primarily to our love of God.

However, a summary does not dispense with the details. I may describe a collection of moulded steel, cast iron, electrical wiring, leather upholstery, reinforced glass, plastic, and an assortment of nuts, bolts and screws. But I summarise all this by telling you that I have just bought a motor car. That simple word 'car' does not destroy the detail, it merely summarises it.

When our Lord was asked which one is the greatest commandment in the law, he replied by offering a short summary: 'You shall love the Lord your God with all your heart and with all your soul and with all your mind. This is the great and first commandment. And a second is like it: You shall love your neighbour as yourself. On these two commandments *depend* all the Law and the Prophets' (Matthew 22:37–40). He made it quite clear that the summary did not dispense with the detail. This is apparent by the word that is translated 'depend'. It is used of leaves that hang from a tree or a door that is hung on its hinges. Some translations actually use the word 'hang'. All the law and the prophets are summarized by the law of love for their full and proper expression. But love no more means that we can do without law than the existence of trees means we can do without leaves or hinges means that we can do without a door.

In John 13:34 Christ did not give his disciples a new command that they should love one another, he was merely quoting—just as Paul did—from the law itself found in Leviticus. What was new in the command that Christ gave was this: 'Just as I have loved you, you also are to love one another.' That is uniquely Christian. Quite simply we need the law to guide and control our definition of love, because love alone is too subjective. Let's be very practical:

Two young people love each other, so they decide to sleep together. Is this right? How do we know? Love does not tell us, but the law does.

A man loves a woman and so he leaves his wife and family to go with her. Is this right? How do we know? Love does not decide, but the law does.

A man is cruel to his wife so her brother kills the brutal husband to protect his sister whom he loves. Is this right? Love does not tell us, but the law does.

Two men, or two women, enjoy intimate sexual relationships because they love each other. Is that right? Again, love does not tell us, but the law does.

A poor man steals to buy his children Christmas presents because he loves them. Is that right? Love may say it is, but it is the law that teaches us otherwise.

A woman lies to protect her friend whom she loves. Is that right? Only the law can tell us.

These moral issues are not answered by love alone. Our moral decisions must be motivated by love monitored by law. The law restrains love from its excesses whilst love releases law from its harshness. It was the law of love that meant Christ could discharge the woman who was taken in adultery from the legal penalty of death. The law condemned her and rightly so. This is a beautiful example of love and law in action: 'Neither do I condemn you; go, and from now on sin no more' (John 8:11). It is the grace of law when it keeps love in check.

## 'Not under law but under grace'

It is clear from the context of Romans 6:14 that far from denying the value of the law, Paul is establishing a higher motivation in our life: 'For sin will not have dominion over you, since you are not under law but under grace'. The law is no longer our master and it no longer condemns us. Christ is our master and his death releases us from all the condemning judgement of the law. More than this, his Spirit enables us to understand the value of the law and delight in applying it to our lives. In a highly significant phrase in verse 17, Paul recognises that whilst we were once slaves of sin, in Christ we have now become obedient, 'from the heart to the standard of teaching to which you were committed'—that must refer to the law. We are now 'slaves of righteousness' (verse 18). In his detailed and careful argument in Romans 7 and 8 about the law, Paul makes clear that the law standing on its own can only increase my sin and condemn me; it can neither give me life nor the power to overcome sin. However, once I am set free from the power and condemnation of the law by the Spirit of life in Christ, that which once was my enemy can become my friend. We are not saved *by* obedience to the law, but we are saved *for* obedience to the law.

## The law written in our hearts

A frequently quoted promise from the Old Testament is Jeremiah 31:33. All are agreed that this refers to the new era of the Spirit after Pentecost: '"This is the covenant that I will make with the house of Israel after those days", declares the LORD: "I will put my law within them, and I will write it on their hearts. And I will be their God, and they shall be my people."'

What does this refer to? Since Jeremiah refers to 'my law' six times and on every occasion it can only refer to the law of God (see 6:19; 9:13; 16:11; 26:4; 31:33; 44:10), it must be the Old Testament law that God writes on our hearts under the new covenant. But are we to assume that none of the Old Testament saints ever kept the law of God joyfully, willingly, and wholeheartedly? Such a conclusion would be hard to square with the psalmist's expressions of love for God's word in Psalm 119 where on ten occasions he declares his 'delight' in the law, on seven he declares how he 'loves' God's law, and further comments how he has stored it in his heart (v 11), kept it with his 'whole heart' (vs 34,69), and 'longs for it' (vs 20,40). The distinction is this: under the old covenant every member of Israel belonged to the people of the promise though not all lived by faith and therefore many obeyed the law grudgingly; however, under the new covenant every member will be a true believer serving God and his law with a glad heart. David in Psalm 119 enjoyed the law in his heart under new covenant blessing.

## The New Testament and the law

In 1 Corinthians 10:6–10 Paul provides us with four cameos of the disobedience of Israel in the wilderness which illustrate four of the Ten Commandments. Commandments 1,2,7,10 are clearly in focus here and Paul concludes, 'these things happened to them as an example, but they were written down for our instruction' (v 11). More significantly is the fact that in Romans 13:9, Paul lists four of the Ten Commandments, embraces the rest by the statement: 'and any other commandment', and then summarises them by quoting, not from the teaching of Jesus, but directly from Leviticus 19:18. He offers not a word of hesitation or warning on the use of Old Testament law. As one writer comments, 'Paul appears to have no problem quoting from the Decalogue and leaving it at that.'

A third passage is 1 Timothy 1:5–11. Here Paul states that the law is good and is to be used—provided it is used 'lawfully'. Therefore there must be a right and a wrong way to use the law of God, and in vs 6–7 he refers to those who teach the law in the wrong way—though Paul does not define in what way they misused the law. However, he does indicate the correct use of the law: it is not needed for those who already obey its dictates (the just or righteous of v 9, and compare with Matthew 9:13 and Philippians 3:6) but it is for those who do not, whether Christian or non Christian. In other words, the law is a clear marker for righteous living; it has little to say to the righteous man—until he steps out of line. To underline this, Paul provides Timothy with a sin-list that follows the order of the Ten Commandments precisely (vs 9–10) and he concludes that these—and anything else that contradicts the law—is 'contrary to sound doctrine'. In other words, adherence to the law is part of what Paul calls 'sound doctrine'.

## The grace of law

Both law and love are the grace of God. We are never to talk of 'grace *or* law', as if they are opposites—Paul tells us that the law is not 'contrary to the promises of God' (Galatians 3:21). Nor should we talk of 'grace *and* law', as if they are compatible differences. But we can speak of 'the grace *of* law'. Law was God's grace to define and confine sin, and it still is because it still does. Keeping in step with the Spirit is never to be divorced from keeping in step with his law.

When Christians 'talk down' the law of God, they do a serious disservice to the God of all grace who gave his rules to us in the first place; they equally do a great disservice to a world living in a moral maze with only the sin-branded conscience of society to guide it. They do a great disservice also to a generation of young Christians struggling to learn just how they can claim that there are in existence standards stamped with God's authority. It is of little help for them to be told that the revelation of the law in the Old Testament is irrelevant for the twenty-first century, or even that though the world needs some of it, Christians need none of it.

King Alfred the Great, who became the first king to unite much of England under his rule, placed the Ten Commandments at the beginning of the law book for his subjects and showed how they should be understood: 'by the love and compassion of the Lord Christ.' The puritan Thomas Watson once wrote, 'They who will not have the law to rule them shall have the law to judge them.' Or, as a wise old Methodist preacher once commented, 'We either keep the Ten Commandments or we illustrate them.' Better still, David in the Old Testament declared: 'I find my delight in your commandments, which I love' (Psalm 119:47). It is remarkably sad that King David could declare: 'Open my eyes, that I may behold wondrous things out of your law' (Psalm 119:18), whilst many Christians three thousand years later can find nothing wonderful in them at all.

HOW CAN THE WAY OF YOUTH BE PURE,
what guiding light can wisdom give?
Their path, O LORD, shall be secure
if by your holy word they live.

2. With all my heart I seek you, LORD;
O let me not from you depart!
To guard my steps from sin, your word
I safely cherish in my heart.

3. All praise, O gracious LORD be yours!
Teach me the truth of your decrees;
so with my lips I speak your laws,
your precepts and your promises.

**4.** As those who in their wealth rejoice
so is my joy to heed your ways;
my ears will listen to your voice,
my mind reflect, my mouth give praise.

**5.** As your decrees are my delight
so shall I not neglect your law;
here is my study, day and night,
here may I walk for evermore.

The Psalter 1912, Alt.
© in this version Praise Trust
*Praise!* 119C Psalm 119:9–16

## FOR GROUP DISCUSSION

1. Can you defend the suggestion that it legitimate to make a distinction between the moral and ceremonial law in the Old Testament?
2. What do you think John Newton meant when he claimed that Christ is the 'transcript of the law'.
3. In Deuteronomy 22 can you find at least three of the laws that provide significant principles to guide us in the 21st century?
4. How would you respond to the claim that 'Love is all we need'?
5. How do you reconcile these two statements by Paul: 'Now we are released from the law' (Romans 7:6) and 'We know that the law is good, if one uses it properly' (1 Timothy 1:8)?

# Justifying grace

'He was delivered up for our trespasses and raised for our justification'
Romans 4:25

When Paul wrote 1 Corinthians 15, his purpose was to convince the Corinthian Christians of the essential reality of the resurrection of Jesus Christ from the dead. He had not hazarded his life riding stormy, pirate-infested seas and trekking across harsh, bandit-ridden wastelands to tell the Corinthians a make-believe tale of fantasies past. So, he taught them why the literal, physical resurrection of Jesus Christ from the dead was so vital to their faith, and he even provided them with a list of those who had seen the risen Christ for themselves to whom they could apply if they wanted to take up references for the truth of his story. At the end of that list Paul declared, 'Last of all ... he appeared to me also' (v 8).

Paul had problems convincing the Corinthian Christians of his authority, and as a result his relationship with them was stormy. The church at Corinth had enough moral, spiritual, and doctrinal baggage to sink a Roman galley, and more than once they rejected Paul and accused him of pulling apostolic rank when he tried to correct the abuses within the congregation. To convince them of his authority as a true apostle, Paul insists that when the Lord had finished appearing to all the others, 'he appeared also to me'. Then, immediately, Paul described himself as one who was 'untimely born'.

Paul used a vivid word here. 'Untimely born' (*ektroma*) referred to an abortion or a miscarriage and it was sometimes used as a word of abuse. First century records show that it would be hurled contemptuously at someone who was despised. It was not unlike our word 'bastard' that started out in life simply as a descriptive word, but in the course of time became an insult. A modern colloquialism would be 'a waste of space', although that is far too gentle as an insult compared with the strength of this word. When used in the Old Testament (Numbers 12:12; Job 3:16; Ecclesiastes 6:3) it was always of something pitiable. Paul didn't come from Palestine or follow around with Jesus like the mainstream apostles. In fact Jesus only appeared to Saul of Tarsus when he was no longer appearing to anyone else. Paul was painfully aware of his past as a violent, bad tempered, arrogant destroyer of Christians. So, when the Corinthians contemptuously referred to him as an inferior apostle—a waste of apostolic space—Paul did not argue with that. He conceded, 'I am the least of all the apostles.'

Seven times in his letters he admits that he once aggressively went after the Christian Church. One example is found in Galatians 1:13 where Paul admits that in his former way of life he 'persecuted the church of God violently and tried to destroy it.' In Acts 26:11 he described his attitude towards the Christians as one of 'raging fury'. It was Saul's all-consuming ambition to be the man who strangled the infant Christian church at birth. He was guilty of the death of the first Christian martyr, and doubtless he could still hear in his mind the words that echoed from the sky outside the walls of Damascus in that life-changing encounter with Christ, 'Saul, Saul, why are you persecuting me … I am Jesus whom you are persecuting.'

## What is sin, really?

Whatever sins Paul had committed—and there were many—this is where everything focussed: Saul of Tarsus was a Christ-rejecter. He fought against Christ. We should never begin by focussing upon our particular sins, however terrible they may be. We may have wrecked our life and the lives of others by addictions or cruelty or greed. But counting up sins is not the place to begin. Preachers can spend many pulpit hours listing sins, but some will go away feeling confident that everybody else had been well and truly lambasted but they themselves are free from accusation. The great issue that should confront everyone is that they have rejected Christ and therefore God.

On one occasion, when Jesus had trounced the Sadducees on a point regarding the resurrection, the Pharisees weighed in. They were glad to see their opponents put down and they came up with a particular question that lay within their field of expertise. It was to do with the law of God, and that was decidedly their territory; no one knew more about the law than the Pharisees did. 'Teacher', they queried, 'Which is the great commandment?' (Mathew 22:34–46). The idea was to force our Lord to be selective with the Decalogue—the Ten Commandments; if he chose one above the others, they could accuse him of undermining the rest. But our Lord, always a step ahead of his opponents, bypassed Exodus 20 and went instead to Deuteronomy 6:5, 'You shall love the Lord your God with all your heart and with all your soul and with all your might.' This, concluded our Lord, is the first and great commandment. In breaking that command—and all honest people must admit that they have—we have broken the greatest commandment and therefore we have committed the greatest sin. But at the same time, our Lord immediately went on to reveal himself as the Son of God. It was his insistent claim that to receive him was to receive God, and to reject him was to reject God. The record in Luke 10:16 makes this clear: 'The one who rejects me rejects him who sent me' (see also Matthew 10:40; John 12:44–45; 13:20; 15:21). As far as Christ was concerned, no one can love God and please him unless they accept the Son of God. To be a Christ-rejecter is to place ourselves outside the Kingdom of God, whether Jew or non Jew.

No amount of preaching against sins would ever have convicted Saul of Tarsus; what finally convinced him were the words from heaven: 'I am

Jesus, whom you are persecuting.' What Saul had to learn was that he was a Christ-rejecter, and that this was his most serious sin. His rigorous religion, his knowledge of the Old Testament law, his zeal as an enthusiastic supporter of Judaism: they all counted for nothing if he was a Christ-rejecter.

John Newton was almost everything Saul was not. His formal education ended before he reached his teens and his future seemed destined for the short, inconspicuous average of an eighteenth century sailor—a bawdy, blasphemous and lecherous drunkard. Press-ganged onto a man-of-war at the age of nineteen, he refined his education with a philosophy to match his lusts and after fifteen months exchanged his Majesty's Navy for the slave trade in Sierra Leone. Within a short while he was a slave himself and his condition was little removed from that of an animal. By a remarkable turn of events Newton, shivering amidst the debris of a sinking ship and a tattered conscience, came to faith in Christ. Saul, on the other hand, was a respectable, well educated and pious Jew convinced that he was serving God and keeping the law of God as best he could. The two men could hardly be more different. But that is a superficial assessment of the two men. The only significant difference between Saul of Tarsus and John of Wapping was seventeen hundred years! Both of them were Christ-rejecters, ignorantly pitting themselves against the Lord himself.

Before we can become a Christian, whoever we are and whatever our background, we must admit that we are Christ-rejecters. We may not have seen it like this, but unless we do see it in this way, we will never understand the meaning of the word grace. This may not fit well with those who have been brought up in a Christian home or a strongly upright and religious environment. Perhaps we have always believed in Jesus and have always been sincere about God and Christian things. We may argue, 'I am not so bad. I am not like Saul of Tarsus or John of Wapping.' Perhaps not. We may not have sunk to the moral depths of

John or risen to the religious heights of Saul, but we must never forget that the devil has his activists and his pacifists, his believers and his unbelievers, his successes and his failures. Grace is only experienced when we recognise that whatever else we thought we were, we have been Christ-rejecters

## Justifying grace

Paul uses the word grace around one hundred times in his fourteen letters. Grace is always God in action. To understand this, let's ask a few questions: How many good deeds are required to wipe away the guilt of Saul of Tarsus by his blasphemy against God, the murder of Stephen, the imprisonment of Christians and the destruction of churches? Or, how many good deeds, are required to cancel the crude, bawdy and blasphemous songs that John of Wapping taught to sailors, his indoctrination of young men into his own unbelieving way of life and his cruel trade on the coast of Africa selling husbands and wives, parents and children continents apart? And how many good deeds are needed to blot out our sin of rejecting Christ? How much penitence is required for total absolution? How much do we have to pay to wipe the slate clean? How many great acts to cancel all the bad?

The answer is—just one! But it is not ours, because we cannot pay. The one act of righteousness that can cancel our sin is that of Christ on the cross. Paul made this plain when he wrote: 'One act of righteousness leads to justification and life for all men' (Romans 5:18). But what is this 'justification'?

Whatever it is, justification has formed the bedrock of Protestant Christianity. The evangelist George Whitefield, wrote in his journal in 1736: 'It is the good old doctrine of the Church of England. It is what the holy martyrs in Queen Mary's time sealed with their blood, and which I pray God, if need be, that I and my brethren may seal with ours.' One hundred and fifty years later the evangelical Lord Shaftsbury wrote in a similar way when he described justification as: 'That grand doctrine, the very life of the Bible and the keystone of the Reformation.'

Each of the great doctrinal statements of the Reformation made a clear assertion on this subject of justification: the Augsburg Confession in Germany (1530), the Second Helvetic Confession in Switzerland (1566), the French Confession of Faith (1559), the Thirty-Nine Articles of the Church of England (1571), The Westminster Confession of Faith of the Presbyterians (1649), the Savoy Declaration of the Independents (1658), and the Baptist Confession (1689). But these confessions were not inventing a new theology; it was clearly the teaching of the first century church led by the apostles, and it had never been lost among many of the great church leaders of later centuries.

The leaders of the Reformation in the sixteenth century across Europe made clear their opposition to the medieval church that viewed salvation as a result of our good works of prayer, penance, charity, the purchase of indulgences, and the ceremonies and sacrifices of the church by which righteousness was infused into the penitent sinner; this righteousness might even be the surplus works of past saints into whose merit we can dip. In a similar way it was taught that we could shorten the stay of our friends and relatives in purgatory by our own good works done on their behalf. All this had been stated plainly by church councils for centuries, and no amount of carefully crafted words, either then or now, could bring together the two opposites of justification by faith alone and justification by works.

What did Paul mean when he wrote that Christ was 'delivered up for our trespasses and raised for our justification' (Romans 4:25)? Justification refers to the declaration by God that, by the sin-bearing death and life-giving resurrection of Christ, the sinner is no longer guilty in God's sight. The great issue at the time of the Reformation in the sixteenth century was the claim by the Reformers that Christ took all our guilt, sin and punishment upon himself at the cross. The result was described in the language of the law court: the guilt of the sinner was passed to the account of Christ, and the Father counted his Son as the guilty one instead. In exchange, the righteousness of Christ was passed to the account of the sinner and thus the just anger of God against sin was satisfied.

The German Reformer in the sixteenth century, Martin Luther, called this, 'the wonderful exchange'. This glorious offer of salvation, as the Reformers insisted, is to be received by faith alone and not by the services or ceremonies of the church. In the autumn of 1528 William Tyndale who, two years earlier had given England its first printed New Testament in English, described this great truth of justification in a powerfully poetic way. He was writing in *The Obedience of the Christian Man*—a book that was intended to persuade King Henry VIII that true Christians were loyal servants of the King, but which took the opportunity of telling the King what the gospel was really about. He described the death of Christ like this: 'God sent him into the world to bless us, and to offer himself for us a sacrifice of a sweet savour, to kill the stench of our sins, that God henceforth should smell them no more, nor think on them any more!' Jim Packer, a modern-day theologian, expressed it more plainly when he wrote, 'Jesus endured and exhausted the divine judgement for which we were otherwise inescapably destined.' In other words, justification has always been understood as having to do with the judgement of God against sin, the suffering and death of Christ and, by his resurrection, the complete acquittal of the sinner in the sight of God. But that is all changing!

A new view today, represented by two theologians Tom Wright and James Dunn, is that the Protestant Reformers got it all wrong. As Wright understands it, in the first century the Jews had a narrow view that grace was confined to Israel only. For the Jew at the time of Jesus and Paul, justification meant two things: membership of the covenant community of Israel—which was open only to Jews—and the ultimate victory of

Israel over her enemies. The key to understand justification, we are told, is all about membership of the covenant community. In his letters, therefore, Paul's doctrine of justification was not about a divine declaration of the 'not guilty' verdict through the sin-bearing death of Christ, but about the fact that membership of the covenant community of God was now open to all. Thus, when Jesus died on the cross, he died as the representative of the whole Jewish nation, and the curse that he bore was the curse upon the Jewish nation for failing to be the light of the world. Wright claims that when Paul wrote in Galatians 3:13 that, 'Christ redeemed us from the curse of the law by becoming a curse for us', the 'us' is not non-Jews, but only the Jewish nation. Similarly the struggle against sin described by Paul in Romans 7:13–25 is not a personal experience but the struggle of Israel with the law. Thus Paul's letters to Rome and Galatia are not about individual salvation, but about who are the people of God. Galatians was written to correct an over-zealous love of Judaism, and Romans was written to correct an over-zealous anti-Judaism. Wright does not use the term 'justified by faith' but prefers to see our justification—membership of the community of God—as the result of our belief that by his death and resurrection Christ fulfilled all that Israel failed to be; we are therefore 'justified by belief'.

This totally reshapes the doctrine of justification by faith as evangelicals have always understood it. Sin as Christ-rejecting rebellion against God, is hardly the issue it seems; and such terms as Christ dying as our legal substitute, God crediting our sin to Christ's account, or sinners acquitted of their guilt, do not form part of the vocabulary of people who hold this view. Paul's statement that, 'a person is not justified by works of the law but through faith in Jesus Christ' (Galatians 2:16) apparently now means no more than that by the works of the law no one will be reckoned among God's people. This may be a pleasant thought, but it is hardly robust—and it meant a great deal more than this for the converted university graduate from Tarsus. We must let Paul himself shape our thinking.

## Justification by faith according to Paul

The first three chapters of Paul's letter to the Christians at Rome is clearly a diagnosis of the personal guilt of everyone. To argue that this is only the guilt of Israel would be suspect to say the least in the light of his clear references to 'all ungodliness and unrighteousness of men' (1:18), to those who sin 'without the law' (2:12) and to the fact that 'none is righteous, no, not one … for all have sinned and fall short of the glory of God' (3:10, 23). His diagnosis is severe and universal, and his conclusion is that 'by the works of the law no human being will be justified in his (God's) sight' (3:20). There is nothing that we can do to save ourselves. This opens the way for Paul to launch into his great exposition of justification by faith alone. We will make it simple.

In order to open up his teaching of sin put to Christ's account and righteousness put to our account Paul introduces a familiar concept: 'To the one who works, his wages are not *counted* as a gift but as his due' (Romans 4:4). But Paul is about to dress up a very common word with a very special Christian meaning. The word for 'counted' is the Greek verb *logizomai*. It was a common word in finance and meant simply to reckon up or calculate. In the first century the word was also used of passing money to someone's account—a direct debit—and the noun from this word was used for a finance office.

Paul begins by employing the word in a normal, commonly used way. You count up the hours that a man works, you multiply it by the hourly rate and then you pay his wages. But, Paul continues, there is a divine reckoning as well, except that the divine reckoning is wholly different. Here are two men called Saul and John, and they have stacked up a great debt—whether ignorantly or knowingly makes no difference. What they need is someone to pass to their account sufficient funds to set them in the clear. The problem is that this debt is not money but wickedness—Christ-rejecting wickedness. At the very best, religious duty might be able to run up a little less debt in future. But the massive past debt, still stays—and that is true of us all. We can turn over a religious new leaf and become more socially acceptable, and by so doing we may think that we can reduce future debt. But if sin is ultimately defined as rejecting Christ, then we have done nothing to reduce that. It is something like this with the debt of modern nations. If a government gets its political and economic house in order, it may slowly reduce the increase of its debt in the future. But what it cannot do is cancel the massive debt of the past. So what is the solution?

The solution is grace—justifying grace—and this is what God does for those who place their trust in Jesus Christ and do not even try to earn their salvation: God reckons righteousness to their account, or, as Paul expresses it: 'To the one who does not work but trusts him who justifies the ungodly, his faith is counted as righteousness' (Romans 4:5). However, there can be no such thing as faith until there is something for faith to rely upon. Faith has to be placed somewhere. In the same way there is no such thing as righteousness apart from a righteous life; righteousness is not some spiritual glue or sacred stardust that is attached to us after religious rituals or sacred services. Righteousness can only be found in a righteous life. So, where can I find such a righteous life that can be credited to me in place of my unrighteous Christ-rejecting life? The answer is that it can only be the righteousness of Jesus Christ. It is his righteousness that is passed to my account.

God justifies us by counting us as clean as Christ himself; he not only sets us free from the punishment our blame deserves, but counts us as no longer guilty of blame at all. On a number of occasions Paul wrote of the Christian as one who will be presented guiltless or blameless before God at the end of time (1 Corinthians 1:8 and Ephesians 1:4 for example).

But there is always a cost involved if one account is to be credited with the value of another, and the language of the Bible to describe this is vividly offensive: '(God) made him to be sin who knew no sin, so that in him we might become the righteousness of God' (2 Corinthians 5:21).

What Paul wrote was quite literally: 'for us he was made sin'. Can it be possible that the eternal and sinless Son of God actually became our sin? The sheer offence of this leads some to conclude that it means only that he became a 'sin offering' for us. But that is not what Paul says. Certainly all the Old Testament sacrifices were sin offerings pointing forward to Christ. The bulls and goats, lambs and pigeons that died in the place of those who offered the sacrifice, could never in reality take away sin because a goat could never take the moral guilt of a human being (Hebrews 10:4). That terrible task was left to Christ alone. The very point Paul is making in the phrase 'for us he was made sin' is that his death was utterly different. He did what all the thousands of animal sacrifices together could not do. Christ became all that we are, so that we could become what he was. The one who was perfectly sinless was counted as a Christ-rejecting rebel so that we might be counted as sinless as he was! The sheer offence of this causes many to back off.

Peter followed the same theology when he pointed to the punishment of our sin that Christ bore: 'Christ also suffered once for sins, the righteous for the unrighteous, that he might bring us to God' (1 Peter 3:18); here the little preposition *for* means literally: 'on behalf of', or 'for the sake of'. He took not only our guilt, but our punishment.

Martin Luther, expressed this in a way as shocking as Paul, and it has caused no little debate among Bible teachers ever since. He was explaining the phrase in Galatians 3:13, 'Christ redeemed us from the curse of the law by becoming a curse for us—for it is written "Cursed is everyone who is hanged on a tree."' Luther explained that Christ was innocent as concerning his own person and therefore had no need to die under the curse of the law of God. But on the cross, in order that he might be a true sacrifice for the sins of the whole world: 'He is not now an innocent person and without sins, is not now the Son of God born of the Virgin Mary; but a sinner who has carried the sin of Paul, who was a blasphemer, an oppressor and a persecutor; of Peter, who denied Christ;

of David, who was an adulterer, a murderer and caused the Gentiles to blaspheme the name of the Lord: and, briefly, who has and bears all the sins of all men in his body, that he might make satisfaction for them with his own blood.'

This was strong stuff! And Luther knew it. He was not claiming that Christ ever ceased to be the Son of God but Luther asks whether it is absurd and slanderous to say that the Son of God became a cursed sinner and concludes, 'Then deny also that he suffered, was crucified and died.' For it is equally absurd and slanderous to claim that the sinless Son of God could become a curse for us and suffer the pains of sin and death; but that is exactly what Paul claims in Galatians 3:13.

Luther was right. This is justifying grace in action. It is a wholly inadequate view of the cross to see Christ only as a representative of rebellious Israel, fulfilling the role that Israel so miserably failed to discharge. But it is equally not sufficient to say only that Christ was punished as our substitute, in our place; he suffered far more than that. Christ did not merely bear our punishment and die under the anger of God against sin; he took our guilt as his own by taking our sin as his own. This is what is meant in those dreadful words of Paul: 'For our sake God made him *to be sin* who knew no sin, so that in him we might become the righteousness of God.' And when Peter writes 'He himself *bore our sins* in his body on the tree' (1 Peter 2:24), this is what he means. For Christ on Calvary, sin was not merely a burden to be born—it was a defilement to be felt. This is God giving himself for us, to do what we could never do—to pay the penalty of Christ-rejecting sin.

Paul made the death of Christ no lighter when he wrote, 'Christ has redeemed us from the curse of the law by becoming a curse for us' (Galatians 3:13). If Christ becoming sin is offensive, this claim by Paul that Christ was cursed on Calvary is more so. It is no casual remark of the apostle; it is the development of a carefully considered theme. In Galatians 3:10 he has claimed that all who fail to keep the law of God are under a justifiable curse of God and this means that all, without a single exception, stand under the judgement of God. The word 'curse' is far more than an expression of divine annoyance—it is a pronouncement of divine judgement. It is the just sentence by a holy God against all who reject his Son and disobey his law. The fearful penalty of *that* was paid by Christ on Calvary when he suffered the anger of his Father's judgement against sin. His agonized cry from the cross: 'My God, my God, why have you forsaken me?' expressed the terrifying depth to which the sinless Saviour felt the wrath of a holy God. To say that he went through hell on the cross has little reference to the physical suffering—many have suffered more lingering and excruciating physical pain than his—but it horribly describes what it meant for the Holy One to smart under the judgement of his Father for sin that belonged to us.

We call justification 'justifying *grace*' because the direction of everything about the subject of justification is from God to us. Our only contribution to justifying grace is to be a Christ-rejecting rebel—beyond that, everything belongs to God. Justification is not a change in us—that is regeneration or new birth—rather, it is a change in how God sees us. This is why Paul can introduce the word 'glorified' after the word justified in Romans 8:30. Justified sinners are as fit for heaven as they ever will be.

## Justification is more than a pardon

Although we say that justification adopts the language of the law courts, in one sense it is far from the language of any human law court. Legal language can cope with the judgement of the guilty and the acquittal of the innocent; but the acquittal of those known to be guilty violates all laws of justice. Yet justification is even more than the acquittal of the guilty: it is a declaration that those known to be guilty are perfectly righteous—and this by the supreme Judge who is always wise, fair and just. At this crucial point all our law court comparisons fail us.

When we speak of Christ paying for our crime we can understand that, because it often happens that someone will pay the fine for another. Similarly, Christ as our substitute has some ring of familiarity about it: there have been heroic stories of a man owning up to the guilt of another and paying for it with his life. But Christ did more than any of this. He did not simply pay for our sins or even own up on our behalf—he became all that we are so that by a 'wonderful exchange' we become all that he is.

Luther once expressed it like this: 'Lord Jesus, you are my righteousness, just as I am your sin. You have taken upon yourself what is mine and have given to me what is yours. You have taken upon yourself what you were not and have given to me what I was not.' This is precisely what Paul meant when he declared to the Christians at Corinth that God made Christ 'to be sin, who knew no sin, so that in him we might become the righteousness of God' in order that he could become, 'our wisdom and our righteousness and sanctification and redemption' (2 Corinthians 5:21 and 1 Corinthians 1:30). We have none of this apart from what we have in Christ. And this justification is final, for ever and complete. It can never be repeated any more that it can ever be undone. This is the reason for the strong note of total assurance that runs throughout the New Testament. Justification means not only that we are pardoned, but that in the sight of God it is as if the guilt was never ours!

A link word that describes this satisfying of the righteous judgement of God is 'propitiation'. It is found only five times in the New Testament, but it is crucial. In Romans 3:25 Paul claims that God put forward Christ Jesus 'as a propitiation by his blood'. The word *hilasterion* was well understood in the first century to mean the turning away of the anger of the gods. But it was always by things we had to do to placate them. For Paul the whole concept was turned about and the propitiation was by God providing the means by which his just anger against sin could be forgiven. What is even more startling about Paul's claim is that all the sins committed before the coming of Christ had been left 'unpunished'

(NIV); if a sacrifice was offered sincerely, the sins were forgiven but no punishment had been borne for them. That waited until Christ on the cross paid the penalty for all forgiven sin.

In a beautiful conclusion to the benefits of justifying grace, Paul took up Psalm 32 and quoted from the first two verses: 'Blessed is the one whose lawless deeds are forgiven, and whose sins are covered; blessed is the man against whom the Lord will not count his sin' (Romans 4:7–8). The theologians have a phrase for this, they call it: 'imputed righteousness' which is another way of saying, 'his righteousness is put to my account and counted as if it is mine'. If we prefer, instead of 'imputed righteousness' we can call it 'reckoned righteousness'. It is when the righteousness of Jesus Christ is credited or reckoned to our account. The debt is wiped out. To be certain of that is the first conscious experience of grace. It is on this ground that God can declare the repentant sinner 'Not guilty'.

## The resurrection and justifying grace

This chapter began with 1 Corinthians 15 deliberately, because there is one other aspect of justifying grace that must never be forgotten. Justification is as much the result of the resurrection of Christ as it is the result of his death. To be true to Scripture, we should never speak of the justifying grace of God as if the cross said it all. In a vital statement on this, Paul claimed, 'Jesus our Lord ... was delivered up for our trespasses and raised for our justification' (Romans 4:25). If Paul means what he says, our justification cannot be complete without the triumph of the resurrection; and for this reason Paul assures the Corinthians that, 'If Christ has not been raised, then our preaching is in vain and your faith is in vain ... you are still in your sins' (1 Corinthians 15:14,17). He says this because the resurrection is God's final 'Amen' to all that his Son accomplished and it is the guarantee of new life in Christ for all who are justified. He stands before the Father as a perpetual reminder that for those who are 'in Christ' there can never again be sin reckoned to their account—they are as innocent as if they had never committed one sin. That is a staggeringly daring claim and one that would be dangerously blasphemous—if it were not gloriously true.

Justification by faith alone in Christ alone through faith alone, was the front line of the Reformation battle, and we must not allow what the Reformers fought and died for to be diluted by a desire for ecumenical peace or theological innovation. A little after the time of Martin Luther, the Swiss reformer John Calvin wrote of this doctrine of justification by faith: 'Wherever the knowledge of it is taken away, the glory of Christ is extinguished, religion abolished, the church destroyed and the hope of salvation utterly overthrown.' Calvin was right.

JESUS, YOUR BLOOD AND RIGHTEOUSNESS
my beauty are, my glorious dress;
mid burning worlds, in these arrayed,
with joy I shall lift up my head.

2. Bold shall I stand on your great day
and none condemn me, try who may;
fully absolved by you I am
from sin and fear, from guilt and shame.

3. When from the dust of death I rise
to claim my home beyond the skies,
then this shall be my only plea:
Jesus has lived, has died for me.

4. O give to all your servants, Lord,
to speak with power your gracious word,
that all who now believe it true
may find eternal life in you.

5. O God of power, O God of love,
let the whole world your mercy prove;
now let your word in all prevail;
Lord, take the spoils of death and hell!

6. O let the dead now hear your voice;
let those once lost in sin rejoice!
Their beauty this, their glorious dress,
Jesus, your blood and righteousness.

Nicolaus L Von Zinzendorf 1700–60
Trans. John Wesley 1703–91
*Praise!* 778 © in this version Praise Trust

## FOR GROUP DISCUSSION

1. Martin Luther called Justification 'The wonderful exchange'. What was so wonderful about it?
2. How would you explain justification for someone who has committed a terrible act that is now crushing their conscience?
3. What is the relationship between justification and the resurrection of Christ?
4. From Romans 4 what do we learn about justification?
5. Can you find the other four uses of the word 'propitiation' in the New Testament and explain its significance?

# Incarnate grace

'You know the grace of our Lord Jesus Christ, that though he was rich, yet for your sake he became poor' 2 Corinthians 8:9

The apostle Paul was a brilliant communicator, and he found some smart ways of letting the churches know exactly what he expected of them. Sometimes he did this by posing a leading question. Here at Corinth, the church was divided over its favourite leaders and best preachers; some preferred Paul, others Apollos, and others Peter. Paul had a simple question for them: 'Was Paul crucified for you? Or were you baptised in the name of Paul?' (1 Corinthians 1:13).

However sometimes, instead of a question, Paul used a comparison. Paul was collecting famine relief for the suffering Christians in Judea, and he knew that the Corinthians could afford to give; in fact they had started well a year earlier but appear to have become pretty tight-fisted more recently, and they had not fulfilled what they had promised. So Paul held up to them the example of the Macedonians who lived close by. In 2 Corinthians 8:2–5, he reminded the Corinthians how their neighbours had given out of their poverty as much as they could, and then a bit more. In fact they had pleaded for the privilege of giving and ended up by giving more than Paul had expected.

We can hear the Corinthians grumbling: 'He's always on about the Macedonians. Give us a break Paul.' So Paul switched attack and in v 8 he told them: 'I'm not commanding you, but I want to test the sincerity of your love by comparing it with the earnestness of others' (*New International Version*)—here come the Macedonians again! But with the masterstroke of surprise Paul continued: 'For you know the grace of our

Lord Jesus Christ, that though he was rich, yet for your sake he became poor.' He was appealing to the Corinthians' grace for giving on the ground of the grace of the incarnation.

That word 'rich', can refer either to earthly wealth or spiritual wealth. Paul loved to link 'rich' with 'glory'—a word that refers to the full character of something or someone. Elsewhere he writes of 'the riches of his glory' (Romans 9:23), and 'the riches of his glorious inheritance' (Ephesians 1:18), and 'according to his riches in glory' (Philippians 4:19). The coming of Christ into this world at the incarnation—a word that means simply 'in the flesh'—is the greatest exhibition of God's grace. And this in turn is the most powerful incentive for Christian humility in the grace of giving.

## Jesus before Bethlehem

To appreciate what Christ became we must understand what he was. Millions are born in dire poverty and millions more live their short lives owning nothing more than a few ragged clothes. Millions have died unjust and horrible deaths with their bodies thrown into common graves at best, without the dignity of being laid in the tomb of a rich man. So, how was the poverty of Christ remarkable? The answer to this is by an understanding of who and what he was. Paul describes the magnificence of Christ's power and authority before the incarnation by the simple claim: 'By him all things were created, in heaven and on earth, visible and invisible … all things were created through him and for him' (Colossians 1:16).

In 330 BC, at the age of 25, Alexander the Great of Macedonia crushed Darius the Great, King of Persia, and in doing so he made himself master of three million square miles and became many thousand times richer than anyone else on earth. Alexander was master of the Greeks, Pharaoh of Egypt and King of Asia. He set out to discover the limits of the world and to conquer it. Seven years later he was dead—Alexander had lost everything and he left little for history except a city bearing his name and the legends of his life.

By contrast, our King spoke a powerful word of command and the earth and heavens were created. Stars and planets spun in space, birds flew in the air, fish swam in the seas, the earth was decked with trees and flowers and animals walked on land; the wealth in every mine and the angelic hosts of heaven are all his. And yet he laid his glory by, and he who was rich, for our sake became poor. That is the grace of incarnation. This is no little prince, president or prime minister tampering with justice and exploiting his subjects.

At 08.15 on 6 August 1945 a single atomic bomb dropped over Hiroshima in Japan obliterated more than half of the city's seven square miles and annihilated over thirty thousand men, women and children in milliseconds. Throughout the history of the human race the largest capital expenditure of nations has been on the effort to produce the most powerful tools to eliminate their neighbours; as a result one hundred million people were killed in war throughout the twentieth century alone. Ultimate human power is always used for maximum human hurt. But our king of unlimited power used his supremacy for ultimate good. For our sake he made himself poor so that through his poverty we might become rich.

When Daniel, 600 years before Christ, desperately needed to be reassured that there was a power more glorious and more powerful than the fierce armies of Nebuchadnezzar of Babylon, God gave him a glimpse of Christ in heaven: 'Behold … there came one like a son of man, and he came to the Ancient of Days and was presented before him. And to him was given dominion and glory and a kingdom, that all peoples, nations and languages should serve him; his dominion is an everlasting dominion, which shall not pass away, and his kingdom one that shall not be destroyed' (Daniel 7:13–14). Every empire known to man comes and goes: the ancient empires of Egypt, Assyria, Babylon, Persia, Macedonia,

Rome, and the modern empires of Britain and Russia all rose to power by the might of their armies and then fell into virtual obscurity. The empire of Christ is everlasting—but he deliberately came into obscurity.

When John the apostle needed to be reminded of a power more powerful and a glory more glorious than the legions of Rome and the emperor Titus—who devastated Jerusalem, and Domitian—who devastated the church, God showed him Christ in heaven: 'I looked and I heard around the throne … the voice of many angels numbering myriads of myriads and thousands of thousands, saying with a loud voice: "Worthy is the Lamb who was slain to receive power and wealth and wisdom and might and honour and glory and blessing!"' (Revelation 5:11–12).

Few leaders willingly give up their power, they have it taken from them. Yet Christ gladly gave up the glory and splendour of heaven. He would always have been who he was even if he had not come to this earth, but he became what he was not—truly man, so that we might become what we are not—children of God. Instead of heaven crying 'Holy, holy, holy', rough mobs shouted 'Crucify him!'. Instead of the honour and adoration of the angels, crude Roman soldiers beat him and spat on him. Instead of the sweet incense of heaven, he exchanged it for the sweat and stench of the place of execution.

## Was he really God?

Some of the earliest heresies of the church centred not around the authority of the Scriptures, or the work of the Holy Spirit, but upon the person of Jesus Christ. Why was this? Not because the doctrine was not clear, but because it was clear. The problem was not what to believe about Jesus being God—the Scripture could hardly be clearer on this— but how on earth could we believe it?

If he had been God alone then he could not have come here because we cannot see God and live. If he had been only man, there would have been no particular value in him coming here; many good men have set us an example before and since. But as both God and man he was unique. To avoid this inconceivable paradox, before the end of the first century the Ebionites claimed that he was only a spirit-filled man—the son of Joseph and Mary. The Docetists believed that Christ came disguised as a man—Jesus was the man who only 'seemed' to be divine. And the Gnostics lost sight of him in a welter of secret knowledge and intellectual enlightenment. Within another one hundred years, Sabellius denied the three persons in one Godhead and taught that Christ was a mere man adopted by God for the occasion—and so Unitarianism was born: God acts in the three modes of Father, Son and Spirit.

No sooner had Constantine—the first Roman Emperor to adopt the Christian faith—painted the Christian *chi-rho* symbol on the shields of his legionaries, than he found himself embroiled in a bitter debate among the Christians over whether or not Christ was truly God. With Arius heading up one side and Athanasius the other, this new convert from worshipping Isis and Mithras was well out of his depth. At Nicea in AD 325 Constantine called the leaders together, alternately threatened and lectured them on the need for unity, tried to force through a compromise, even offered a few definitions of his own, and invited them to supper in his palace. The apostle Paul would not have recognised it—times were certainly changing! But how to declare simply and plainly that Jesus of Nazareth, the uncreated Creator, was eternally God and, of the same nature and character, co-equal with his Father, seemed beyond the Emperor—and beyond most of the bishops as well!

The mysterious doctrine of the Trinity has always been a significant hallmark of Christian orthodoxy. To maintain the monotheistic faith of one God alone yet expressed in three distinct Persons each fully God, co-equal and in perfect and eternal harmony with one another, has always been too much for some to accept. But so has the wonder of the virgin birth, the miracles of Christ's ministry, the effectiveness of his death as our substitute in order to reconcile sinners to God, and the powerful event of the literal, historical resurrection. The day we can clarify every part of our faith to the satisfaction of a cynical world, we will have no one left before whom we stand in awe—God will have been reduced to the size of our imagination and explanation.

The Scriptures rarely explain Christ's deity, but they frequently state it. In the Old Testament he is referred to as 'the Mighty God' in that undeniably Messianic verse in Isaiah 9:6, where the Hebrew *el el gibor* (literally: God, God the Mighty One) can never be made to refer to anyone other than the almighty, transcendent Creator; compare the same expression in 10:21. In the New Testament John plainly identified the one whom the seraphim worshipped with the cry 'Holy, holy, holy is the LORD of hosts; the whole earth is full of his glory!' as Christ himself—compare Isaiah 6:3, 10 and John 12:40–41. When Paul wrote to the Colossians that in Christ 'the whole fullness of deity dwells bodily' (2:9) he could hardly have expressed himself more plainly. Although possibly Hebrews 1:3, where it can be translated literally, 'He is the exact character of the actual reality of God himself' comes nearer the mark than anywhere.

The true deity of Christ may be a mystery—but mystery is not inconsistency. Of course we will find it hard to grasp the idea of two natures perfectly at ease in one person—especially when those two natures are as opposite as deity and humanity—but that makes it neither irreconcilable nor impossible. The wonder was not so much that Jesus of Nazareth was God, but that God became Jesus of Nazareth! But why did God become a man? That is explained only in the miracle of incarnate grace.

## Why the incarnation?

When Anselm, the Archbishop of Canterbury in the eleventh century, tackled this question in his work: *Cur Deus Homo?* (Why did God become Man?) he came up—though at length as most theologians do—with two simple answers: first, only God could make the way of salvation on behalf of sinners; no one else was either good enough or powerful enough. And second, since the human race was the offender and rebel, only mankind could put right the wrong. Thus, the one who made the way of forgiveness on behalf of sinners had to be both God and man.

No doubt this is true. But if God had chosen another way then that too would have been right. God *might* have come in the person of his Son without taking human nature; he *might* have come in the appearance of a man only; it *might* have all been a make-believe humanity. And if God had declared that that is what he was prepared to accept in place of the just punishment of rebel sinners, then that would have been enough. If God had decided that an angel was sufficient, then an angel would have been sufficient. God was not under an obligation to choose a particular way of salvation; he was not captive to some law beyond his control that demanded the life and death of the innocent on behalf of the guilty. If there is such a law—and there is—it is because God himself decreed it to be such.

A better way of understanding the grace and necessity of the incarnation is that Jesus of Nazareth had to be God to show us what God is like and to reassure us that the salvation he offers has the stamp of God's power and authority upon it. Equally he had to be perfect man to show us just how holy God's standard is—and therefore how far we fall from it—and to reassure us that as the God-Man he can perfectly sympathise with us in all things. The grace of the incarnation is for our sake, not for God's sake.

All religions are groping after God—and well they might. Nothing is more human than to search for God; that is what makes humanity human. Paul recognised this in Athens when he reminded the great debaters that they were seeking God 'in the hope that they might feel their way towards him and find him' (Acts 17:27). Religion is human, but when religion arrives at its own conclusion it is a dead end. We can never know God or understand God on our own. We cannot focus on God because his unapproachable holiness would blind us. Snow blindness is caused by the ultraviolet rays of the sun reflecting from the pure whiteness of the snow. In the vast expanse of a white snowscape, there is nothing for the eye to focus on, and nothing to protect the delicate eye from the searing rays of the sun. Just so, we cannot focus on God and his dazzling holiness—but Christ came to show us what the Father is like. There was no other way.

The apostle described Christ here on earth like this: 'He is the radiance of the glory of God and the exact imprint of his nature' (Hebrews 1:3). 'The radiance of glory' is not a dazzling reflection, like the rays of the sun bouncing off a mirror or a wet road. *That* was the reflection of the glory of God that shone out from Moses' face when he came from the presence of the Lord (Exodus 34:29–35); his face shone with reflected glory, and therefore it was a fading glory. On the contrary, Christ's life does not *reflect* the glory of God, it *is* the glory of God. The writer goes further and underscores that Christ is: 'the exact imprint of his nature' (*New International Version* has 'exact representation of his being'). Paul chose the Greek word *character*. A literal translation of this verse would be: 'He is the radiance of the glory of God and the exact character of the actual reality of God himself.' Christ is none other than in reality God, and that whatever we see, hear and learn about him during his life on earth, we see, hear and learn about God himself. In Christ, we are watching and hearing the very heart of God:

When we read of his love for little children

His tender dealing with the woman at the well in Samaria

His sympathy for the poor widow whose son had died

His healing of the lepers and the lame

His compassion for the hungry crowds

His tears over Jerusalem and at the grave of Lazarus

His pastoral comfort to Peter before and after his denial
His passionate warning to Judas before the betrayal
His prayer for the soldiers at Golgotha
His promise to the thief who died beside him
His loving care for his mother and disciple as he hung on the cross

This was the heart of the one who created the entire, unfathomable infinity of the universe, and who stood at the centre of the adoration of heaven. But he laid it aside because it was not appropriate that he should be seen like that here. What he had always been was masked by what he had become because that is what we needed to see and that is how we could understand God. He changed his appearance but not his nature. Christ did not cease to be God, but now we see him as man, confined to space and time; a man who knew hunger and thirst, weariness and aloneness. His emotions were stirred, his heart was broken, his spirit was crushed, his body was racked with pain. He became poor so that we could understand what God is like.

## Never to his own advantage

Christ never used his character as God to his own advantage. This is a point Paul seems to be making in Philippians 2:6, 'Though he was in the form of God, he did not count equality with God a thing to be grasped'. That phrase 'a thing to be grasped' translates an uncommon word found nowhere else in the New Testament and not often outside the New Testament. It is not a reference to something seized or grasped—like a prize or booty. For Christ, equality with God was not a prize for doing well or a booty to be snatched; on the contrary it was his by eternal right. More recently it has been shown that the reference is to something he had but did not use to his own personal advantage. This fits well with the truth of the incarnation. Our Lord was equal with his Father, but here on earth he never used that reality for personal advantage.

When the crowd picked up stones to throw at him in Jerusalem: 'Jesus hid himself and went out of the temple' (John 8:59). Similarly, just two chapters later, the Jews attempted the same thing: 'But he escaped from their hands' (John 10:39). At Nazareth, when they ran him out of town and up to the brow of a hill to throw him over, Luke records almost absurdly: 'But passing through their midst, he went away' (Luke 4:30). In each case he refused to turn on those who abused him, and he used his silent sovereign power to still his enemies—but only because the appointed time, place and manner of his death had not yet arrived.

When the time did arrive, he was still in full control. In Gethsemane 'a large crowd with swords and clubs' came to arrest him. What followed would be amusing if it had not been set against the sinister back-drop of the power of the prince of darkness. Jesus stepped forward and quietly opened the interview: 'Who do you want?' A bold chorus came back: 'Jesus of Nazareth'. When he responded: 'I am he', 'They drew back and fell to the ground.' Jesus encouraged the soldiers to arrest him! A still silence hung over the olive grove as the Son of God repeated his question: 'Who do you want?' This time I suspect the reply was little more than a whimper: 'Jesus of Nazareth'. Is there now a note of scorn in his voice: 'I told you that I am he. So, if you seek me, let these men go.'

A few remembered their duty, gathered their courage and grabbed at Christ. Peter lost his cool, struck out with his sword and, in an ill-judged swipe, lopped off the ear of an unfortunate servant. This desperate and defiant act should have sparked a furious mêlée as the soldiers ripped into the small party of almost defenceless disciples. Instead, with apparently everyone rooted to the spot and Peter wondering what on earth he had just done, our Lord calmly walked across, healed the servant's ear and then, with a side glance to the rough gang, turned on his own well-meaning disciple: 'Do you think that I cannot appeal to my Father, and he will at once send me more than twelve legions of angels?'—more than seventy thousand regimental angels! Such a claim ringing out in the still and shadowy darkness of the olive grove, with the clear authority of the powerful voice of the Son of God whose veiled glory had sent the arresting party grovelling in the dust, must have been a scary experience for the quivering mob from Caiaphas. I can imagine them looking around nervously to see from which direction the first cohort of celestial soldiers might appear! For a moment a carpet of uneasy silence covered the scene. But no angels came. In the next moment the disciples lost their courage and fled, and the gang, having found theirs, closed in on Christ. The grace of the incarnation would never by-pass the cross.

Before Caiaphas they spat, punched and cursed Jesus of Nazareth— but he remained silent. And when the Roman governor warned him: 'I have authority to release you and authority to crucify you', the only response Pilate received was: 'You would have no authority over me at all unless it had been given you from above.' He only ever used his power for our sake.

Significantly, some of the false gospels that appeared during the second and third centuries following the close of the New Testament, created fanciful stories of Christ's childhood. In a false Gospel of Matthew we read two stories of the childhood of Jesus in which he cursed a child who interfered with his game, and in each case the child died. Another story describes him throwing clay birds into the air so that they might fly away and amuse his friends. A *Gospel of Thomas* relates the story of Jesus killing a Pharisee who interfered with his game. All this is precisely what our Lord did not do. He never used his power and glory for his own benefit; never as a final triumphant throw of his trump card over his enemies, but only so that, 'The Son of Man must suffer many things and be rejected by the elders and chief priests and scribes, and be killed, and on the third day be raised' (Luke 9:22).

All this Christ did so that we could understand the compassionate heart of the Son of God who, though he was unimaginably rich, became poor for our sake. In the record of his life 'we have seen his glory, glory as of the only Son from the Father, full of grace and truth' (John 1:14). This is the grace of the incarnation.

## He chose to die

However, there is another reason why Christ became poor, and that is so that we might find God and enjoy him for ever, secure in the knowledge that the one who came to die for us and who rose again to be a living and loving Friend and Saviour is perfectly able 'to sympathise with our weaknesses' (Hebrews 4:15). He suffered and celebrated, endured and enjoyed, just as we do—yet always without sin. The one who knew temptation and pain, and experienced all the human emotions that are common to us is the one best able to assist us in our need. To know that a friend cares and understands is a great comfort in times of need, but to know that that friend is God is a thousand times better. This is in part what Paul means when he adds: 'So that you by his poverty might become rich.'

At the time of his death, Alexander the Great was well advanced in his plans to conquer the Asian world. Part of his greatness lay in his ability to plan. His forces were assembling, the baggage collected and the summer campaign almost ready. The advance army was on its way. And beyond that, Alexander planned to conquer and conquer until the world ran out! Plans. Great plans. Well-made plans. Then, perhaps it was a little mosquito that achieved what all the armies of the world had failed to do—it drew the blood of Alexander the Great and killed him. All his plans ended with his death. He lived in splendour and was buried with honour, but his plans came to nothing.

He who was a million times greater than all the world's great leaders laid plans and chose the time and fulfilled the detail. He who was immortal chose to die. Christ was the only man ever to walk this earth who chose to die. Many have volunteered for desperate and hopeless missions; others have willingly given their lives for a cause—good or bad;

some choose suicide in the false hope of ending pain or gaining paradise. But no one chooses to die. They may choose the time and manner and place, but sooner or later death is the inevitable end of everyone who is born into this world. We have no choice. Death was only inevitable for Christ because he chose it—not because he deserved it.

He came to conquer the lives of men and women like us; and to carry this out he became poor—rejected, betrayed, despised and crucified in his body and his character. And the shedding of his blood was all part of the plan. It was the most important part of his plan. The death of world rulers always brings their finest moment to an end. Whether they die in battle or in old age loaded with riches and honour, all is at an end. For the year AD 1087, the Anglo-Saxon Chronicle recorded the death of William of Normandy and concluded: 'Alas, how deceitful and untrustworthy is this world's prosperity. He who had been a powerful king, and lord of many a land, had then of all the land only a seven foot measure; and he who once was clad in gold and gems, lay then covered with earth.'

But this King was never more glorious than in his moment of death. On the cross was revealed for us the true heart of God. That was his finest hour and the moment of his greatest power. On Golgotha Jesus carried our sin and guilt and punishment so that the anger of his Father against us would be deflected against the Son instead. His purpose was to defeat sin—the cause of all suffering—and to reconcile us to God. He came to make us friends of God and by his resurrection to guarantee all who trust in him a place in heaven: 'so that you, by his poverty, might become rich'—that is wealth beyond the treasures of this world.

The novelist E M Forster foolishly claimed: 'When I realised that the main aim of the incarnation was not to stop war, or pain or poverty, but to free us from sin, I became less interested.' What a blind conclusion! It is like a man saying: 'When I realised that the main aim of medicine was not to treat symptoms but to destroy the cause of disease and death, I became less interested.'

## How poor was poor?

When he who was the centre of adoration and worship in heaven came to this earth, he was born as a helpless baby and laid in a haybox. For a moment the hosts of angels announced his birth in a fanfare of heavenly glory to a handful of poor shepherds—then both angels and shepherds left him. Wise stargazers from a foreign land were led to the place where his parents lodged; they presented a few gifts to tide over the simple family—and then they left him too. Next on the scene were the merciless soldiers from Herod who massacred all the two-year-old boys in Bethlehem—but their quarry had gone. And ever since, the name of that child and the cause of his followers have been the object of hate and bitter opposition across the world. He who was rich became poor.

They called him a glutton and a drunkard, a collaborator with quislings and a friend of the vilest scum in society ( Matthew 11:18–19). They mocked that he was a sinner, demon possessed, a despised Samaritan (John 8:48; 9:24), even a traitor to the Emperor himself (John 19:12), and a blasphemer (Matthew 26:65). Crucifying an innocent character can be a cruel form of persecution, and for the sinless Son of God—who had lived always in perfect harmony with his Father—to be accused of treacherously siding with the dark enemy and of hurling insults at the Father, must have been a bitter hurt.

But he asked for it! Joseph and his mother fled to Egypt—a long-time enemy of Israel—and returned to live in Nazareth. Contrary to a Christian tradition, there is no firm evidence that Nazareth was particularly despised—though there are some grounds for thinking that it was looked upon with suspicion. Nathaniel's often-quoted comment: 'Can anything good come out of Nazareth?' may express no more than his surprise since Nazareth is never specifically mentioned in the Old Testament and therefore would seem to have no claim to the Messiah. Certainly the city was remote in a high valley and perhaps aloof. What was significant, however, is the fact that when the crowd announced him as: 'Jesus, the prophet from Nazareth in Galilee' (Matthew 21:11), it was a comment of surprise—whoever heard of a prophet from Nazareth?

Why did he not return to Bethlehem? That was his birthplace and the town dignified with royal connections as the hometown of the great King David and with Messianic connections (Micah 5:2). Surely it would have been more telling if he had been announced as 'Jesus from Bethlehem'. But he never was. Even Pilate knew him only as 'Jesus of Nazareth, the King of the Jews' (John 19:19).

Even more to the point was the way he rode into Jerusalem, not on a fine horse or in a glittering chariot, but on the colt of an ass. The donkey was the most widely used beast of burden in the ancient East, and often still is, and it was no shame to ride on a donkey—unless you were claiming to be a king! In that case it would be ridiculous. The Roman persecutors later ridiculed their Christian victims by referring to them as *assinari*. When he submitted himself to the cruel indignity of crucifixion it only compounded the mockery of his claims. For the Romans, crucifixion was the death reserved for the lowest common criminal; and it gave first century graffiti artists a field day to scrawl on walls pictures of a donkey-headed man spread out on a cross. For this reason Christians were not in a hurry to use the cross as a symbol of their faith, and they preferred the fish, or the letters alpha and omega (from Revelation 22:13—the first and last letters of the Greek alphabet) or the *chi-rho* monogram (the first two letters of the word *Christ*).

The way the Triune God chose to make salvation possible was by the greatest act of grace. In a simple phrase the apostle summed up the before and after when he wrote, 'After making purification for sins (the *New King James Version* rightly adds the phrase 'by himself'), he sat down at the right hand of the Majesty on high' (Hebrews 1:3). In order to make purification for our sins, God chose the hardest way possible. He chose to send his Son to die.

The incarnation was the hardest thing the Father and the Son ever did, and the one thing they did not have to do. It was not hard for the Son of God to create the world by a powerful word of command, and it is not hard for him to uphold the whole of the universe by that same powerful word. But it was desperately hard for him to become what he was not and suffer the scorn and ridicule of his creatures and submit to death in the jaws of Satan's final throw, and to come here knowing that for a few terrible hours he would be rejected by his Father because he would become our sin in our place.

God chose a way of salvation that, beyond all doubt, demonstrated that the whole cost was born by himself; we could pay nothing. The incarnation was the only way. In the incarnation God stooped down to meet us at our point of need. How else could we know what God is like? How else could we be assured of his love and care? How else could we be certain that salvation was possible and secure? He did not do it for his sake, for he could have chosen any way he preferred; there must have been an easier way. But this way was the only way for us—though the most costly for him. That is the grace of the incarnation.

LET EARTH AND HEAVEN COMBINE,
angels and men agree
to praise in songs divine
the incarnate Deity;
our God contracted to a span,
incomprehensibly made man.

2. He laid his glory by,
took form in mortal clay;
unseen by human eye
the hidden Godhead lay;
infant of days he here became,
and bore the meek Immanuel's name.

**3.** See in that infant's face
the depths of Deity;
endeavour, while you gaze,
to probe the mystery;
let even angels gaze no more,
but bow and silently adore.

**4.** Unsearchable the love
that has our Saviour brought;
his grace is far above
the reach of human thought:
it is enough that God, we know,
our God, is manifest below.

**5.** He deigns in flesh to appear,
widest extremes to join;
to bring our vileness near,
and make us all divine:
and we the life of God shall know,
for God is manifest below.

**6.** Made perfect by his love
and sanctified by grace,
we shall from earth remove
and see his glorious face:
then shall his love be fully showed
and we shall be complete in God.

Charles Wesley 1707–88
*Praise!* 364 © in this Version Praise Trust

1. Discuss all that Christ was and enjoyed before the incarnation.

2. From Isaiah 6:1–3 and 9:5; Philippians 2:5–11; Colossians 1:15–20 and Hebrews 1:3 how would you defend the Christian belief that Jesus Christ was truly God?

3. Anselm claimed that since the human race was the offender and rebel, only mankind could put right the wrong. Is this the best explanation for the incarnation?

4. How did Christ demonstrate that he never used his authority as God to his own advantage?

5. What is the pastoral value of the incarnation?

# Invincible grace

'He who had set me apart before I was born and who called me by his grace'
Galatians 1:15

Throughout his life Paul frequently looked back in sorrow and in amazement. Sorrow at what he once was—proud, self-confident, narrow-minded and arrogant; a bitter, Christ-rejecting, Christian-persecuting and Church-destroying extremist. And amazement at what he now is—the acknowledged leader of the Christian community, the privileged receiver of revelation from God, the model first century church planter, and above all a man with a passion to know Christ, a willingness to suffer for the faith he once laboured to destroy, and with a total conviction of the reality of heaven.

John Newton also provides us with a clear example of invincible grace, so we will use him often in this chapter. Like Paul, he was equally amazed at the change in his own life. When he first published his autobiography in 1764, shortly after he had settled as curate-in-charge at the parish church in Olney, he found himself the object of great interest. He wrote that from all over the nation: 'People come to stare. I am a mystery to them. Indeed, I am a mystery to myself.' What amazed Paul and John more than anything, was how they came to shift from their total unbelief and opposition, to their total commitment to Christ.

Over the centuries, Christians have debated the process of conversion. What makes a man or woman 'wake up' to the call of the gospel and turn to Christ in repentance? Most would agree that the answer lies somewhere in the word 'grace'. Paul leaves no room for doubt in Ephesians 2:8, 'By grace you have been saved through faith. And this is not your own doing; it is the gift of God.' Conversion is through the undeserved mercy of God who applies the righteousness of Jesus Christ to our account so that we can be justified—declared free from our guilt of Christ-rejecting sin. This is why grace is one of the most beautiful words in the Bible.

Whilst justification by faith has been called a hallmark of true Christianity, I would suggest that grace is the true hallmark, because grace comes before justification. Justification is God's verdict when all the merits of Christ's righteousness are put to our account, but grace is God's *willingness* to do so; in fact grace is God's eagerness and joy in doing so. Grace is not wrung from God reluctantly, it is given gladly. And what is more important, grace begins in eternity. Without grace in eternity there would be no justification in time. But exactly when does grace 'kick in'? If grace describes God's eternal purposes to save me and justify me, when does it all take effect, and how?

## How can we respond to God?

Some assume that we have to exercise our will to respond to God. God stands back and waits, and only when we call does he respond. It is our initiative and God waits patiently. We are told that God would never command us to do what we cannot do, so the fact that he commands us to repent and turn to him must mean that we can do this without his immediate aid.

One obvious problem with this position is that there certainly *are* some things God calls us to do that he knows we cannot achieve. He commands us to be holy because he is holy (Leviticus 11:45; 1 Peter 1:15), but on this side of our transformation in heaven that is not fully possible. The standard is set before us as an incentive to holy living and a reminder that God does not reduce his standards to suit our convenience. However, some have done just that, and they suggest that what God is really expecting is an 'all-round integrity and sincerity' and no more. But when our Lord defined the greatest commandment as: 'You shall love the Lord your God with all your heart and with all your soul and with all your mind', and the second as: 'You shall love your neighbour as yourself' (Matthew 22:37–39), he meant exactly what that appears to mean.

Others conclude that whilst it is true that the first faltering move towards God is ours, as soon as we cry for help, God sends his Holy Spirit to sharpen our understanding and strengthen our faith. The American evangelist Charles G Finney wrote in the middle of the nineteenth century: 'It is mine to be willing to believe and it is the part of God's grace to assist.' We have to make the first call. The problem with this is that it demands of us the hardest part—responding from our stubborn and rebellious mind and will—and it leaves for God the easiest part of assisting our progress. In reality, our predicament is that we don't want God to start with—we are spiritually dead. It takes more power to start your car from stationary than it does to keep it moving. The initial turn of the ignition to wake up the vehicle draws massive energy from the battery; but once the engine is running, the battery can relax.

Others disagree with both these wait-and-see and cooperative agreement positions, and claim that as we are so very sinful we *must* have the Holy Spirit to take the initiative. To continue the automobile illustration, we need the Holy Spirit for a 'jump-start'. However, once we are alive to God, it is all up to us. We may resist even to the point of final rejection of the truth. In fact we may, and many do, surprise God by our stubbornness, and God is willing to have it this way because he loves this sort of 'open' relationship with us by which we choose the what, when and if of receiving grace. This is an increasingly popular approach today. It is known as 'open theology' or, with a slight variation, 'process theology'. God, we are assured, cannot ever be certain of our response to him but he enjoys relying upon our cooperation and will never compel us to do anything that we do not want to do.

In contrast to each of these views, the position taught by evangelical

Christianity at the time of the Reformation in the sixteenth century and beyond, was that our response to God is all due to his grace from start to finish. We do not receive the Holy Spirit *when* we believe, but we receive the Holy Spirit *so that* we can believe.

This conviction is especially seen in Galatians 1:15–16 where Paul expresses his gratitude and amazement that it was grace alone that set him apart 'before I was born' and 'called' him and revealed Christ to him. Such a view is also based upon our helpless condition before conversion. Paul describes it this way: 'You were dead in the trespasses and sins in which you once walked' (Ephesians 2:1). Before our conversion we were living a spiritual death even in an active life. Therefore in a real sense our freedom was lost. We could make many moral and ordinary choices, and at times good ones—not all religious or non-religious morality is bad morality—but in responding to God we are helpless.

In 1517 Martin Luther, the German Reformer, wrote a book entitled *The Bondage of the Will*; it was an argument against the Dutch theologian, Desiderius Erasmus, who believed that we could respond to God by our own power. Commenting upon our Lord's words: 'No one can come to me unless the Father who sent me draws him' (John 6:44), Luther wrote, 'Christ declares not only that the works and efforts of "freewill" are unavailing, but that even the very word of the gospel is heard in vain.' He went on to assert that we have no power of our own to respond to God. It is not just that we *will not* respond, the reality is that we *cannot* respond. To word this another way: before the Fall mankind was free not to sin, but after the Fall mankind was not free not to sin. Or, in the words of the apostle Paul: 'The natural person (that refers to someone who is without the Spirit of God) does not accept the things of the Spirit of God, for they are folly to him, and he is not able to understand them because they are spiritually discerned' (1 Corinthians 2:14).

In Romans 8:5–8 Paul expressed the hopeless helplessness of what he called the 'flesh'; in this context the word refers to our sinful nature: 'Those who live according to the flesh have their minds on the things of the flesh … To set the mind on the flesh is death … For the mind that is set on the flesh is hostile to God, for it does not submit to God's law; indeed, it cannot. Those who are in the flesh cannot please God.' This is all very plain even though not pleasant. In his first chapter in Romans, Paul presented a bleak picture of humanity. He wrote of a will in rebellion against the truth (v 18), and without a love for God (v 21), a futile mind and a foolish heart (v 21), emotions out of control (vs 24–27), a life filled with all kinds of wickedness and a conscience corrupted so that it is no longer reliable (v 32). When we package all this with the fact that we are dead towards God (Ephesians 2:1), hostile to God (Romans 8:7), blind to the truth (2 Corinthians 4:4) slaves to sin and Satan (Romans 7:14; 2 Peter 2:19), and incapable of responding to God (John 6:44). It is all very depressing and hardly surprising that modern religions and sociologists are not comfortable with such a diagnosis.

So, if our nature is helpless, is it all hopeless? That is exactly the point at which Paul's claim in Galatians 1:15–16 comes in: 'He who had set me apart before I was born … called me by his grace (and) was pleased to reveal his Son to me'. That is invincible grace.

## The eternal grace of God's choice

This grace that determined our salvation was according to God's own purpose—not ours—before time began. Elsewhere Paul expressed it another way when he told the Ephesian Christians that they were 'chosen in Christ before the foundation of the world' (Ephesians 1:4); and he made the same claim in 2 Timothy 1:9, 'Called … not because of our works, but because of his own purpose and grace which he gave to us in Christ Jesus before the ages began.' Twice in the Revelation of John we learn that our names were written in the book of life before 'the foundation of the world' (13:8; 17:8).

This is the meaning of that striking word 'predestined' that Paul uses in Romans 8:29–30 and Ephesians 1:5, 11. The Greek word is made up from a little preposition that means 'beforehand', and another word from which we gain the English word 'horizon'. The verb *horizo* originally referred to the act of dividing or separating one thing from another. For us the horizon refers to the dividing line between earth and sky; in the New Testament it is used of a boundary or limit (Acts 17:26). So, the word predestined means that we have been brought within God's horizon from before the beginning of time. God plans what he will see and sees all that he has planned.

The God who created the universe of stars and planets, who planned the laws of science and the exact regulation of this complex world, the God of the infinity of space and the eternity of time, of majestic holiness, fearful justice and sovereign power, is the God who, before time began, chose those who would be saved, and he credited grace to their account. He determined even then, to deal with them favourably and not as their sins deserved. He keyed in their names to the database of citizenship in heaven. Paul can confidently claim that the solid foundation of God's kingdom has a seal that reads, 'The Lord knows those who are his' (2 Timothy 2:19). It was not that God woke up when he heard us call but we woke up when he gave us grace to call. There is a world of difference between the two.

No one knew this better than John Newton, and writing to a friend on this subject he drew his attention to John 3:27, 'A person cannot receive even one thing unless it is given him from heaven.' The converted blasphemer went on to encourage his correspondent by reminding him of the broad road to destruction that once we were all walking: 'Were not you and I in this road? Were we better than those who continue in it still? What has made us differ from our former selves? *Grace*. What has made us differ from those who are now as we once were? *Grace*. Then this grace … must be differencing or distinguishing grace; that is, in other words, electing grace.' Newton was well aware of his own state at the time of his remarkable conversion to Christ and so he continued, 'We know that the Lord foresaw us in a state utterly incapable either of believing or obeying, unless he was pleased to work in us to will and to do according to his own good pleasure.'

Newton had in his congregation a wise old lady who, when challenged on the subject of predestination, responded, 'Oh, I settled that long ago. If he had not chosen me before I was born, he certainly would have seen nothing in me worth choosing me for afterwards.' And Saul of Tarsus was not ashamed of grace like that. In the same way God told the young prophet Jeremiah: 'Before I formed you in the womb I knew you; before you were born I consecrated you; I appointed you a prophet to the nations' (Jeremiah 1:5). That purposeful grace of God was not peculiar to Jeremiah, it is true for all who find Christ as Lord and Saviour.

Many Christians spend too much of their time either arguing or worrying over this great truth of predestination, when all that God intends for us is that we should bask in the light of it. To change the picture—it is a comfortable armchair to relax in. For all who have sincerely turned from their sin to Christ, this is one of the most reassuring doctrines found in the Bible. Luther expressed his enjoyment of this grace of God like this: 'I have the comfortable certainty that I please God, not by reason of the merit of my works, but by reason of his merciful favour promised to me; so that, if I work too little, or badly, he does not reckon it to me, but with fatherly compassion pardons me and makes me better. This is the glorying of the saints of God.'

When the sun finally breaks out after a long, miserably cold and wet winter, I suppose there may be some people who are so terrified by the thought of skin cancer from the harmful ultraviolet rays of the sun that, before they venture out, they dress themselves in their winter coat, scarf, hat and gloves for protection. For most of us, however, we are so delighted at the rediscovery of all the benefits of God's sunshine that we throw off our winter clothes and enjoy the warmth and light of God's gracious gift. Over this great truth of God's electing grace, we are to go out and take pleasure in its warmth, strength and security. All that God wants us to do with this great truth of election is to enjoy it.

## The preparing grace of God

The grace that knew us from eternity, determined our salvation, and settled our names in the database of heaven was also the grace that maintained a watchful care over us long before our conversion; in fact, from the moment of our birth. The Puritans had a word for this; they called it 'prevenient' grace. That word is from the Latin *praevinire* which means 'to come beforehand or precede'. Our English word 'prevent' came from this Latin word, and originally it referred to someone who precedes or goes before us. 'Prevenient grace' refers to God's preparation in our lives when he prepared the way before our conversion. We may call it 'preparing grace' if we wish. Certainly at times he 'got in our way' to ensure that we kept to the path that he had chosen for us, even though we did not know this. Our birth, family, education, friends—even our decisions—were all in the hands of the One who had chosen us for salvation.

Saul of Tarsus was a well-educated Jew from one of the best universities of his day; highly regarded and with good connections, he was a Roman citizen and possessed a sharp mind, a strong will and a firmly disciplined life. This was all true long before he became a Christian, but it meant that once converted, Paul had easy access into the synagogues throughout the Roman Empire and this formed the basis of his strategy when he became a Christian evangelist. This was all part of God's prevenient grace in the life of one who would be 'a chosen instrument of mine to carry my name before the Gentiles and kings and the children of Israel' (Acts 9:15).

As a young boy, John Newton had his mind stored by his godly mother with Bible verses and hymns from the collection of Isaac Watts. This was later used by God in his experience of conversion when those verses came flooding back to his memory. John possessed a very retentive mind—he learnt to read at the age of four and began Latin at six—enjoyed a gift of putting thoughts into verse, and he was a natural leader. All this prepared him for his later service for God.

If we look back at our own lives, it is not difficult to see the plan of God in our family connections and upbringing, our natural ability and interests, perhaps also our enjoyment of reading, studying or just arguing! We may have been 'open to religion', or impressionable, or naturally sceptical, even cynical. Many roads closed, or opened, that at the time were frustrating or forwarding our plans; then we could see no purpose, but much later on we could see how everything worked towards our conversion and subsequent Christian service. Whatever our background, personality or interests, we can now see how it was all being used by God to prepare the way for our future.

Prevenient grace is not only God's preparation, but also his providence. Those 'unseen footprints' of God (Psalm 77:19) by which he protects and guards us until the time of our conversion—and beyond— are all part of invincible grace. Our lives are full of occasions of remarkable protection and the strange coincidences that brought us first into touch with the message of the gospel. We know very little about the early life of Saul of Tarsus, though we do know of his presence at the death of Stephen which clearly made an impact on his conscience. Of John Newton we know much more. As a boy he narrowly avoided death on several occasions, and as a godless sailor he was more than once remarkably preserved, though at the time he never recognised the hand of God in these 'lucky' escapes from death.

Perhaps the greatest evidence of prevenient grace in Newton's life was the series of coincidences that finally brought him back from the coast of Africa. John was by now trading for slaves on the coast of New Guinea and was preparing for a mission inland. Before he set out, a ship passed the point where Newton and a colleague were working and, being in need of some items, they sent up a signal for trade. It was unusual for ships to pass this part of the coast at this time of the year, and the captain at first decided that since his ship was already past the convenient point for returning he would simply ignore the signal; however, on a whim he hove-to and received Newton's trading partner on board. Almost the captain's first question was to enquire whether the young man knew of a John Newton anywhere on this coast! He had received orders from Newton's father that if he ever located Newton, he was to bring him back to England at whatever cost. John had not been heard of in England for more than eighteen months. The same happens to all who are chosen for faith in Christ—though we are mostly unaware of these unseen footprints and they are not always dramatic.

## The invincible grace of God

For those predestined to eternal life, there is always a time when God's grace 'gets through'. For Saul of Tarsus that moment was outside the walls of the city of Damascus in the year AD 30, for John of Wapping it was on a broken ship in mid Atlantic in March 1748. Whenever we hear the call of God with ears that are listening and a mind that can understand, it is at a moment God has planned from eternity. This is what is meant by the phrase 'called according to his purpose' in Romans 8:28. It is that moment when God speaks personally and we must respond. This does not mean only that we ought to, but that we cannot do other than respond; there is a divine compulsion about this call. God is speaking to us personally—and we know it! For Saul it came in a vision and an audible voice, for John it came through a terrified conscience and the recollection of many verses from the Bible. For each it is personal and particular.

Some refer to this as the 'irresistible' call of God. John Newton preferred the word 'invincible' because he knew that we can resist the call of God—and he often did—but finally we cannot win; God always has his way. Saul had obviously been resisting the nagging of his mind and conscience and that is why the Lord told him, 'It is hard for you to kick against the goads' (Acts 26:14).

In *Grace Abounding*, Bunyan traces the invincible grace of God's call in his own life. He tells of the occasion when he was in the town of Bedford and overheard a group of women sitting at their doorway and talking about religion. His conscience was already troubling him and he deliberately listened-in to their conversation. Their talk both intrigued him and troubled him because they seemed to have found a new world that he was a complete stranger to, and their experience of God and salvation was well beyond anything he himself could understand. He slipped away and went on with his business but he commented, 'Their talk and conversation followed me.' He could not get out of his mind the things they had been saying, and the assurance and joy that they had. Bunyan's conscience was troubling him. Invincible grace was at work in his life. In his case the path to salvation was a long and hard one; he went through an agony and torment of conscience before finally he found peace with God.

In his poem *The Hound of Heaven*, Francis Thompson, a Roman Catholic in religion, described the work of this invincible God as a great beast (he did not mean that in a bad sense) following relentlessly the one he loves even though that person is struggling to get away from him. Thompson, who died in ill health and poverty in 1907 at the age of forty-eight, began his powerful poem in this way,

'I fled Him, down the nights and down the days;
I fled Him, down the arches of the years;
I fled Him, down the labyrinthine ways
Of my own mind; and in the mist of tears

I hid from Him, and under running laughter.

    Up vistaed hopes I sped;

    And shot, precipitated,

Adown Titanic glooms of chasmèd fears,

From those strong Feet that followed, followed after.

    But with unhurrying chase,

    And unperturbèd pace,

Deliberate speed, majestic instancy,

    They beat—and a Voice beat

    More instant than the Feet—

"All things betray thee, who betrayest Me."'

God would not let him go but followed him in all his attempts to break free. Francis Thompson continued by describing the man who runs from God, turning to the world for its pleasure, longing to find love, and then, hungry, thirsty and discontented, he is stripped of all he hoped would satisfy him; his life crumbling around him:

'In the rash lustihead of my young powers,

    I shook the pillaring hours

And pulled my life upon me; grimed with smears,

I stand amid the dust o' the mounded years –

My mangled youth lies dead beneath the heap.

My days have crackled and gone up in smoke,

Have puffed and burst as sun-starts on a stream.'

Finally, with the Hound of Heaven never giving up the chase, he discovers that the heavy hand of suffering and pain that he thought was for his harm, was in reality the only love that he, unworthy as he is, could ever expect. He hears the voice of the one who reminds him that human love has to be merited, but that he has merited nothing:

"How little worthy of any love thou art!
Whom wilt thou find to love ignoble thee,
    Save Me, save only Me?
All which I took from thee I did but take,
    Not for thy harms,
But just that thou might'st seek it in My arms.
    All which thy child's mistake
Fancies as lost, I have stored for thee at home:
    Rise, clasp My hand, and come!'"

How much Francis Thompson understood of the theology behind his poem we can only guess, but Paul of Tarsus and John of Wapping would not only have appreciated the theology, they would have recognised how very closely it expressed their own experience. Paul referred to himself as the 'foremost of sinners', and John certainly knew a 'mangled youth grimed with smears' the details of which he once longed could be 'buried in eternal silence'.

But this work of the Spirit is not simply external impressions. Peter wrote of Christians being 'partakers of the divine nature' (2 Peter 1:4), and that is one of the most significant phrases in the New Testament. If all that we have said about the tragic state of human nature after the Fall is true, then God must not only take the initiative but he must also provide all that is necessary for us to be able to respond to him. In biblical terms this is the new birth, or regeneration, without which, according to our Lord himself, no one can see the kingdom of God (John 3:3); and again by our Lord's own claim this is a sovereign work of the Spirit (v 8). It is not for us to be fussy over the time-sequence of regeneration and conversion, or to know precisely the moment of the Holy Spirit's first work in our life or the exact time of our new birth; but we must surely agree with Luther that, 'Through the drawing of the Holy Spirit, God makes willing men out of the obstinate and unwilling.'

## Grace to be willing

It is natural to object to the idea of God forcing us against our will to bow to Christ in repentance. But whoever believes that God forces men and women unwillingly into the Kingdom of God? He will not frog-march or press-gang people into his kingdom; he is not argumentative and belligerent. On the contrary, he seeks willing volunteers for his service. Matthew illustrated this by borrowing a lengthy quotation from Isaiah to reveal that Christ will not break a bruised reed or quench a smouldering wick (Matthew 12:18–21). In his determination God is gently firm and kindly resolute.

The fact is that God works upon our will by his Spirit, sometimes by gentle wooing and at times by the harsh treatment of our circumstances; sometimes he leaves us to run and we try the world and all its pleasures—like the man in Thompson's *The Hound of Heaven*; sometimes we suffer pain and disappointment. At times we cry out *against* him; but always that Hound of Heaven pursues us, until at last we long *for* him and cry out *to* him. From all who have been 'appointed to eternal life' (Acts 13:48) he will ultimately and inevitably win willing repentance, devoted love and believing trust. This is no new teaching, because as far back as the time of Moses the nation of Israel was encouraged to believe that God would work in their lives: 'So that you will love the LORD your God with all your heart and with all your soul' (Deuteronomy 30:6). God is a great huntsman—he always hits his mark.

God's agency in this prevenient grace is twofold. He uses the Holy Spirit and the word of God—by which we mean the Scriptures. The human will is not a third agent in cooperation, as if God cannot succeed by his Spirit and his word unless we agree to allow him. Lazarus had been four days dead and, in a warm climate, Martha wisely pointed out that there would be an offensive smell if the tomb were to be opened. Nevertheless the stone was rolled from the mouth of the cave and

Lazarus 'came out, his hands and feet bound with linen strips' (John 11:44). But Lazarus did not come out of the grave because the stone was removed, still less because he considered it an attractive option, or because he decided not to be dead any longer. There were just two forces that combined to bring Lazarus out of the tomb: The commanding voice of the Son of God and the reviving power of the Spirit of God. Nothing less and nothing more is required for our new birth.

The way that God applies grace is not by the Spirit alone as some would suggest, or by the word alone, as others propose, but by the Spirit *and* the word. It is not that God sometimes uses the Spirit instead of the Scriptures; so-called spiritual illumination that comes apart from God's revealed word is often very dangerous. Equally it is not that at other times he will use the word instead of the Spirit, as if we can rely upon the moral force of the truth of the Bible to awaken sinners. On the contrary, it is God's normal way to use the word by his Spirit to convince of sin, of righteousness and of judgement. No spiritual experience or persuasive argument is sufficiently powerful to awaken a Christ-rejecting sinner to new life.

I said the word and the Spirit are God's 'normal way' of applying his grace to a sinner, because I recognise that where there are no Scriptures, and no evangelist either, then God may send his Spirit to employ other ways to bring the knowledge of his Son. I do not doubt the stories of those across the world of Islam where the Bible is unknown, who are introduced to Christ through a dream or vision; God is free to reach into the lives of his elect in any way he chooses, but it will always be through his Holy Spirit. And his way of saving sinners and of growing Christians, in normal circumstances is always by his Spirit through the word.

This is why the Scriptures are called 'the sword of the Spirit' (Ephesians 6:17); and for this reason, 'walking in the Spirit' and 'keeping in step with the Spirit' (Galatians 5:16, 25) are to be defined as obedience to the Bible. When Peter encouraged the young churches that, 'His divine power has granted to us all things that pertain to (are relevant for) life and godliness' (2 Peter 1:3), the 'all things' are described in the next verse when he writes of the promises of God and the Christian being a 'partaker of the divine nature'. That is the word and the Spirit. With those two we have all that we need to become a Christian, and all that we need to continue as a Christian.

There was a time when Christians often seized the opportunity to review the invincible grace of God in their lives both before and after their conversion. We sadly neglect this today, and this is partly because we have been given the impression that we are somehow smart to respond to the call of God and that the first inclination of our heart and mind towards the Creator was more our work than his. We have wandered a long way from the theology of the old hymn by W Spencer Walton:

O the love that sought me!
O the blood that bought me!
O the grace that brought me to the fold,
wondrous grace that brought me to the fold!


MY LORD, I DID NOT CHOOSE YOU
for that could never be;
this heart would still refuse you
had you not chosen me:
you took the sin that stained me,
you cleansed and made me new;
for you of old ordained me
that I should live to you.

2. Unless your grace had called me
and taught my opening mind,
the world would have enthralled me,
to heavenly glories blind:
my heart knows none above you;
for you I long, I thirst,
and know that if I love you,
Lord, you have loved me first.

Josiah Conder 1789–1855
*Praise!* 691

**FOR GROUP DISCUSSION**

1. What are the attractions and the problems with the 'free will' approach of our response to God?
2. How would you defend God's electing love from the Bible?
3. 'All that God wants us to do with this great truth of election is to enjoy it.' What are the pastoral benefits of a belief in the electing grace of God?
4. Share together the evidence of 'prevenient grace' in your own lives.
5. Discuss how providence, the word of God and the Holy Spirit work together in conversion.

# Forgiving Grace

'Forgive, as the Lord forgave you' Colossians 3:13

Well into the Middle Ages the study of mathematics was regarded with either suspicion or derision. Abelard, the French philosopher of the twelfth century wrote of it as 'a nefarious [evil] study'. Long before that, in the time of the Roman Empire, the Theodosian Code of AD 394 passed the sentence of death upon all 'mathematicians'—mainly because of their alliance with astrology, fortune telling and divination. As a schoolboy I had different reasons for agreeing with the Emperor Theodosius!

When King David took up the study of maths it was one of the greatest mistakes of his life. 2 Samuel 24 records that he ordered a census of his fighting men, and for that act of arrogance both he and the nation suffered. Almost immediately David owned up to his sin: it seemed to lay like a terrible weight upon him. He vividly expressed the experience of a man under conviction in Psalm 32 when he complained of the heavy hand of God: 'my bones wasted away through my groaning all day long' and 'my strength was dried up as by the heat of summer' (vs 3–4).

One thing David was acutely aware of was that the mathematics of God is perfect. He must have felt that if God counted up his sins they would amount to far more than the million and a quarter men he had counted under arms. But David also knew that the happiest man on earth was the one 'whose transgression is forgiven, whose sin is covered … against whom the LORD counts no iniquity' (vs 1–2).

Forgiveness is when God stops counting up our sin. When sin is forgiven by God it will never be recalled, neither in time nor in eternity.

God adorned his promise of forgiveness with picture after picture to convince his people that it is not a mere passing mood or transient warm feeling, but that forgiveness is final and for ever:

He will replace their scarlet sins with the whiteness of snow (Isaiah 1:18)

Cast their sins behind his back (Isaiah 38:17).

Sweep them away like a dissolving cloud or mist (Isaiah 44:22).

Tread them into the ground without trace and cast them into the depths of the sea (Micah 7:19).

But of all his pictures, one is understood far more today than when David first passed it on:

'The Lord is merciful and gracious,

slow to anger and abounding in steadfast love.

He will not always chide,

nor will he keep his anger forever.

He does not deal with us according to our sins,

nor repay us according to our iniquities.

For as high as the heavens are above the earth,

so great is his steadfast love towards those who fear him;

as far as the east is from the west,

so far does he remove our transgressions from us.'

Psalm 103:8–12

When David looked up into the sky, he could see around 4,500 stars on a clear night. What he did not know was that in the great splash of light across the heavens that we call the Milky Way, there could be in excess of thirty thousand million stars. And beyond that? The only certain knowledge that we have added since the time of David almost three thousand years ago is that there is far more universe beyond our furthest probes. That is how far God removes forgiven sin from us.

The earth is not quite round. The equatorial diameter is greater than the polar diameter—it is a bit fatter by around twenty-seven miles than it is tall. There is no west pole or east pole. Our psalmist, knowingly or unknowingly, measured the greatest distance, which is from east to west. Here there are no fixed points; to travel from east to west is endless. That too is how far God removes forgiven sin.

## Paul's view of Forgiveness

In the New Testament the pictures are no less powerful. God has, 'forgiven us all our trespasses, by cancelling the record of debt that stood against us with its legal demands. This he set aside, nailing it to the cross' (Colossians 2:13–14). That is typical of Paul tumbling over himself with imagery. The phrase 'the record of debt' translates just one word in the Greek (*cheirographon*), and although this is the only use of the word in the New Testament, it was commonplace in the time of Paul. It referred to a certificate of debt written with one's own hand—a promise that in due time the debt would be repaid. Once paid, the bill would be literally crossed out and cancelled. God has cancelled and obliterated the charge sheet.

That language is not too strong, because the simple word 'cancelled' was used of the practice of washing out the writing on a papyrus scroll so that it could be used again. Technically it is called a *palimpsest* which means 'scraped again'. Our grubby and smeared life is washed and scraped clean so that God can write with us a new life. The Christian has a brand new recycled life. Palimpsest Christianity!

The word 'forgiven' in Colossians 2:13—the verb is *charizomai*—is derived directly from our beautiful noun 'grace' (*charis*), and it means 'to show oneself gracious'. However, in Ephesians 1:7–8 Paul uses an altogether different word: 'In him we have *redemption* through his blood, the *forgiveness* of our trespasses, according to the riches of his grace, which he lavished upon us, in all wisdom and insight ...'

Here 'forgiveness' translates a word meaning to release or set free and it was a common word for the release of prisoners. The vivid picture of the prison doors opened and the captive walking free may be what was in the mind of the apostle—who at the time of writing was under house arrest in Rome! But, once more, the freedom is not due to anything we have done, it is a freedom gained by the blood of Christ—much as Barabbas was released in exchange for the death of the Man whose blood the mob screamed for (Matthew 27:16–26). Linking 'forgiveness' with 'redemption' is no coincidence for Paul. Redemption was common enough in the first century, but Paul chose a form of the word that occurs ten times in the New Testament and fewer than that in all other known literature of the time. Perhaps he deliberately chose an irregular word to press home a Christian distinctiveness.

There is an ongoing debate about whether Paul's use of the word 'redemption' applies chiefly to the slave market, prisoners of war, or to the Jewish practice of redeeming the first-born. But whichever picture is intended, and perhaps the slave market would be chiefly in the mind of the congregation at Ephesus, the picture was certainly one of release from captivity or death as a result of a payment made. In this case Paul is insistent that the payment is nothing less than the blood of Christ.

However deep the dye, however ingrained the stain, however hurt our conscience may be and whatever guilt may plague our mind and soak into our soul, forgiveness by the blood of Christ is full, free and for ever.

When we know our sins are forgiven, we can be sure that they are blotted out, no longer reckoned against us, sealed up and cast away from God's sight; they are forgotten by God, trodden into the ground, cast into the deepest ocean, removed as endlessly as the equator and as distantly as the infinity of space; the record is removed, the slate wiped clean and all is replaced by the pure whiteness of snow. We are set free from the penalty and imprisonment of sin. And all through the blood of Christ on Calvary.

But there is a condition attached to forgiveness!

## Conditional forgiveness!

There is a condition attached to the experience of receiving God's forgiveness, and it is called *repentance*. In the New Testament the word 'repentance' is made up from two words: a little preposition plus the noun for 'mind'. Repentance means to change our mind—to turn and return to God. To do this, we own up to our sin of rejecting Christ, hate the sin that sent him to the cross, and return to the God who made us.

Forgiveness and salvation are never offered by God—either to his backsliding people or to a pagan world—without repentance. Repentance is an invariable condition for forgiveness. Speaking to Israel God promised, 'If my people who are called by my name humble themselves, and pray and seek my face and turn from their wicked ways, then I will hear from heaven and will forgive their sin and heal their land' (2 Chronicles 7:14). The 'if' is a condition attached to restoration.

At the time of the exile God commanded, 'Repent, and turn from all your transgressions, lest iniquity be your ruin' (Ezekiel 18:30, see also 14:6). Two verses later: '"I have no pleasure in the death of anyone", declares the LORD God; "so turn and live."'

Through Jeremiah God urged his people in exile: 'If you return, I will restore you, and you shall stand before me' (Jeremiah 15:19).

Not once in the Old Testament did God ever forgive without first demanding repentance. There is a phrase used in the time of Jehoiakim that makes this frighteningly clear. A run of bad kings in Judah had left God with no choice but to bring severe judgement upon the nation. The Babylonians swept across the land in their slaughtering tradition and they were followed by bands of Syrians, Moabites and Ammonites who mopped up all that was left. There was no let up. But clearly God was waiting for the people to turn, and they did not. There was no sorrow, no repentance, and no change of mind or heart. And then comes the awful phrase: 'The LORD would not pardon' (2 Kings 24:4) or, as another translation has it: 'The LORD was not willing to forgive.' God will never pardon if we do not repent. That is his condition attached.

The same theme is even more evident in the New Testament where the Greek word *metanoeo* means a complete change of mind for the better. John the Baptist came with a straightforward message: 'Repent, for the Kingdom of heaven is at hand' (Matthew 3:2). And in case we suggest that Jesus had a softer message, almost his first words at the commencement of his own ministry were, 'Repent, for the kingdom of heaven is at hand' (Matthew 4:17). And nothing had altered when he sent his disciples to preach: 'So they went out and proclaimed that people should repent' (Mark 6:12).

At Pentecost Peter followed his Master's example: 'Repent and be baptized every one of you in the name of Jesus Christ for the forgiveness of your sins' (Acts 2:38). It was the same in Peter's next sermon: 'Repent therefore, and turn again, that your sins may be blotted out' (3:19).

Paul carried forward the same message. When preaching at Athens he uncompromisingly declared, 'God commands all people everywhere to repent, because he has fixed a day on which he will judge the world in righteousness' (Acts 17:30–31). He later reminded the Ephesian elders that his invariable message to both Jews and Greeks was that they must turn to God in repentance and have faith in Jesus Christ (Acts 20:21).

Paul was just as consistently insistent in his letters. He reminded the Christians at Rome that the goodness, forbearance and longsuffering of God was 'meant to lead you to repentance' (Romans 2:4). Likewise the believers at Corinth were encouraged not to forget that it is only repentance that can lead to salvation (2 Corinthians 7:9). Repentance, like faith itself, is a gift of God.

Three words can never be divorced: *Repentance, forgiveness and reconciliation.* These three can never be separated; you cannot have one without the others, you cannot even have two without the third. All three must be present and they must be present in this order: Repentance, forgiveness and reconciliation.

God's grace is undeserved, unending, unlimited, invincible and eternal—but not unconditional. 'Repentance' is our part, and to miss this is to misunderstand the character of God and the nature of true conversion.

## How are we to forgive?

Unfortunately, Christians have allowed the word 'forgive' to be defined by the world rather than by the Bible. On this subject society, generally speaking, believes in unconditional grace. Most have never heard the phrase and they have no idea what it means, but they believe it.

In January 1999, Stewart Staines and his two sons aged 8 and 10, were burnt to death as they slept in their jeep in Manaharpur, India. He and his wife Gladys had been working among leprosy sufferers. Gladys immediately decided to stay on with her thirteen year-old daughter. But the other thing she did immediately was to forgive her husband's killers, and she claimed that it was, 'A spontaneous act'. She went on to say that it took away the bitterness from her heart.

That was very commendable, and I do not doubt at all that it took away the bitterness from her heart. I have no criticism of Gladys Staines. But not all can rise to that, and my question is, did she have to forgive? Was she under an obligation to forgive? Was she even right to forgive? Was it essentially Christian for her to forgive?

In the cruel and violent world in which we live there seems to be plenty of opportunity for Christians to show forgiveness, but not just Christians. After the latest terrorist outrage or senseless drink-drive murder, the public waits for the early response of the bereaved: 'I forgive the people who did this terrible thing.' That is trumpeted as a great example to us all, a great victory. But if they cannot muster the emotional courage to utter those saintly words, society reckons they have failed.

Society doesn't say as much, but it has implied it by extolling those who do manage to 'forgive'.

Consequently Christians, not wanting to be morally wrong-footed by an unbelieving world on the subject of forgiveness, have convinced themselves that a public announcement of forgiveness is the right thing to do.

I will set out my response to this in five statements.

### First, God in Christ is our pattern for all responses in life

This should hardly require proof for the Christian. One great purpose of the incarnation was that we could more easily focus upon what God is like and what he expects of us. Christ 'suffered for you, leaving you an example so that you might follow in his steps' (1 Peter 2:21). Christ is always our example. He is our model in holiness, service and priorities and he must therefore be our model in this whole question of forgiveness as well. In the pattern of our forgiving others it can be no different, we are to forgive: 'as God in Christ forgave you' (Ephesians 4:32 and Colossians 3:13). This can only mean that in every respect, the way we are to forgive is to be modelled on the forgiveness we receive from God in Christ.

### Second, in Scripture God never forgives unconditionally

As we have already seen, God's forgiveness is dependent upon repentance. Certainly this is a repentance that is won from us by the invincible grace of God, but it is nevertheless a repentance that is a condition if we are to receive God's grace in forgiveness. If God is our pattern, and that pattern is seen most clearly in Christ, then we must ask why we are expecting mere men and women to forgive those who sin against them regardless of the offender's response. God himself never forgives in this way.

This is a significant pastoral issue. When a man's child is killed by a drunk driver or by the deliberate act of a terrorist we are asking him to do what we expect of no one else. Society does not forgive but demands justice and God does not forgive but demands repentance first. Yet we expect the emotionally bruised to muster with superhuman courage the devout words: 'I forgive'.

### Third, in Scripture forgiveness always involves reconciliation

In his book *Total Forgiveness*, R T Kendall claims that on our part there must be, 'Total forgiveness even when there is not a restoration of relationship. One must totally forgive those who will not be reconciled.' The problem with this statement is that we must ask, where in the Bible did God ever forgive like this? Never did God forgive and still allow those forgiven to remain his enemy. God may not deal with them as their sins deserve but that is mercy or compassion, not forgiveness. Every day the atheist enjoys the benefits of health and strength, beauty and pleasure; this is all part of God's mercy. But that is not forgiveness. The little ditty found in some gardens well expresses this confusion:

The kiss of the sun for pardon;
The song of the birds for mirth.
One is nearer God's heart in a garden
Than anywhere else on earth.

The kiss of the sun and the song of the birds is God's universal grace of mercy, but it is not pardon for sins. No one is reconciled to God through a good day's gardening.

To overlook the essential element of reconciliation in forgiveness denies all that this word forgiveness means in the Bible. This truth is perhaps best seen in a passage that is so often used to support forgiveness regardless of response. In Matthew 18 Peter complains to our Lord about his brother and asks how often he must forgive him; our Lord's reply is often held up to us as a clear lesson of forgiveness without regard to reconciliation. But this entirely overlooks the context of Peter's question. Peter did not ask his question 'out of the blue'. His question and our Lord's answer in Matthew 18:21–35 immediately follows Jesus' teaching on what to do when 'your brother sins against you' (vs 15–17). Here our Lord requires us to 'go and tell him his fault, between you and him alone', and if he 'listens to you' then you have won him over. That 'listening' must imply at the very least an admission of guilt, because if he refuses to hear what is being said, the offended brother must report him to the church; if he refuses to listen to the church then he must be treated 'as a Gentile and a tax-collector' (v 17). Whatever that means it does not sound much like forgiveness!

At this point in the narrative Peter came up with his question: 'Lord, how often will my brother sin against me, and I forgive him? As many as seven times?' The parable that our Lord told in response to Peter's question clearly portrays a debtor who pleads for compassion (vs 23–35). On another occasion Jesus made this very clear when he repeated the same teaching and added, 'If your brother sins, rebuke him, and if he repents, forgive him, and if he sins against you seven times in a day, and turns to you seven times, saying, "I repent", you must forgive him' (Luke 17:3–4).

It could hardly be clearer that Jesus is not teaching unconditional forgiveness. Our Lord is expecting reconciliation: but only on the back of repentance by the offender and forgiveness by the offended—any number of times. This is our pattern.

It is surely against the background of this clear teaching that Matthew 6:14–15 must be interpreted, 'If you forgive others their trespasses, your heavenly Father will also forgive you, but if you do not forgive others their trespasses, neither will your Father forgive your trespasses.' As God will always and only forgive us when we repent, so we *must* forgive others when they repent. Similarly the phrase in the Lord's prayer: 'Forgive us our debts as we also have forgiven our debtors' (Matthew

6:12) must be understood in the same way; the very offering of this prayer implies an admission of guilt and a sorrow for it.

The story of Joseph in the land of Egypt is told in Genesis 43 to 50, and the closing order of events is very instructive. When Joseph first realised who these travellers from the distant land of Canaan were, we are not told that he forgave them—and it is not for us to implant our reconstruction into the mind of Joseph. But he did show them mercy. In fact he proceeded to test their integrity before he revealed his identity to them. And even when at last he told them that he was their brother, there is still no word of forgiveness in the biblical text. Forgiveness came much later in the story. It is not until Genesis 50:16–17, after the death of their father, that the brothers fully own up to the enormity of their sin and plead for forgiveness (v 17).

'They sent word to Joseph, saying, "Your father left these instructions before he died: 'This is what you are to say to Joseph: I ask you to forgive your brothers the sins and the wrongs they committed in treating you so badly.' Now please forgive the sins of the servants of the God of your father." When their message came to him, Joseph wept. His brothers then came and threw themselves down before him. "We are your slaves," they said. But Joseph said to them, "Don't be afraid. Am I in the place of God? You intended to harm me, but God intended it for good to accomplish what is now being done, the saving of many lives. So then, don't be afraid. I will provide for you and your children." And he reassured them and spoke kindly to them.'

At this point Joseph was committed to forgive, and not before. However, it is evident from the whole story that Joseph had long before divested himself of any bitterness and anger at his brothers' action, so that when they turned up on his doorstep many years after their murderous treatment of him, Joseph could instantly show them mercy. That distinction between mercy and forgiveness must never be overlooked or else we downgrade the word forgiveness.

## Fourth, in Scripture forgiveness always implies repentance as a condition and reconciliation as a consequence

This point is, of course, proven by the previous two. If repentance is understood as a hatred and rejection of sin, and if forgiveness is understood in the vigorous way that we have seen earlier in this chapter, then reconciliation between the two parties follows inevitably. It always does when God forgives us, and we cannot assume any different meaning to the three words—repentance, forgiveness and reconciliation—when *we* are called upon to forgive. God, in Christ, is our pattern. But where did the Father or the Son ever forgive without any interest in repentance, a changed life or reconciliation? He said to the woman found in the act of adultery, 'I do not condemn you', but this was followed by an insistence upon a repentant life: 'Go and stop your life of sin.'

There is a striking pastoral illustration of this in Paul's letters to the Corinthians. In 1 Corinthians 5 Paul refers to a serious moral issue in the church that the leaders had apparently overlooked; an issue that even the pagans would not tolerate: 'a man has his father's wife' (v 1). The apostle demanded rigorous discipline: 'Deliver this man to Satan … Purge the evil person from among you' (vs 5,13). From 2 Corinthians 2:5–11 it would appear that this action had its hoped-for effect and the man repented of his sin, because Paul refers to his 'excessive sorrow' (v 7). The issue now was how should the Christians respond to him? However grave his wrongdoing and however serious the scandal, there could now be only one response from the church: 'For such a one, this punishment by the majority is enough, so you should rather turn to forgive and comfort him, or he may be overwhelmed by excessive sorrow. So I beg you to reaffirm your love for him' (vs 6–8). This love would be displayed in wholehearted *forgiveness*—a word that Paul uses three times in verse 10—and that would mean full reconciliation. Significantly there was also repentance on the part of the church for tolerating the sin in the first place; and their repentance is described in 2 Corinthians 7:9–13.

Where there is repentance on the part of the offender there must always be willingness on the part of the offended to forgive and be reconciled. And we have already seen just how bountiful and extensive the forgiveness will be if it is a reflection of God's forgiveness. It may not always be easy, but it is essential; it is a reflection of the unlimited grace of God.

## Fifth, therefore, forgiveness is not appropriate where there is no repentance—but something more valuable must take its place

If I do not have to forgive where there is no repentance, do I have to stay bitter and resentful with a poisoned heart like the Warsaw ghetto leader who said, when he had seen such brutality by the Nazi regime, 'If you were to lick my heart it would poison you.'? Of course not! C S Lewis wisely commented that: 'Everyone says that forgiveness is a lovely idea until he has something to forgive.' Forgiveness is not always easy or pleasant, but it is made so much more easy and pleasant when the condition is met.

Corrie ten Boom, the Christian from Holland who spent much of the war in a concentration camp wrote, 'You never so touch the ocean of God's love as when you forgive and love your enemies.' And she should know. Years after the war Corrie met one of her prison guards.

At the close of a meeting the man approached her: 'You mentioned Ravensbruck in your talk', he began, 'I was a guard there; but since that time I have become a Christian. I know that God has forgiven me for the cruel things I did there, but I would like to hear it from your lips as well. Fraulein, will you forgive me?' Corrie recognised him at once as one of the most cruel guards in that terrible camp. She hesitated as all the vivid memories of those dark days leading to her sister's death flooded back into her mind and she admitted, 'I stood there with the coldness clutching my heart.' Then, woodenly, mechanically, she put out her hand and grasped his, 'I forgive you, brother. With all my heart.' That is precisely what out Lord wanted her to do; that is exactly what he does when we come in repentance and faith. That is abundant, forgiving grace. At that moment—confronted with the repentance of the prison guard—Corrie ten Boom *had* to forgive. But she did not have to forgive until her prison guard was repentant.

## In place of forgiveness

When there is no sorrow or repentance on the part of my enemy—when they do not want reconciliation and cannot see that they have done anything wrong—what does God expect of me then? To exercise a massive effort of will and forgive may help *me*, but it actually does nothing for the offender. He may continue to scoff at God and revel in the misery he has caused. To forgive is meaningless to him. What then should be our response?

Remember, the Lord is our pattern in this subject as in all things. So what do we learn from him? When he looked out over the crowds, we are never once told that he forgave them; but what we are told is that he was moved with 'compassion' for them (Matthew 9:36; 14:14; 15:32).

That is a very strong word because it refers to him being moved with all his inner being. The result of this compassion was that he healed their sick or fed them, as the occasion demanded. That was mercy. This is exactly the distinction that we have already made. Interestingly, in that parable of the unforgiving servant recorded in Matthew 18, the word 'pity' is used in v 27, but the result in v 33 is described as 'mercy'; some English translations have 'compassion' in both verses, but this is not accurate because two distinct words are used. That gives us the answer we are looking for. Our response must be one of compassion or pity and this will lead to mercy. Mercy is compassion in action. The Oxford English Dictionary defines *compassion* as 'pity inclining one to help or be merciful', and it defines *mercy* as 'the quality of compassion'.

This pattern is set for us so beautifully in the story of Christ at the cross in Luke 23:33–34. Throughout his ministry, when he was spitefully abused—verbally and physically—never once do we read of him forgiving his enemies. When Dr Kendall in his book pleads for unconditional forgiveness, even he recognises that at the cross Jesus did not say 'I forgive you', and he explains that omission in this way: 'Such words would have been misinterpreted and wasted. It would also have been casting his pearls before pigs' (Matthew 7:6). That is a wise understanding, but such an admission undermines the whole argument that there must be forgiveness without repentance. To forgive those who do not want to be forgiven and who are unconcerned about reconciliation, devalues the meaning of 'forgiveness' and throws pearls at pigs.

So, if our Lord did not forgive, what did he do? He prayed for them. And he could only do that if he had a heart of compassion. That is our model when we are sinned against and when repentance is entirely lacking. To pray for our enemies is far more valuable both to us and certainly to them than to announce a public forgiveness.

This is exactly what our Lord taught his disciples. He did not promise, 'Blessed are those who forgive' but 'Blessed are the merciful' (Matthew 5:7). In the same way—though this fact may be very surprising to some— the Bible nowhere commands us to 'Forgive your enemies'. Our Lord commanded his disciples to 'love your enemies and pray for those who persecute you' (Matthew 5:44) and 'Love your enemies, do good to those who hate you … pray for those who abuse you' (Luke 6:27–28 and 35– 36). So much is said about loving and doing good to our enemies, but not a single word about forgiving them. Is this an oversight or what?

Significantly, in 1 Corinthians 13—a whole chapter devoted to Christian love—the word forgiveness does not occur once. In the long list of qualities of true Christian love—patience, kindness, humility, selflessness, endurance, not seeking revenge, or rejoicing in the calamity of the wrongdoer, or harbouring a grudge—nothing is said about forgiveness. This absence is not because all these virtues are the inevitable result of forgiveness but because they must be present even if the conditions for forgiveness are not met. They reflect the character of God. Just as God's compassion and mercy are intended to lead *us* to repentance for forgiveness, so our compassion and mercy on those who sin against us are intended to lead *them* to repentance. The words 'love' and 'compassion' are much greater words than 'forgiveness', because that is where forgiveness begins.

In society and the church, the big reason to forgive is too often to make the victim, and the rest of us, feel better. But does God forgive repentant sinners in order that *he* might feel better? The object of forgiveness is to make the *sinner* better, and he never will be better until he repents. On the other hand, compassion sheds tears. Healing for the Christian comes not from forgiving those who have sinned against you, but by trusting in the wisdom and the love of God, humbly accepting his wise ways, and yearning with a compassion that leads to prayer, for the forgiveness by God of those who have wronged you.

If we can learn anything from the psalmist on this subject it is that not once did he forgive his enemies; on the contrary, he left them to the mercy or judgement of God (for example Psalm 1:5–6; 6:8–10; 7:6). There is still such a thing as divine retribution, and it is remarkably odd to imagine that I am required to forgive someone for an offence for which God promises them only judgement. Do I really have to forgive those whom God himself will not forgive?

So, the opposite of forgiving is not bearing a grudge, seeking revenge, remaining bitter, nursing a hatred or storing up a list of wrongs done. It is asking for a compassionate heart that pities those who have been so cruel; a compassion that leads to prayer, and action that leads to their repentance so that I may forgive them. As the proverb reminds us: 'Hatred stirs up strife, but love covers all offences' (Proverbs 10:12).

At the cross our Lord's prayer, 'Father, forgive them, for they know not what they do' set the pattern for us: 'When they hurled their insults at him he did not retaliate. When he suffered he made no threat, instead he entrusted himself to him who judges justly' (1 Peter 2:23). Stephen, at his own martyrdom, followed his Master's example when he prayed, 'Lord, do not hold this sin against them' (Acts 7:60). It was not for Stephen to forgive them; he knew that was not his prerogative, but he offered a final compassionate prayer for those who crushed his skull.

God's grace is undeserved, unending, unlimited, invincible and eternal—but not unconditional. 'Repentance' is our part, and to miss this is to misunderstand the character of God, the nature of true conversion, and completely to misread what Paul meant when he wrote, 'Forgive, as the Lord forgave you'

NOT WHAT THESE HANDS HAVE DONE
can save this guilty soul,
and nothing that this flesh has borne
can make my spirit whole.

2. Not what I feel or do
can give me peace with God;
not all my prayers or sighs or tears
can bear my awful load.

3. Your work alone, O Christ,
can ease this weight of sin;
your blood alone, O Lamb of God,
can give me peace within.

4. Your love to me, O God,
not mine, O Lord, to you,
can rid me of this deep unrest
and all my heart renew.

# Chapter 8

5. Your grace alone, O God,
speaks pardoning love to me;
your power alone, O Son of God,
can set my spirit free.

6. I bless the Christ of God,
I rest on love divine,
and with unfaltering lip and heart
I call this Saviour mine.

Horatious Bonar 1808–89
*Praise!* 701 © in this version Praise Trust

**FOR GROUP DISCUSSION**

1. Can we distinguish between compassion and forgiveness, and if so, what practical difference does it make?
2. Read Luke 23:33–34. Did Christ forgive those who crucified him? What does your answer tell us about forgiveness.
3. Does Romans 2:4 help us to understand they way we are to forgive?
4. If a friend admitted that they were bitter and resentful against someone, how would you counsel them from Scripture?
5. From 1 Corinthians 5:1–5 and 2 Corinthians 2:5–11 what can we learn about forgiveness?

# Eternal grace

'Now may our Lord Jesus Christ himself, and God our Father, who loved us and gave us eternal comfort and good hope through his grace, comfort your hearts and establish them in every good work and word' 2 Thessalonians 2:16–17

The church at Thessalonica made Paul's heart sing. With all the problems and pressures of the first century world and the tragic failure of many young Christian communities, this was one church that Paul had consistent cause to be grateful for. All the churches were talking about how the Thessalonians had turned to God from their idols (1 Thessalonians 1:8–9), and had immediately recognised the authority of the gospel not as the words of men but as the word of God (2:13). These were certainly marks of true conversion. But Paul was grateful also for their hard work which he refers to as their 'work of faith and labour of love' (1:3). He was also grateful to God for their beautiful relationship together (2 Thessalonians 1:3); theirs was a love that spilled over to all throughout Macedonia, and Paul had experienced it himself (1 Thessalonians 4:9 and 3:6). Equally, Paul was glad because of their endurance in suffering. He boasted about them among all the churches because of their: 'Steadfastness and faith in all your persecutions and in the afflictions that you are enduring' (2 Thessalonians 1:4).

But there was something more that encouraged Paul and which probably underlined all else. It was their 'steadfastness of hope' that he refers to in 1 Thessalonians 1:3. This is explained more fully here in 2 Thessalonians 2:16–17. Paul was always very specific in his prayers. There was never any sloppy thinking with Paul because he knew that these young Christians would pick up his words and take them as truth. Paul only prayed for things that may or may not happen, he never prayed for that which is a certainty since that would be both unnecessary and unbelieving. So, when Paul prayed that God would comfort and establish them in every good work and word, it was because he knew too well that you can be a Christian and not experience and enjoy those two things.

There is a world of difference between the *reality* of something and the *enjoyment* of it. There have been and there still are some very rich people in this world. They have all that money can buy and all the money to buy more—but many of them are not happy. Sometimes they live miserably fearful lives. One of the saddest examples of this was Howard Hughes. When Hughes died on Sunday April 4 1976 at 1.27 pm, he left behind an estate worth an estimated $2.3 billion. But for all his wealth and power, he lived his closing years, as one reporter described it: 'a sunless, joyless, half lunatic life … a virtual prisoner walled in by his own crippling fears and weaknesses.' Hooked on heroin, distrusting everyone, and with a pathological fear of contact with the world of germs, Hughes died miserable and alone—yet the boss of an empire more wealthy than many African states. That is the difference between the reality and the enjoyment of the reality.

Many Christians are exactly like Howard Hughes. Every Christian is infinitely wealthy. Notice carefully that Paul does not pray that the Thessalonians might *have* eternal love, comfort and good hope. He knows very well that they each have all that. But what he prays for is that they may be *comforted and established* in those three things. Let's be sure that we understand what those three things are:

### Every Christian is loved

That is not just *how* we came to salvation, it is the reason *why* we came to salvation. That was a love that was both eternal and invincible. It was a love that not only chose us to be saved (v 13), but a love that conquered our rebellion when he called us through the gospel (v 14). That is invincible grace. In the distant corridors of eternity, the Father and the Son and the Spirit—all three are here in vs 13 and 14—planned our salvation. What an incredible privilege. What a glorious security that should give us.

If we want to know the measure of God's love, we will find it in these words: 'God so loved the world that he gave his only Son ...' (John 3:16). If a Christian ever doubts God's love or wonders whether they really matter to God; or if they ever question their personal value in the scheme of eternity and infinity and among the billions of people who have already lived on this tiny planet earth, then they have only to look again at that cross on the hill Golgotha on which the Prince of Glory died, and at the same time recall, 'The son of God, *loved me* and gave himself *for me*' (Gal.2:20). Could God express his love any more powerfully than that?

Every husband wants to be loved by his wife, and every wife by her husband; every child wants to be loved by their parents and every parent wants to be loved by their child. And good families find a thousand ways to express their love to each other. The privilege of every Christian is that they are loved by Christ. We don't have to pray for it, long for it or hope for it. To be loved by Christ is our most prized possession because it is our most valuable possession—it is beyond price. It is worth more than all the worldly wealth of all the earthly billionaires together. But the question is, do I enjoy it? That is what Paul is praying for here.

## Every Christian has an advocate

The *Oxford English Dictionary* defines 'comfort' as 'relief in affliction', and that fits quite well the word that Paul uses here in 2 Thessalonians 2:16, though the word 'encouragement' found in some translations might be better. It is derived from the noun *parakletos,* and was a strong word used largely, though not exclusively, of tribunals and law courts. It is made up from two Greek words that together mean: 'called to the side'. For the Greeks, the *paraklete* was the one who accompanied the accused person to the tribunal and supported him by testifying and interceding on his behalf. He was their relief in affliction and was something equivalent to our barrister today. It was quite natural therefore, that the Jews should use the same word in their synagogue worship to refer to the daily sacrifice that secures divine forgiveness; it became their advocate to appease the anger of God against their sin.

That is exactly the word we would expect to be used of Jesus, who stands before God the Father on our behalf and meets the just demands of God's holy anger against our sin. So, we are not surprised to find that John used the word in just this way when he refers to our 'advocate with the Father, Jesus Christ the righteous' (1 John 2:1). The word 'advocate' is this same word *parakletos*. Our eternal comfort and encouragement is that Christ is in heaven for ever as a perpetual reminder to the Father that everything necessary for our salvation has been done. In fact *he himself* is our eternal comfort, our relief in affliction and our advocate with the Father. Christ is our barrister who has never lost a case yet—and he never will. Paul uses another, though similar word when writing to Timothy: 'There is only one mediator (an arbiter or surety) between God and men, the man Christ Jesus' (1 Timothy 2:5).

When we sin, will we allow the devil to accuse us or will we, in the words of that well-loved hymn by Charitie Bancroft: 'look to heaven and see him there, who made an end of all my sin'? He is our eternal advocate. In non-legal jargon, he is our backer, our sponsor, our supporter; and with Jesus Christ at our side we cannot lose. Only once did the Father turn his face away from his Son, when Christ hung on the cross guilty with our sin and rebellion and in that hour of terrible abandonment cried out: 'My God, my God, why have you forsaken me?' But he will never reject his Son again. Our security lies in the fact that Christ is our perfect and eternal advocate with the Father.

However, what is of particular interest to us is the fact that four times in John's Gospel the same word *parakletos* is used of the Holy Spirit: John 14:16,26; 15:26; 16:7. Since it is such an appropriate word to use of Christ as our advocate with the Father, it may seem strange to apply it to the Spirit. But the Holy Spirit can also be said to be an advocate. Jesus himself tells us that the Spirit, as our *parakletos,* has come 'to convict the world concerning sin and righteousness and judgement' (John 16:6, 7). Lord Hailsham died on Sunday 7 October 2001. He had been a leading lawyer in England for half a century and had served under six Prime Ministers. Not long before his death he commented, ' I hope, when I stand before my Maker, that I shall have sufficient skill to plead guilty and cast myself on the mercy of the court.' Only the Spirit can make a man wise enough in this life to realise that his only hope is to cast himself wholly upon the mercy of God and discover in Christ complete salvation. In other words, like a representative of the law, the work of the Spirit is to convict the guilty of their sin and its terrible consequences by convincing them of the nature of true righteousness and the fearful judgement of God. As an honest attorney, the Holy Spirit persuades us that our case is hopeless, that we have nothing to plead in our defence, and that the course of wisdom is to cast ourselves wholly upon the mercy of the court. He is the King's Counsellor.

But the Spirit does more than this as our advocate. He first brings us to that condition where we know our desperate need of Christ and forgiveness. It is at this point that the King's Counsellor tells us just what to say—or how to say it: 'The Spirit helps us in our weakness. For we do not know what to pray for as we ought, but the Spirit himself intercedes for us with groanings too deep for words' (Romans 8:26). These are not his groans, but ours. It is the Spirit breaking our spirit until we cry, desperately and at times incomprehensibly: 'Oh God!'. These are some of the most profound prayers we will ever utter. Our King's attorney has persuaded us to cast ourselves entirely at the mercy of God, and the King himself stands there to present our case to the Father with his own guarantee of the secure outcome. Those are two powerful advocates. That is the Christian's privilege. We do not have to pray for this. It is unquestionably, undeniably and eternally ours. But do we live in the happy enjoyment of it?

## Every Christian has hope

This can only be the expectation of heaven based upon the sure foundation of the reliable promises of a completely reliable God. But what a hope! When this life is over, Christians will be forever like their Saviour for they will see him face to face and the mortal will be swallowed up in immortality. There will be joy and peace and an appreciation of God's grace and all his created beauty in a way unimaginable here. And the promise of that for every true Christian is unconditional and is guaranteed by the character of God himself. Riches that far surpass the total of all the wealth that the entire history of this world has ever known. But are we enjoying the expectation of that now?

When Paul sums up the unbelieving world, he describes it as having 'no hope and without God' (Ephesians 2:12). It is incredible how resilient people can be. They can suffer the lost of virtually everything and often still remain buoyant and purposeful. But when all hope goes, life becomes meaningless. Suicide is the third cause of death among under 25s after cancer and accidents. Suicide is always when all hope has evaporated.

God's love, God's eternal advocates, and God's hope, are all certainties for the Christian. We need not pray for what we already have. The Thessalonians entered into the reality of all that the very moment they were converted. And so does every Christian. And notice that they all came through grace (v 16). That is the whole point. We deserved nothing but received everything.

So what *does* Paul pray for? He prays that God would help this young church to experience the 'comfort' of those three great truths and therefore 'establish' them in all that they do and say for Christ (v 17). The word 'establish' is used of our Lord himself when: 'He *set* his face to go to Jerusalem' (Luke 9:51). Some translations have 'steadfastly set', and that well emphasises the idea of a clear and definite purpose.

But what is particularly interesting is the word 'comfort'. It is the verb from our noun *parakletos*—comforter, encourager or advocate! In other words, Paul is praying that God will help these young Christians to experience the reality of those three great facts—God's love, God's eternal advocacy and God's good hope—in such a way that in any and every situation those three eternal facts will themselves act as advocates, reassuring them that they are safe in Jesus, and thus making them stable, strong and steadfast. Comfort is sometimes offered with empty or even deceiving words and assurances. In bereavement; too many false comforters are ready to offer vacant hope in vain words. But there is nothing empty or vain in the reassurance that comes from God's love, God's eternal advocates and God's good hope.

Just as the great work of Jesus was to die on Calvary so that he could stand beside us at the tribunal and, as our advocate, present our cause as his own and so assure us of acquittal, so one great work of the Spirit is to remind us of that powerful advocate. And this, together with the knowledge of God's love for us and our ultimate good hope of heaven, will provide all the relief we need in affliction. It is an incredible privilege to know that grace is eternal, and a great joy to live in the light of it and work in the confidence of it.

## Good hope and assurance

Some Christians believe that it is not possible to have assurance, and they conclude that only the proud and self-confident will express certainty in ultimate salvation. For those who believe that salvation depends significantly upon human action or endeavour this is a reasonable conclusion; it would be extreme arrogance to claim that we are sure of a place in heaven. Who, on earth, could ever be *that* certain?

John Newton once wrote against this theology of self-effort in what was for him an unusual understatement: 'To have nothing to trust to for our continuance in well-doing, but our own feeble efforts, our partial diligence and short-sighted care, must surely be distressing.' But for those who believe that we are saved by grace through faith and that this is not our own doing but it is the gift of God, not a result of works, so that no one may boast (Ephesians 2:8), it is the most sincere act of humility to lay claim to eternal grace. Everyone has to decide whether they will try to earn their way to heaven and live with the uncertainty of knowing whether or not they have ever gained sufficient merit, or whether they will accept the reality that they can never gain heaven by merit and that faith in Christ alone is the only hope.

In 1788 Newton was asked to give evidence against the slave trade before the Privy Council in the British Parliament. Few men knew that miserable trade better than him since he had been a trader himself for nearly ten years. On that day he surveyed his life and his salvation and wrote, 'O Lord, it is all thy doing; to thee be also the praise. To me belongs the shame and confusion of face, for I am a poor vile creature to this hour.' A man like that clearly was not relying upon his own efforts to provide him with eternal comfort! His only confidence was in the eternal grace of God, his advocate in Jesus Christ, and the promise of a good hope for the future.

### Salvation found and lost

Others do not trust in any human merit or effort for salvation; for that they rely upon Christ alone. However, they believe that it is possible for us to lose our salvation. This was the theology of John Wesley, the founder of Methodism. What this means is that whilst I may have complete assurance of salvation at the moment—because I am trusting wholly and only in the death of Christ for my forgiveness—I cannot be sure that I will not lose my faith tomorrow and fall away from grace. There cannot be any 'eternal comfort' for me. Life is a constant round of watching, waiting and striving for fear that I may finally lose my salvation. The weakness here is discovered in the whole doctrine of beginnings: if I come into my faith largely through my own effort, so I may go out again in the same way.

That may be a strong doctrine to encourage my diligence as a Christian, but it is no comfort when I fall. As a young teenage Christian no one had told me that salvation once gained could not be lost or, which is more likely, if they had I wasn't listening; as a consequence, whenever I sinned I would come back to God and pray, 'Lord, if I have never been a Christian before, I want to become one now.' My intentions were sincere but my theology was poor. It was good that I really hated my sin, but it was hardly the way to progress in my Christian life: every time I sinned I felt I had to start all over again.

Our Lord promised, 'The one who endures to the end will be saved' (Matt. 10:22), but that is to be taken as an encouragement to keep on, rather than as a warning against falling away from eternal grace. Those who have received eternal grace *will* endure to the end. After all, it was the same Lord who promised, 'I give them eternal life, and they will never perish, and no one will snatch them out of my hand. My Father, who has given them to me, is greater than all, and no one is able to snatch them out of the Father's hand' (John 10:28–29). But the real confidence is that if God has chosen those who are his, and has given them to Christ as the trophy of his sacrifice, then he cannot and will not lose even one of them.

## Careless Christians

Does such security encourage us to be careless and slack? Perhaps, but if anyone thinks that they can take advantage of the promise of eternal grace and live as they please then they are only proving that they have never truly met with Jesus Christ in a saving way. Salvation is far more than a detached theology. It is a radical and far reaching change. Conversion means precisely that: nobody converts their mortgage, their garage or their business, and leaves everything just as it was before. Conversion is a transformation.

Paul met this very challenge when he wrote to the Christians at Rome: 'What shall we say then? Are we to continue in sin that grace may abound? By no means! How can we who died to sin still live in it?' (Romans 6:1–2). He went on to explain that the Christian is someone who has died with Christ and has been raised to a new life with Christ; as a result we live in 'newness of life' (v 4), our old self has died (v 6), we are set free from inevitable slavery to sin and we are under the Lordship of Christ from now on (v 7, 12–14). Far from the enjoyment of eternal salvation providing an excuse for sloppy living, the New Testament constantly sees it as an incentive for holiness.

## Too good to be true

Is the idea of eternal grace too good to be true? To which my best reply is that it would be—if anything was impossible for God! It is understandable that in this world of transience, where nothing lasts for long, we find it hard to believe in a promise of salvation that is eternal and that can never be lost or taken from us. But let God himself reassure us with his own promise: 'Lift up your eyes to the heavens, look at the earth beneath; the heavens will vanish like smoke, the earth will wear out like a garment, and its inhabitant will die like flies. But my salvation will last for ever, my righteousness will never fail' (Isaiah 51:6 NIV).

## Timid Christians

Some have a natural timidity of character and every decision of significance in their life sends them into a panic. They are never sure about anything. So when it comes to the subject of faith, they are always analysing their faith and examining their lives to see whether they have sufficient faith to justify assurance. How often I have been asked, sometimes almost despairingly: 'How do I know whether I have enough faith to believe?' It is as if faith is some kind of good work that is rewarded by salvation. I can tell such people immediately that they need not trouble to examine their faith any more—I can assure them that they certainly *do not* have sufficient faith.

The Bible is far less concerned about the *quantity* of faith as it is about the *object* of faith. It is not a matter of whether you have sufficient faith but who you put your faith in. I may be facing major heart surgery, and I am naturally very anxious about it. But when they tell me that the country's leading heart surgeon and his entire specialist team will undertake my operation then I am somewhat relieved and have far more confidence and less fear. I have no confidence in myself, but significant confidence in my physician. However, my apprehension will soon return if I am informed on the morning of the operation that my consultant is unavoidably sick and that his team have been drafted to another case—I will have a junior houseman in charge of my surgery after all. I had no more confidence in myself either way, but understandably I had much more hope when I knew the excellent reputation of my physician. We surely know the excellent reputation of our great spiritual physician.

It matters more than anything *where* we place our confidence for eternity. We have all seen the evidence of those who, with massive faith in their religion, will carry out the most despicable actions. They are so convinced that by giving their lives for the cause of Allah, they will certainly receive instant admission into paradise and enjoy all the sensuous pleasures that their imams promised them. I am quite sure that they have far more certainty and less doubt than many Christians have. But it is tragically misplaced. It is unswerving faith in a false religion.

Someone may be beset with doubt—'fighting without and fear within' as Paul describes it in 2 Corinthians 7:5—but if we are trusting in Christ alone, he has promised eternal salvation. What matters most of all is not how strongly we are on the side of God, but how certainly he is on our side. Christ is the one who defeated Satan on the cross and made an open show of him (Colossians 2:15). Christ promised his disciples that all those he called he would keep. Like sheep following the shepherd, they would hear his voice and they would 'never perish, and no one will snatch them out of my hand' (John 10:28–29). What is more, he gave the reason for this certainty: 'My Father, who has given them to me, is greater than all, and no one is able to snatch them out of the Father's hand. I and the Father are one.' Have you watched a small child holding the hand of its parent in a crowd? Whose grip was the most firm—that of the child or that of the parent?

The faint-hearted and timid have only to keep in mind a well-worn promise of Paul. Having dealt with the great theology of justification by faith alone in the death of Christ alone, and having reassured the Christians at Rome—who may at any time be hauled off to the butchery of the arena—that the Spirit will help them in their weakness and that there is a glorious new creation waiting for them ahead, the apostle then laid out a question and answer: 'If God is for us, who can be against us?' Paul was utterly convinced that nothing can ever separate us from the love of God in Christ so he ran through a list of possibilities: tribulation, distress, persecution, famine, nakedness, danger, sword, death, life, angels, rulers, things present, things to come, powers, height, depth, or anything else we can imagine in all creation, and then he concluded that none of this 'will be able to separate us from the love of God in Christ Jesus our Lord' (Romans 8:31–39). Is there any argument against this? The response that suggests the only exception to this list is my own weak faith is a remarkably weak argument. Can we really believe that Jesus Christ went through hell on Calvary in order to reconcile us to God and fit us for heaven, only to let us slip through his hands at the last? Is Christ no more reliable than the careless parent who allows a child to wander off and get lost in the crowd? Is that what we think of him?

Few men were more aware of their wicked past than John Newton. As a blasphemous infidel who had deliberately abandoned the faith his mother taught him, he worked hard to undo the faith of others; as a debauched, drunken sailor he threw himself into the vile slave trade. Even after his conversion he was only too aware of the weakness of his own heart. But here was his conclusion on the matter of eternal grace when he wrote a letter on the subject: 'While Christ is the Foundation, Root, Head and Husband of his people, while the word of God is yea and amen, while the counsels of God are unchangeable, while we have a Mediator and High Priest before the throne, while the Holy Spirit is willing and able to bear witness to the truths of the gospel, while God is wiser than men and stronger than Satan—so long the believer in Jesus is and shall be safe. Heaven and earth must pass away, but the promise, the oath, the blood, on which my soul relies, afford me a security which can never fail.'

## A conscience plagued with guilt

Understandably, some believe that either before or since their conversion, they have committed something so bad that God cannot possibly forgive them. They are usually tortured with the conviction that they have committed the blasphemy against the Holy Spirit. To this I can only respond by asking this question: 'Would you claim that during his earthly ministry Jesus Christ was in league with the prince of demons?' I think I can fairly anticipate the response! Well, that is precisely the context of our Lord's warning about the blasphemy against the Holy Spirit in Matthew 12:31.

One of the earliest verses I learnt soon after I became a Christian was Hebrews 7:25, 'He (Christ) is able to save to the *uttermost* those who draw near to God through him, since he always lives to make intercession for them.' I remember that it was common at that time to explain the verse like this: 'Christ can save from the guttermost to the uttermost.' It was one of those slick little phrases that at least had the merit of being memorable. In reality that is perhaps not the best way to explain the word, *panteles*. William Gouge took it as completeness and liked the translation 'uttermost'—and he should know because in the first half of the seventeenth century he spent thirty-three years and one thousand sermons expounding this book of Hebrews to his congregation at Blackfriars, in London! On the other hand, in the sixteenth century John Calvin preferred a reference to time, and therefore translated the word as 'for ever'—and he should know because he was the greatest Swiss Reformer and theologian. But perhaps a poor disabled woman can help us here, because the only other occasion this word is used in the New Testament is in Luke 13:11 where the crippled woman 'could not fully straighten herself' and here the word 'fully' is our word *panteles*—and it must mean 'completely'.

Either way, there is a for ever fullness—an eternal completeness—about our salvation. Back in Hebrews 7:25 the apostle gives us the reason why our salvation is so complete and for ever: 'Since (because) he always lives to make intercession for (us)'. Our confidence that God's forgiving grace can embrace the foulest, and for ever, is in the fact that Jesus Christ is alive and his presence in heaven guarantees our safe arrival. This is exactly why Paul tells the Corinthians that if Christ did not rise from the dead then all the preaching since Calvary and all our feeble faith has been in vain; we are still lost in our sins (1 Corinthians 15:14,17).

The Puritans in the seventeenth century used to say that sometimes God puts his children to bed in the dark. There is hardly a clearer and sadder example of this than the experience of our national poet, William Cowper. Suffering throughout his life from manic depression, his conversion to Christ only brought a temporary respite for his tortured mind. Although he wrote some of his finest poetry during his period of extreme spiritual depression, this was little comfort for the man who considered himself to be, in his own words 'buried above ground'. Before his conversion Cowper had more than once tried to take his own life and he thought that this must be a sin God could never forgive. John Newton, his faithful friend and pastor, spent many hours trying to help him, and at one time he and Mary had Cowper living with them for eighteen months. The poet was convinced that Christ had died for everyone except himself. But John Newton knew that the poor suffering bard had trusted Christ alone for salvation and he was sure that Cowper would arrive in heaven by the secure grace of God. He told William this many, many times.

Sadly, Cowper was not alone in his fears. There have been, and still are, many Christians who would love to enjoy the assurance of salvation and find strength in the experience that Paul was praying for on behalf of the Thessalonians; but somehow they can't. They stagger round in a never ending circle of doubt finding a little hope here and there but unable to grasp the full benefit of all that Christ has done for them as their advocate. There are many reasons for this. Perhaps it is because the way the gospel was first presented has left them with the idea that they must never be certain, or that salvation can so easily be lost. Or perhaps our own hesitant, brooding personality never allows us to be confident in anything. On the other hand, it may be that we can never forgive ourselves for some particular sin we have committed in the past, and we are always doubting whether God can therefore forgive. For this very reason John encouraged us that 'whenever our heart condemns us, God is greater than our heart' (1 John 3:20).

The enjoyment of confidence in eternal grace depends upon the great unchanging certainties of the gospel, not upon how you felt when you woke up this morning; or what kind of week it has been in the factory, office, workshop or classroom; or whether we feel a complete failure as a parent or husband or wife; or whether we messed-up our Christian testimony yesterday.

William Cowper died cheerless and hopeless on Friday 25 April 1800 in East Dereham, Norfolk. John Newton was now seventy-five, and when he heard the news of his friend's death, John picked up his pen and wrote a few lines imagining that he himself had just arrived in heaven and found, as he expected, that William was already there. Looking back over the long years during which he had tried to convince the doubting poet that God's eternal grace could be trusted, John could not resist saying, 'I told you so'. Here are the closing two verses as John meets William in heaven:

My friend, my friend! and have we met again,
Far from the home of woe, the home of men;
And hast thou taken thy glad harp once more,
Twined with far lovelier wreaths than e'er before;
And is thy strain more joyous and more loud,
While circle round thee heaven's attentive crowd?

Oh! let thy memory wake! I told thee so;
I told thee thus would end thy heaviest woe;
I told thee that thy God would bring thee here,
And God's own hand would wipe away thy tear
While I should claim a mansion by thy side,
I told thee so—for our Emmanuel died.

That is eternal grace. Trust it, believe it, be comforted, strengthened and encouraged by it—and enjoy it.

SOVEREIGN GRACE AND LOVE ABOUNDING
over sin and death and hell!
Sing its depth that knows no sounding;
who its breadth or length can tell?
On its glories,
on its glories
let my soul for ever dwell.

**2.** What from Christ that soul shall sever
bound by everlasting bands?
Once in him, in him for ever,
thus the eternal covenant stands.
None shall tear us,
none shall tear us
from the Strength of Israel's hands.

**3.** Heirs of God, joint-heirs with Jesus,
called and chosen in the Son!
To his name eternal praises
for the wonders he has done!
One with Jesus,
one with Jesus,
by eternal union one.

**4.** On such love, my soul, still ponder,
love so great, so rich, so free;
say, while lost in holy wonder,
'Why, O God, such love to me?'
Hallelujah!
Hallelujah!
Grace shall reign eternally.

John Kent 1766–1843
*Praise!* 671 © in this version Praise Trust

# Chapter 9

1. What is the difference between the knowledge and the enjoyment of our Christian faith?
2. Discuss the reasons why many Christians lack assurance and how you would respond to each.
3. How will you counsel someone whose conscience is plagued with guilt?
4. In the light of John Newton's pastoral care of Cowper, can it ever be right to persuade someone that they really are a Christian?
5. In the light of Romans 6:1–25 how would you refute the suggestion that a belief in eternal salvation encourages a careless Christianity?

# Purposeful grace

'To me this grace was given, to preach the unsearchable riches of Christ'
Ephesians 3:8

P aul had good reason to consider himself 'the least of all the apostles' because he knew that he had been a Christ-rejecting rebel. From his past he deserved nothing, and if he was now an apostle—with the added privilege of seeing Christ after his resurrection and ascension—then he knew it was only by the grace of God. Paul was under house arrest in Rome when he wrote to the church at Ephesus, and at the beginning of his letter he addressed them as 'the saints who are in Ephesus' (1:1). Who are they? This is not the only time Paul used that word in his letter. The Greek word in the singular is *hagios* and it refers to one who is religiously holy or clean. In the first century it was a common word used chiefly as a description of the gods who were different from the commonplace; they were set apart from that which was ordinary. The only other beings who could claim this word were the priests whose ministry brought them into touch with the holy gods. As he did so often, Paul clothed this common word with a very special Christian meaning.

## Who are the saints?

Both 'saints' and 'grace' were devalued words in the middle ages. The church imagined that certain Christians of the past had lived more holy lives than was necessary and therefore had accumulated a hoard of good works into which ordinary mortals could dip in order to add to their own diminishing supply. Those long dead pious celebrities were adorned with the title 'saint', and that use spoiled it for the true meaning of the New

Testament word. The Church of Rome invented a word to explain this: they were known as works of 'supererogation' which came from two Latin words *super* and *erogare*—which meant 'beyond requirement'. As a result, the penitent could use the super abundance of righteousness by the saints to help pay off their own debt of sin—and that was thought to be grace. Praying to these saints is still a common practice within the Church of Rome. They are depicted in stained glass windows and they jockey for the honour of becoming patrons of this or that. This false use of the word is heard whenever someone explains the misdemeanours of another with the comment: 'He is no saint'.

For the apostle Paul 'saint' referred to all who have received the undeserved grace of God by faith, having the righteousness of Christ alone reckoned to their account; and on that ground they are declared holy. In other words, every true Christian is a saint in New Testament terms. For Paul there are two clear implications of the word. First, it refers to those who have been declared righteous by God on the ground of Christ's death alone, and secondly it implies that these people have been set apart for the service of God. It is this second meaning that is so important for our present chapter.

In his letter to the Ephesians Paul uses the word saint five times (1:1,15,18; 2:19; 3:8). Read those verses and imagine that the word refers to a club of superior Christians, and test your reaction. Sometimes Bible translators have lost their nerve and insert 'God's people' instead of the word 'saints' (see for example the NIV at 2:19 and 3:8). It is true that all the saints are God's people, but Paul deliberately used the word *hagioi* to demonstrate that all Christians, without a single exception, are holy in the sight of God and set apart for his service. This was as surprising to the first century pagan world as it is to parts of twenty-first century Christianity, for in both cases the word was reserved for a special class of religious people above the normal, and Paul was now applying it to all Christians.

## Less than the least of all saints?

In his attempt to explain how he sees himself, Paul threw together a comparative formed on the back of a negative superlative. That needs explaining! In verse 8 he wrote, 'I am less'. That word is a comparative word. He is comparing himself with others, and he says 'I am looking at the other saints (Christians) and I want you to know that I am less than them.' But Paul went on to say, 'I am less than the least'. The word 'least' is a superlative, and I call it a negative superlative because he did not say I am the best, he said, I am the least, I am the worst. You can be less without being the least but when you are the least you cannot be any less. However, that is exactly what Paul claimed to be: 'less than the least'! That he was a Christian—a saint—is not in doubt; but he felt so strongly about his unworthiness that he could not be content merely to say that he is less than any, or even that he is least of all; instead he breaks all the rules of grammar and claims to be less than the least.

In some respects John Newton and Saul of Tarsus had similar testimonies. The only significant difference between the spiritual condition of the two men was seventeen hundred years. In 1764, when he was curate in charge at Olney in Buckinghamshire John Newton published his autobiography, *The Narrative of a Surprising Conversion*'. Now, at last, everyone could read the incredible story of this Church of England clergyman who had once been a drunken, debauched, hard-swearing sailor, impressed onto a man-of-war in His Majesty's navy, beaten for deserting his ship and finally a slave dealer in Africa before his remarkable conversion to Christ during a violent Atlantic storm that almost wrecked his ship. Shortly after the publication of his biography, Newton discovered that people were travelling to Olney, a small out-of-the-way village, to meet this strange man, and he claimed that he felt like a monkey in a cage as people came to view this amazing sight. 'They find me a mystery', John declared and then added, 'I am a mystery. I am a mystery to others, I am a mystery to myself.' He could not understand how God could have loved him or how it could be possible for such an unclean man to be become a saint.

Saul of Tarsus faced the same dilemma himself; he could not understand how God could have loved him: 'I persecuted the followers of this Way to their death, arresting both men and women and throwing them into prison … I went (to Damascus) to bring these people as prisoners to Jerusalem to be punished' (Acts 22:4–5 *New International Version*). And elsewhere: 'Many a time I went from one synagogue to another to have them punished, and I tried to force them to blaspheme' (Acts 26:11 *New International Version*). That is precisely what John of Wapping did; on each ship he served before his conversion to Christ, he encouraged young sailors to profane the name of God and to sing bawdy and blasphemous sea shanties. He taught them to abandon whatever faith they came on board with and to join him in freethinking and free-living. For his part, Paul had an obsession with persecuting Christians and even went from city to city to hound them. Both men looked back in shame. Those who do not look back in shame cannot look forward with hope.

Both Paul of Tarsus and John of Wapping knew that, undeserving as they certainly were, they were now through Christ clean in the sight of God and, what was just as amazing, they were made holy for the purpose of serving God. From now on, every circumstance in their life would be with the one chief end that God would be served whether by their life or their death (Philippians 1:20).

## Purposeful grace

Paul was keenly aware that the word 'saint' that he had newly minted for the purpose of instructing the young Christians, not only referred back to the undeserved grace of God, but it looked on to the purposeful grace of God. Saints are not static memorials to God's grace, but living examples for his service. Saints are declared holy by God so that they may serve wholly for God. What amazed Paul, and what never ceased to amaze John Newton, was that God's plan was to make use of a man like him—and that is true of every saint. Towards the end of his life Paul wrote, 'God saved us and called us to a holy life, not because of our works'—that is undeserved grace—'but because of his own purpose and grace which he gave us in Christ Jesus before the ages began'—that is purposeful grace (2 Timothy 1:9). Two verses later Paul described that purpose: 'I was appointed a herald and an apostle and a teacher' (*New International Version*).

Paul was told at the outset of his new spiritual life that he was God's chosen instrument: 'to carry my name before the Gentiles and kings and the children of Israel' (Acts 9:15). Here in Ephesians 3, Paul picked up on that, and having received the undeserved grace of God he now recognised that he was a servant (v 7). The precise purpose for Paul he explained as, 'to preach to the Gentiles' (v 8). That is not preaching in our formal sense of the word; it is the word from which we get our English 'evangelise'. What Paul was claiming was that he was saved and received the undeserved grace of God so that he might evangelise the nations. When Paul wanted to write about preaching in a more formal sense, he used the word 'herald' (see for example 2 Timothy 1:7 in the *New International Version*).

Clearly, the purpose of anyone receiving grace is that they may bring glory to God; but the issue here is *how* do we bring glory to God? When God gave Paul undeserved grace, it was accompanied by purposeful grace. Grace that would enable him to serve God and fulfil God's plan for his life in any and every circumstance. His purpose in being saved, his purpose in receiving undeserved grace was that he might evangelise the nations with the gospel. But that was not an end in itself. To suggest that the purpose of the church, and therefore of the Christian, is mission, is only the first half of the answer to the question: 'What is the purpose of the church?' *The* great purpose of the church, and therefore of every saint, is to glorify God. But how do we do that?

The content of our evangelistic message, the content of our good news that we have to share with the nations is beyond discovery! We can never fully explain it. It is the 'riches of Christ' (Ephesians 3:8). Notice that it is not the riches *in* Christ, but the riches *of* Christ. If they are riches found in Christ then we may preach about the riches, but if they are the riches of Christ, then we have to preach Christ himself. And what is that? It is the wealth of undeserved grace. Undeserved grace is not just to be personally enjoyed, it is to be prodigally shared. The moment we receive undeserved grace we receive purposeful grace. We have to do something with the grace we have received; we have to evangelise the nations by being a witness. The task of the church is to reveal the otherwise undiscoverable riches of Christ which are described in verse 10 as 'the manifold wisdom of God'. The word 'manifold' means 'many sided', and poetically it has the meaning of colourful or variegated.

So, how did Paul, and how do we, throw light upon the many-sided and variegated wisdom of God, to entice men and women into the community of those who enjoy the undeserved grace of God? That is easier than we could ever imagine. God has already done it for us, because if we are a true Christians—saints—we are the answer to our own question. Each one of us is a story of God's many-sided wisdom and grace. The infinite diversity of his dealings with us is all part of God's manifold wisdom. The way he prepared us for the gospel and the providence that preserved our life for the moment when we found Christ as our Lord and Saviour; and the way that he has led us every step of our life since then; all this should be a sparkling story of God's wisdom and grace. That is why Paul could write, 'Oh the depth of the riches of the wisdom and knowledge of God'. Our story—our quality of life, miracle of conversion, transformation from rebel to servant and from Christ-rejecter to Christ disciple and discipler—is all part of God's purposeful grace and should be our best evangelism. Every saint—without a single excuse of age or infirmity—can evangelise like that.

This is what Paul means when he wrote to the Corinthians and assured them that in Christ, God 'always leads us in triumphal procession, and through us spreads the fragrance of the knowledge of him [Christ] everywhere' (2 Corinthians 2:14). The preaching and verbal witness of Christians, however vital that is, cannot spread the attractiveness of Christ in this world half so effectively as the kaleidoscopic beauty of the wisdom of God lived out in the lives of a countless myriad of Christians in the cities and farmlands, deserts and jungles, offices, factories, workshops, classrooms, and neighbourhoods of this world.

The purpose of our election and calling—invincible grace—is that we might be, 'conformed to the image of his Son' (Romans 8:28). In other words, everything that happens in the life of the Christian is for the purpose that we might become moulded more into the likeness of Jesus Christ, God's Son, *so that* others will be brought into the fellowship of the unimaginable grace of God, *so that* God will be honoured by more and more people. This may make us feel a little uncomfortable in the knowledge that God should stake the knowledge of his glorious undiscovered wisdom upon people like us. This may help us to understand why the apostle Paul could call himself 'less than the least of all saints'. Perhaps we are beginning to jockey with him for that position!

## A twist to purposeful grace

If the purpose of purposeful grace is for every saint to bring the light of the gospel to those who are in darkness, and by this means to bring glory to God, have we said all? Typically Paul adds an unexpected twist to his argument. Instead of leaving us with the obvious conclusion that the more people who are saved the more glory there is to God, Paul takes us one step further. In verse 10 he informs us that 'through the church the manifold wisdom of God might now be made known to the rulers and authorities in the heavenly places.' Who are these? We might expect him to refer to the town council at Ephesus, and no doubt he was concerned for them. On the other hand, since he is imprisoned at Rome, Paul may be thinking of the imperial household of the Roman Emperor Nero. But that is not his conclusion here.

These 'rulers and authorities in the heavenly places' are referred to earlier in Ephesians 1:21, and whilst some suggest that this is the demonic realm—and there can be no doubt that to their shame they will see the glorious grace of God in the lives of his saints—that is unlikely to be Paul's reference here. Paul appears to be speaking of all the host of heaven; those angels who, Peter informs us, all through the history of God's redemption, right up until the coming of Christ, have been longing to understand what the message of the prophets was all about (1 Peter 1:12). Now they understand fully because at last in the church they can see the wonderful undeserved grace of God.

Compare this with the words of our Saviour: 'There will be more joy in heaven over one sinner who repents … There is joy before the angels of God over one sinner who repents' (Luke 15:7,10). With the conversion of every saint, the angels worship the Lord God for such wonderful, undeserved and purposeful grace. Therefore purposeful grace brings glory to God not only because the transformation of a sinner into a saint demonstrates his grace on earth, but because it demonstrates it to all heaven as well. Whenever a sinner is saved, all heaven explodes with worship and adoration of such a God who planned such a way of salvation. This is Paul's plus factor in purposeful grace.

## Purpose in natural suffering

But let's take a broader look at purposeful grace. It would be quite wrong to assume that purposeful grace is found only in those good things that happen in the life of the Christian. There is purposeful grace in everything that happens to everyone in this world. That is certainly a massive claim.

Not even the most grotesque events or circumstances are beyond the purposeful grace of God. Here is one hard example: AIDS is referred to as the 'silent holocaust' and it is an international emergency of pandemic proportions; tragically many innocents suffer, including widows and orphans. The fact is that obedience to the law of God would eradicate the HIV virus within a twenty year time scale; even the World Health Organization recognised in 1991 that the most effective way to prevent the spread of AIDS was for two uninfected partners to remain faithful to each other. But HIV is not a nasty virus that God drops in on godless lifestyles, any more than he manipulates liver failure for the alcoholic, lung cancer for the smoker, brain damage for the heroin addict or heart failure for the obese. Rather, any lifestyle that cuts across God's law will bring tragedy, because when we refuse to operate according to the Maker's instructions, pain and misery always result.

When Achan disobeyed the command of God: 'He did not perish alone for his iniquity' (Joshua 22:20 and see 7:1–5; 24–26). This was a terrible lesson that Israel would never forget. The tragic results of natural suffering like this are not beyond the knowledge or control of God; they are part of his purposeful grace. AIDS did not begin by infecting millions; it began small and limited as a serious warning. But the warning was ignored—and it still is by far too many—and as a result the terrible virus spread. It is so simple to prevent and would be so easy to eradicate, but the world has chosen a lifestyle against the revealed purpose of God and it is reaping the consequences. If ever there was an example of sowing the wind and reaping the whirlwind (Hosea 8:7), HIV and AIDS is that example.

In a similar way, we will have to learn the hard way that when a nation chooses to set aside God's wise law concerning one day of rest in seven, it triggers a natural law that the health of the people will suffer in every respect. And when we are content for our marriages to break up at the current alarming rate and parents drift in and out of relationships, we need not be surprised that our children will grow increasingly wild and lawless. There are natural laws that govern all these results.

Imagine a society composed of homes where God is first, where husbands and wives keep themselves only for each other, where children honour and respect their parents, and where parents love and care for their children, where gossip is unheard, blasphemy unknown, lies are never told, coveting and stealing always resisted, and where love reigns. Is that an impossible dream? Perhaps, but it would certainly be the blessing of conformity with the master plan of God. Let no one blame the Creator if we do not enjoy the fruit that would follow from obedience to his laws. In the chapter on sovereign grace we established that God is in control of all events on earth; but much more than this, that he has a purpose behind all those events that he controls.

## Purpose in spiritual suffering

When king David, against the command of God, ordered a census of his fighting men, God allowed him to choose his own punishment: famine, military defeat or plague. We do not always connect sin and its punishment, but God warns that he will always punish sin—sooner or later. His punishment is not always immediate. Adam was warned that the day he disobeyed the command of God he would die, and he did—though the process took another 930 years to complete! God never closes a case on unforgiven sin.

Similarly, the blessing of obedience does not always come at once. It is a lie when 'prosperity' preachers promise immediate health, wealth and happiness for all who trust Christ. That is untrue to the Bible and to two millennia of Christian experience. The second generation of children out of Egypt suffered forty years for the unfaithfulness of their parents before they themselves could inherit the Promised Land (Numbers 14:33); and in Hebrews, the apostle listed some of the great heroes of faith, none of whom received the promised blessing but 'greeted them from afar' (Hebrews 11:13). God frequently delays reward just as he defers judgement. Let no one take advantage of this—it always comes.

Paul wrote of being 'utterly burdened beyond our strength (so) that we despaired of life itself' (2 Corinthians 1:8) and of being 'afflicted in every way, perplexed, persecuted and struck down' (2 Corinthians 4:8). But he understood the purposefulness of grace; he knew that even at such times there were lessons to be learnt, not least the provision of God to help in times of need so that the experience of God's purposeful grace can be passed on to others (2 Corinthians 1:4, 9).

## The reality of purposeful grace

At one time armies fought set piece battles during the day. The opposing forces would line up facing each other, and at a given time battle would commence. If there was no result by sundown, the two sides would generally retreat to their camp and sort it out in the morning. Armies rarely fought at night simply because no one could see in the dark. Today, with his electronic communications, global positioning and night sights, the modern soldier is as well equipped to fight at night as in the day. He can see in the dark. If physical suffering taught Paul to trust more in Christ, he also learnt that imprisonment opened new doors for the gospel. It is this ability to watch for the unfolding plan of God when all around is dark that is the unique privilege of the Christian. Christians are a people who can not only bask in the sunlight of God's evident grace, but they can also see in the dark.

Let me show you how this works. In Romans 15:4 Paul encouraged the young converts in the great metropolis of the empire that 'Whatever was written in former days was written for our instruction.' This means that all Old Testament events are with this purpose in view, though not all the Old Testament characters recognised the fact. For example, Joseph was sold into slavery by his brothers and when, towards the end of the story, they came grovelling to him in sorrow, repentance and fear, Joseph came up with that magnificent statement of faith: 'You meant evil against me, but God meant it for good' (Genesis 50:20). Joseph had no idea of the full significance of what he was saying. He thought, and rightly so, that the story of his time in Egypt was good for his family, and good for Egypt—and so it was. But the purpose was far bigger than this. Countless generations have learned from the story of Joseph's integrity and purity, as well as from the aggressive cruelty of his brothers. Just so, with Moses' anger, David's tragic moral slide, Jonah's disobedience, and Hezekiah's pride, all of these have a greater purpose than any of them understood. Their story was meant to teach *us*. The same is true with the successes and triumphs recorded in the Old Testament: Joseph's honour, Ruth's loyalty, Samuel's faithfulness, Nehemiah's courage—all these have a purpose well beyond the immediate life of the character involved.

This is exactly how Paul saw his own life. And so must every Christian. Even in sickness and the death of a loved one; there is purpose in our weakness and in our failure; there is purpose when our plans crash and when our circumstances fall out the 'wrong' way. For those who will only listen, they will hear the reassuring voice of God: 'I will instruct you and teach you in the way you should go; I will counsel you with my eye upon you' (Psalm 32:8). We do not always discover the purpose, but we must always believe there is one. When Jesus was told that Lazarus was ill, he responded 'it is for God's glory'; *we* know that, because we can read the end of the story, but immediately Mary and Martha could see no point in it. When Paul left Trophimus, who was ill, at Miletus, we still do not know the purpose in this, but there certainly was one (2 Timothy 4:20). The well-worn promise of Isaiah 29:11 had been comfortably applied by generations of Jews before Christians took it over: 'I know the plans I have for you, declares the LORD, plans for wholeness and not for evil, to give you a future and a hope.'

Let me take you a little further. One of the most quoted verses from Paul's letters must surely be: 'We know that for those who love God all things work together for good, for those who are called according to his purpose' (Rom 8:28). That phrase 'according to his purpose' is crucial.

Paul believed that was the purposeful grace of God. He meant that in everything there was a plan and purpose designed by God for the ultimate benefit of his people and the certain honour of his name through the proclamation of the message of Jesus. But did Paul really believe this?

Writing from house arrest in Rome about the same time as his letter to the Ephesians, Paul wrote, 'I want you to know, brothers, that what has happened to me has really served to advance the gospel' (Philippians 1:12). Paul had the audacity to write about 'advance' when he was actually confined to quarters! And later he told the Philippians that he had 'learned in whatever situation ... to be content' (Philippians 4:11); this was not a reluctant resignation that 'whatever will be will be', but a confidence in the fact that God had plans—better plans—than immediately appeared. For this reason he was always on the lookout to see how those plans would be fulfilled.

But did this really work for Paul? Being under house arrest in Rome could have been utterly frustrating for the itchy feet of a pioneer evangelist who longed to reach the unreached with the good news of Christ. Yet, writing to the church at Philippi he revealed that he had discovered at least a two-fold purpose in his confinement: 'I want you to know, brothers, that what has happened to me has really served to advance the gospel, so that it has become known throughout the whole imperial guard and to all the rest, that my imprisonment is for Christ. And most of the brothers, having become confident in the Lord by my imprisonment, are much more bold to speak the word without fear' (Philippians 1:12–14). His imprisonment had not only taken the gospel into the very centre of the Emperor's palace guard, but it had put new courage and new life into some of the wavering converts.

For this reason, Paul prayed that whenever he spoke on behalf of his King, he would fearlessly make known the gospel of Christ 'for which I am an ambassador in chains' (Ephesians 6:20); an ambassador in chains? So much for diplomatic immunity! Similarly, he urged the Christians at

Colossae to pray that 'God may open to us a door for the word, to declare the mystery of Christ, on account of which I am in prison' (Colossians 4:3); it is certainly an expression of Paul's confidence in purposeful grace that he can write in the same sentence of an open door whilst he is in prison! Backed by the example of his own faith and experience, Paul expected the young churches to follow the same route. To the Philippians he urged: 'Whatever happens (to me or to you), conduct yourselves in a manner worthy of the gospel of Christ' (Philippians 1:27 *New International Version*).

For all who are saints—declared holy by God to serve wholly for God—God has a purpose to bring honour to his name, and what is more, we can fulfil that purpose. We may try to excuse ourselves by the plea that we are not gifted, lack strength, are not muscular in faith, or that we are elderly, frail, or alone. When Paul claimed, 'I can do all things through him who strengthens me' (Philippians 4:13), he was not so stupid as to believe that this meant he could swim the Mediterranean backstroke or rid it of pirates! What he meant quite simply was that he could accomplish all that God had purposed for him.

William Carey is well known as the 'Father of modern missions' and the Baptist pioneer in India who sailed from England in 1793 and died forty-one years later without ever returning home. His prodigious contribution to India—and the world beyond—in the realms of botany, engineering, economics, medicine, communications, literature, education and social reform were eclipsed only by his outstanding work of Bible translation. Carey was responsible for overseeing translations of the Bible or parts of it into forty Indian languages and dialects. Which was not bad for a Northamptonshire cobbler who once earned fifty pence a week making and mending shoes!

But it is the story of one of his sisters, Mary, which is even more significant for us here. Mary was born with a diseased spine and few expected her to live very long. William led her to Christ and she was cared for by her sister Ann. All through his time in India, William sent money home to help towards Mary's support. By the age of twenty-five, Mary was paralysed, and for the next fifty years she was confined to her room. For eleven years she could not speak, and her right arm became the only limb in her body that she could move. Yet, we are told that her face shone with the joy of Christ, and she taught Ann's children the Bible by writing on a slate; in fact for years she led a Bible Class this way.

When Carey went to India, Mary wrote letters to him regularly. She told him all the family news—all the things distant missionaries really want to know. But best of all, she was described as the mission's chief priest whose ceaseless prayer was a fragrant offering to God. One nephew learnt the heart of mission work from his Aunt Mary, and in 1828 a niece wrote, 'Aunt's sufferings were a few weeks ago very distressing; yet we could not give her up. We do all love her so dearly; to part with her would tear us asunder. Her late affliction was enough to kill a person in good health. She is merely skin and bone, and not much of that, and so weak as to be hardly able to sit pillowed up in her chair, while her bed is made. Yet she continues the same sweet-tempered, humble Christian she ever was, feeling for others more than for herself, and always fearful lest mother should debar herself anything for her comfort.'

Incredibly, Mary lived to the age of seventy-four. In her own way her work was as great as that of her illustrious brother. His achievements belonged to her. Only eternity will reveal just how much Mary accomplished in India by her prayers. Without a doubt she had learnt the meaning of purposeful grace by discovering God's plan for her life.

This is how saints are to see their lives and circumstances. What he commands we can do. Where he sends we can go. What he brings we can endure. Because purposeful grace is the ability to do what God's purpose has planned. Why then do we duck his claims, avoid his call, hold back from his work, and make excuses? He has a plan, and purposeful grace will be given to fulfil it, abundant grace for an abundant purpose. In a superb expression of this Paul wrote to the church at Corinth: 'God is able to make all grace abound to you, so that having all sufficiency in all things at all times, you may abound in every good work' (2 Corinthians 9:8). This is one of Paul's many extravagantly precise claims: all grace for all things at all times providing all you need for all your work. That is purposeful grace for all his saints.

YOUR WAY, NOT MINE, O LORD,
whatever it may be;
lead me by your own hand,
choose out the road for me.

2. Smooth let it be or rough,
your path will be the best;
direct or winding, still
it leads me to your rest.

3. I dare not choose my life,
I would not if I might;
choose for me, O my God;
your choice is sure and right.

4. Then fill my cup, O Lord,
according to your will,
with sorrow or with joy;
choose all my good or ill.

5. And choose my friends for me,
my sickness or my health,
choose for me my concerns,
my poverty or wealth.

**6.** Not mine but yours the choice
in things both great and small;
Lord, be my guide, my strength,
my wisdom and my all.

Horatius Bonar 1808–89
*Praise!* 874 © in this version Praise Trust*

**1.** How best can the Christian share 'the riches of God's grace'?

**2.** How can we explain purposeful grace to a friend in great tragedy or suffering?

**3.** Think through some of the 'disasters' in the Bible and discover the ultimate purpose in them. Can you recall any Christians in the story of the church who were like Mary Carey?

**4.** Can you share anything similar from your own experience of those known personally to you?

**5.** Read Ephesians 3:1–13. Paul encourages the Ephesians not to be discouraged by his suffering. What basis for this encouragement does he give?

# Sufficient grace

'My grace is sufficient for you' 2 Corinthians 12:9

Commentators argue over the precise nature of Paul's 'thorn in the flesh' that he refers to in verse 7—their views range from poor eye-sight to a poor choice of wife! Whilst it is true that the phrase almost certainly refers to a physical ailment, for Paul it must have been the effect rather than the cause that especially troubled him. Paul had suffered much in his Christian life, but this seems to have come into an altogether different category.

He calls it simply his 'thorn in the flesh', and three times he pleaded with God to take it away. Paul felt that it came directly as a satanic attack and he was 'harassed' by it. That is the same word used of the fist-beating that our Lord suffered (Matthew 26:67). It must have been something out of the ordinary. However, each time Paul pleaded with God, he knew that the same answer was coming back to him: 'My grace is sufficient for you.' Whatever this grace was, Paul clearly did find it to be sufficient, because to these same Christians at Corinth he promised that God was able to provide ample grace: 'So that having all sufficiency in all things at all times, you may abound in every good work' (2 Corinthians 9:8). When Paul writes about sufficient grace, I want to know what he has experienced in his Christian life that has enabled him to prove the reality of sufficient grace. It is not difficult to discover the answer.

### Paul's physical pain

Much of Paul's suffering is discovered in 2 Corinthians 6:4–10 and 11:23–27. He had been imprisoned more times than he could recall, five times lashed with thirty-nine strokes until bleeding furrows were cut into his flesh, three times beaten with rods and once stoned by the mobs and left for dead. His broken body, lacerated back and resulting limp he carried with him to the grave. In addition he was shipwrecked three times— including a night and day adrift in an open boat—and was frequently in danger from floods, bandits, Jews and Gentiles, and even false Christians. In summary, Paul knew the meaning of endurance, afflictions, hardships, calamities, beatings, imprisonments, riots, labours, sleepless nights, hunger, dishonour, slander, exhaustion, hunger, thirst, and exposure. He certainly understand the meaning of being poor and living constantly close to death.

That is an impressive list of suffering for thirty years of missionary work, and if Paul really found the grace of God sufficient then he has something to teach me. However, apart from all else, there was the daily pressure on him of his anxiety for all the churches (2 Corinthians 11:28–29). That word 'anxiety' referred to a distraction from the main task.

## Painful churches

The churches in Galatia were among some of the first to be won for Christ and among the first to be led astray by error. No sooner was his lacerated back turned than the 'Judaeizers' came among them and told them that as Gentile (non-Jewish) converts they had to submit to some of the old Jewish ceremonial laws if they wanted to be real Christians. And they swallowed the line! Paul sent off an urgent letter pleading for them to come to their senses and not reject the Saviour who had paid the price for their salvation.

The Christians at Colossae and Laodicea, were in danger of being enticed away by fine-sounding empty philosophy and futile religious observances—even the worship of angels! There had been petty squabbles at Ephesus and Crete; and the Hebrew Christians, who knew their Old Testament perfectly, were making very little progress in their faith and still needed to be taught the elementary things of the Truth. In the church at Corinth, divisions and party spirit, toleration of heresy, immorality and lawsuits, and a lack of love and care for one another, wrecked their witness to the world. It took Paul at least three letters and one very painful visit, during which the church told him to mind his own business and stop pulling apostolic rank on them, finally to sort them out. No wonder Paul was distracted from the main task. There were better people in the world than some of those in the church.

## Painful people

Painful above all were those individuals who either caused so much trouble or who could not be relied on when the pressure mounted. There were men in Asia who seemed only to be preaching in order to parade their superior gifts against Paul (Philippians 1:15–18) and some in Greece who did all that they could to assassinate his character with barbed innuendos against him (2 Corinthians 10:2, 10). Paul wrote sadly to Timothy that in Asia everyone had deserted him when he needed them most, including Phygelus and Hermogenes (2 Timothy 1:15). Demas, who had once been so eager, had deserted the gospel because of the attractive pull of the world (2 Timothy 4:10). Hymenaeus and Philetus were claiming that the resurrection was past, and their beguiling message acted like gangrene in the body of the church (2 Timothy 2:17); and Alexander was well known as the troublesome blacksmith who hammered away at Paul and did him so much harm (2 Timothy 4:14).

Writing from house arrest in Rome in AD 62 Paul was clearly feeling abandoned by many when he informed the church at Philippi that so many: 'Seek their own interests, not those of Jesus Christ' (Philippians 2:21); and we can sense his disappointment in the lament to the Colossians that of all the converts from Judaism, only Aristarchus, John Mark and Jesus Justus were currently with him (Colossians 4:10–11). It was a lonely role for Paul as the spearhead of gospel expansion.

Paul used the Greek word *catastrophe* in 2 Timothy 2:14 to describe the effect of 'quarrelling about words'. And not even the women were exempt from some of the trivial quarrelling in the churches that could do such severe damage. At Philippi, Euodia and Syntyche would work hard, long and fearlessly—just so long as they were not working together (Philippians 4:2–3). The sharp disagreement with Barnabas over John Mark was hurtful enough (Acts 15:36–40), but nothing like the issue that forced him to confront Peter and 'even Barnabas' a few years later over the heresy of the 'Judaeizers' (Galatians 2:11–21). Happily it all ended with Peter and Barnabas admitting their error, but it was a very painful experience at the time.

There were even workers who, through no fault of their own, caused Paul anxiety. Poor Trophimus was so ill that he bravely offered to be left behind at Miletus (2 Timothy 4:20); Epaphroditus nearly died in Rome, and when he eventually recovered Paul felt obliged to send him back to his home church (Philippians 2:27). Suffering did not take Paul by surprise, though the relentless scale of it might have done. He was warned right from the start: 'How much he must suffer' for the name of the one who has saved him (Acts 9:16), and in turn he warned the young churches he established that, 'After my departure, fierce wolves will come in among you, not sparing the flock' (Acts 20:29, 30).

## Sufficient grace

How do we know that Paul found grace to be sufficient? He assured the Philippians: 'I have learned in whatever situation I am to be content. I know how to be brought low, and I know how to abound. In any and every circumstance, I have learned the secret of facing plenty and hunger, abundance and need. I can do all things through him who strengthens me' (Philippians 4:11–13). To the Corinthians he wrote, 'We are afflicted in every way, but not crushed; perplexed, but not driven to despair; persecuted, but not forsaken; struck down, but not destroyed'

(2 Corinthians 4:8–9). And to these same Christians who caused Paul so many headaches, he could assure them: 'Thanks be to God, who in Christ always leads us in triumphal procession, and through us spreads the fragrance of the knowledge of him everywhere' (2 Corinthians 2:14). The church at Rome was reminded that, 'We are more than conquerors through him who loved us' (Romans 8:37). The Philippians were given the seemingly impossible command: 'Rejoice in the Lord always' (Philippians 4:4), and an even more impossible example: 'I can do all things through him who strengthens me' (4:13).

What is the bridge that spans the gulf between, on the one hand, all that suffering and disappointment and, on the other hand, Paul's incessant optimism? It is called, sufficient grace. Paul described it in 1 Corinthians 15:10, 'I worked harder than any of them, though it was not I, but the grace of God that is with me'. Whatever this grace was, it enabled Paul to be glad in his weakness, and to delight in insults, hardships, persecutions and difficulties. He says it was grace that enabled him to be strong when he was weak, to accomplish all that God wanted him to achieve and to glory in his confidence in God (2 Corinthians 12:11).

## Paul's belief in the passion of God was sufficient grace

When God encouraged Paul, 'My grace is sufficient', that was a very personal promise. No man ever had a greater understanding of the character of God than Paul, and his God was not remotely distant. His was a God who *felt*. The Old Testament pictures a God who is grieved, concerned, and angry. He is a loving husband (Jeremiah 31:32), a caring mother (Isaiah 66:13), a compassionate father (Psalm 103:13), a watchful shepherd (Psalm 23:1), and a faithful friend (2 Chronicles 20:7). These are all pictures of a God of compassion. God cares, and cares deeply. Paul knew this, and therefore he could write to the Corinthians: 'No temptation has overtaken you that is not common to man. God is faithful, and he will not let you be tempted beyond your ability, but with the temptation he will also provide the way of escape' (1 Corinthians 10:13).

When theologians speak of God as 'immutable', they mean that he is unchanging. To speak of strong emotion or passion in *us* always implies a change; our moods shift. But this is not so with God. He does not change in any way. Unlike us, God is always all that he is. We may sometimes observe his wrath and at other times his mercy, but still he is always both. This is why we must never suggest that one attribute or characteristic of God—like love for example—is more significant than another.

However, could God really appreciate Paul's pain? Could God suffer? To say 'no', means that Paul went through experiences of which God himself had no understanding. To say 'yes' appears to bring God to the level of flinching in agony with each lash across Paul's back! But neither of these responses is quite true. In order to avoid the danger of suggesting that God is fickle, when such words as passion, compassion, love, anger and mercy are used of God, it is common to assume that they must be what is called 'anthropomorphisms'—that is, attributing human emotions to God only as a picture to help us understand God. But perhaps there is no need for this defensiveness.

To assume that because words of emotion imply change in us they are therefore not appropriate to use of the unchangeable God, is to view them the wrong way round. In reality, God is the most perfect expression of all true emotion, and ours is the pale sin-spoiled reflection of this. We are created in *his* image and likeness, he does not express himself in *our* image and likeness. Therefore all that is good in us is perfect in him, because that is where our goodness comes from. It is this very fact that makes humankind distinct from animals. In other words, it is not that God's passion is unlike ours, but it is ours that is a poor and tainted reflection of his. Viewed like this, we can certainly talk of God's passion—his ability to feel and experience.

We must hold together in harmony the two apparent contradictions that God is both *transcendent* (that is, so unlike us) and *immanent* (that is, so close to us). It was one purpose of the coming of Christ into this world (the incarnation) to show us how human nature was intended to be; he alone was wholly without sin (Hebrews 4:15). It is in Christ that the transcendent God reveals that he is immanent. God did not *become* immanent in the incarnation he simply *demonstrates* his immanence; in the same way that God did not *become* love when he sent his Son into this world, he *shows* his love (Romans 5:8)—a love that was always there. God has always been and always will be closely and immediately active in his world.

Similarly, Christ did not come to earth in order to experience our suffering and then return to heaven to tell the Father what suffering is like; on the contrary, he came here to tell us what God is like. So the real physical suffering of Christ expresses the real understanding of the Father. God the Father cannot suffer physical pain, but as God he fully understands physical pain and can enter into our experience of it *perfectly*. Christ was not the Father's experiment of passion, he was the Father's expression of passion.

God is most certainly a passionate God. The psalmist claimed that God is a 'merciful and gracious God, slow to anger and abounding in steadfast love and faithfulness' (Psalm 86:15 see also 103:8; 111:4; 112:4; 145:8). And when Isaiah promised Israel that, 'In all their affliction he was afflicted' (Isaiah 63:9), he was telling them something profoundly relevant. When Christ wept at the tomb of Lazarus, that not only reflected what the incarnate Word felt, it was a true expression of the heart of God. God felt the agony of Job who cried out in his torment of body and spirit: 'Why is light given to those in misery, and life to the bitter of soul, to those who long for death that does not come, who search for it more than for hidden treasure' (Job 3:20–21 *New International Version*).

The subject of the passion of God is a mystery, and we must beware of trying to explain our Christian faith so adequately that there are no more mysteries left. Equally we must be aware that we can so protect the revelation of God's character that we deny the very things that he wants us to enjoy. It *is* possible to believe in a God who feels and understands our suffering and pain to the fullest extent of his passionate compassion, and at the same time to maintain a God who knows and plans all things beforehand and who is sovereign and unchanging in his character. Paul was perfectly understood by a God who was infinite in his compassion and eternal in his watchful care.

## Paul's trust in the promises of God was also part of this sufficient grace

When Paul wrote to Timothy and sadly commented that at the first hearing before the Emperor Nero everyone deserted him, he added, 'But the Lord stood by me and strengthened me ...' (2 Timothy 4:17). What Paul does not tell us is just how the Lord stood beside him. Whether he felt, saw or heard anything we can only guess; but what we do know for certain is that Paul held to the promises of God. Writing in Hebrews 13:5–6 the apostle referred to both Deuteronomy 31:6 and Psalm 118:6 to remind the Christians that God will never abandon them and that with the Lord as their helper, they need never fear whatever man does to them. The psalmist held the same firm conviction: 'Even though I walk through the valley of the shadow of death ... you are with me' (Psalm 23:4) and God promised the same through Isaiah 'When you pass through the waters, I will be with you' (Isaiah 43:2). It was similarly Jacob's confidence: 'I will not leave you' (Joshua 1:5).

It was on this ground that Paul was firmly convinced that the outcome of his trial meant that either way, God would 'rescue me from every evil attack and bring me safely to his heavenly kingdom' (2 Timothy 4:18 NIV). Like Daniel and his three friends five hundred years earlier and in a not too dissimilar predicament, the outcome of the threat of fire or lions was guaranteed to bring them safely into heaven. The stories of Hananiah, Mishael, Azariah and Daniel are certainly stories of courage and victory, but they are primarily stories of faith in the trustworthiness of God. The accounts of their daring defiance of pagan persecution would have been equally well-worth telling even if the three friends had been burnt to ashes and if Daniel had been ground to meal—except that we would not have been so eager to recount them to the Sunday School! Their trust was in God to be with them, though not necessarily to deliver them from death. They knew that if he wished, their God would deliver them through death safely into heaven; that is exactly what lies behind those remarkable words of the friends: 'But if not ... we will not serve your gods' (Daniel 3:18). It was this trust that enabled the psalmist to declare without a fear of contradiction, 'Many are the afflictions of the righteous, but the LORD delivers him out of them all' (Psalm 34:19).

That bold promise of God recorded in Isaiah 43:1–3 has presented a problem to some Christians because in reality Christians do drown and they do burn. It is a promise that flood and fire will never have the final word for the Christian. God will always bring his people safely through—one way or the other.

Paul must have been aware of some of the most reassuring words of our Lord just before he left the disciples: 'I am with you always, to the end of the age' (Matthew 28:20). However, these words have rarely been rendered in English translations with all the strength that Matthew recorded it. William Hendriksen accurately paraphrases it: 'I am with you day in day out to the close of the age.' Paul lived in the light of that promise—day in and day out.

John Newton's wife, Mary, died on Wednesday 15 December 1790. Ten days later the heartbroken pastor entered his ornate pulpit at St Mary Woolnoth in the City of London and announced his text: 'Although the fig tree shall not blossom, neither *shall* fruit *be* in the vines;

the labour of the olive shall fail, and the fields shall yield no meat; the flock shall be cut off from the fold, and *there shall be* no herd in the stalls: Yet I will rejoice in the LORD, I will joy in the God of my salvation. The LORD God *is* my strength …' (Habakkuk 3:17–19 *Authorised Version*). In all his ministry John had never preached on this verse before, but thirty-six years earlier he had written a letter to a friend and referred to these verses from Habakkuk and concluded, 'Oh the name of Jesus when we can speak of him as ours; this is the balm for every wound, the cordial for every care; it is an ointment poured forth, diffusing a fragrancy through the whole soul, and driving away the hurtful fumes and fogs of distrust and discontent.'

It is sad how many Christians claim to believe that the Bible is God's sufficient revelation, and yet are looking for additional revelations. At the close of a meeting, a man related how hard the previous year had been for him and added that at the start of the year someone had given him a word of prophecy that included the promise of God's help; he concluded, 'Without that prophecy I really do not know how I would have got through the year'. He might have relied upon the promises of God in his word as a better alternative!

### Paul's confidence in the purposes of God was sufficient grace

Because Paul believed in purposeful grace, as we saw in the previous chapter, he was convinced that all that God had called him to do, he would be able to accomplish. That is exactly what he meant when he told the Philippians, 'I can do all things through Christ who strengthens me'. We have said before that he was not so foolish as to imagine that he could swim the Mediterranean back-stroke or rid it of all the pirates that Rome was battling against with its galleys, but Paul firmly believed that he could accomplish all that God had planned for him to do. He knew that he had been called according to God's 'own purpose and grace' (2 Timothy 1:9).

However, for us all there are times when our circumstances change, often suddenly and radically. It is not always to our liking or to our understanding and, like Paul with his 'thorn in the flesh' we argue that there is surely a better way; how much more useful we could be if … Sufficient grace is when we accept his wisdom and plans in place of our own. Paul also believed that in all the circumstances of his life there was a higher purpose than may appear immediately. Writing to the first century Christians the apostle expressed his confidence like this: 'Therefore, let us be grateful for receiving a kingdom that cannot be shaken, and thus let us offer to God acceptable worship, with reverence and awe' (Hebrews 12:28). God alone can give us grace to accept the purposes of God in our life and to believe that whatever our situation or suffering he has a plan for us and therefore a place for us in the work of his Kingdom. In the words of Samuel Medley, God is 'too wise to be mistaken and too good to be unkind.'

There is always purpose in life. More than once Paul struggled with the dilemma of longing to be away from this world of injustice and pain and be with Christ which is 'far better'; but he checked himself with the knowledge that for the sake of the churches it was better that he should remain here a while longer (Philippians 1:23–24). He learnt in Asia that the severe suffering that caused him to despair of life was always for a purpose and would teach him to rely more upon the Lord and less upon himself (2 Corinthians 1:8–10). Even the frustration of a closed door at Mysia proved to be the means of an open door to Philippi (Acts 16:6–10).

Across the world today there are tens of thousands of Christians who are persecuted for their faith: Fathers taken away from their families and daughters taken away from their parents; brothers and sisters in Christ denied justice and tortured. Harassment, arrest, interrogation, imprisonment, fines, torture and death are some of the ways that religious and atheistic governments pursue their vain attempt to stamp out the Christian faith. In two thousand years of Christian history such methods have failed to destroy entirely the community against which Christ promised that the gates of Hades would not prevail (Matthew 16:18). Yet still persecution and injustice appear to prevail. Paul experienced this, but in his own case the persecutor became the persecuted. Every rock thrown at his head, every lash that ploughed across his back and every chain that chafed his wrists and ankles had a meaning in the purposeful grace of God.

Paul was convinced that packed into his almost unbearable suffering in Asia was not only benefit for himself as he experienced the comfort that Christ could give, but also benefit for the Corinthians as they too learnt from him how to find consolation in Christ, 'For as we share abundantly in Christ's sufferings, so through Christ we share abundantly in comfort too. If we are afflicted, it is for your comfort and salvation; and if we are comforted, it is for your comfort, which you experience when you patiently endure the same sufferings that we suffer' (2 Corinthians 1:5–6).

## Paul's pleasure in the people of God was sufficient grace

In 1783 John Newton, with a small group of fellow evangelical ministers, commenced a regular meeting to discuss matters of common concern. They called it 'The Eclectic Society' and John kept a notebook of the issues they discussed. In December 1795 one of the subjects on the agenda was, 'How may we best introduce religious conversation in company?' There was a history behind that question. When John had arrived to begin his ministry in the City of London in 1780 he soon discovered that his evangelical views were not at all acceptable among many in the fashionable society of his new parish. He wrote sadly to a friend that he received very few invitations into homes, and when he did, the conversation was simply polite and no more; it seemed almost impossible to steer the conversation onto profitable subjects, and yet he was dissatisfied simply to be there and be of no value to them. To join in their trivial conversation in order to bring them up to his, 'would be a rather hazardous experiment'. He felt very much alone.

Paul also knew what it was to be alone. He often found himself in aggressive company; deserted even by those who shared the same message. Sooner or later every Christian will know what it means to be on the edge of a crowd, outside the chattering conversation, snubbed by colleagues because their views do not fit the current topic. Or else there is the loneliness of being the only one in the home to serve Christ, the only one in the office to refuse the lottery, or the only one in the classroom not sleeping with her boyfriend.

We began with a very black portrait of people in the first century church: those who reneged on the truth, quarrelled over trifles and abandoned Paul in his need. But not all were like this. One of Paul's greatest joys was the fellowship he had with Christians, and their progress in the gospel. Here is Paul writing to some of the churches:

'Because I have heard of your faith in the Lord Jesus and your love towards all the saints, I do not cease to give thanks for you' (Ephesians 1:15–16).

'I thank my God in all my remembrance of you, always in every prayer of mine for you all making my prayer with joy, because of your partnership in the gospel from the first day until now' (Philippians 1:3–5).

'We always thank God, the Father of our Lord Jesus Christ, when we pray for you, since we heard of your faith in Christ Jesus and of the love that you have for all the saints' (Colossians 1:3–4).

'We give thanks to God always for all of you, constantly mentioning you in our prayers, remembering before our God and Father your work of faith and labour of love, and steadfastness of hope in our Lord Jesus Christ' (1 Thessalonians 1:2–3).

'We ought always to give thanks to God for you, brothers, as is right, because your faith is growing abundantly, and the love of every one of you for one another is increasing. Therefore we ourselves boast about you in the churches of God for your steadfastness and faith in all your persecutions and in the afflictions that you are enduring' (2 Thessalonians 1:3–4).

Ah, that's better! There is much to encourage us, providing we keep our eyes on the faithful Christians who work so hard, so long and so loyally for Jesus Christ. The doctor who assesses the whole of society by the people he meets in his surgery each day will have a miserably jaundiced view of life; let him go out to the local sports field on a fine Saturday morning and he will gain an altogether different and far more encouraging perspective. So Paul, ever the model of balanced Christian theology and experience, was sufficiently realistic to admit both the tragedy of fallout and the encouragement of faithful workers. They are all part of sufficient grace. In the course of my ministry I see so much petty squabbling, unnecessary divisions, harsh criticism, and downright sinful behaviour among Christians. Sometimes those who have been battered and bruised by 'brothers' tell me it is always like this—sadly that's just the way Christian are. But I can tell them that it does not have to be like that. For many decades I have been part of a caring and united local church where love and a happy respect for leadership reigns; and there are many others like it across the nation—and beyond.

Let me introduce you to some of Paul's best encouragements.

There was 'My dear friend Epaenetus', who was the first convert to Christ in the province of Asia (Romans 16:5), and hard-working Epaphras 'A dear fellow servant and faithful minister' who, like Aristarchus, was prepared to stand by Paul even when it meant that he became a 'fellow prisoner' (Colossians 1:7; 4:10), and Epaphroditus Paul's 'brother, fellow worker, and fellow soldier' who nearly gave his life for Paul's sake and who should be held in high esteem by everyone

(Philippians 2:25–30). Then there was Luke 'the beloved physician' (Colossians 4:14), and Onesiphorus, the prison visitor who searched all over Rome until he found where Paul was being held and, at great risk to himself, so often encouraged Paul (2 Timothy 1:16–18), and Onesimus who, as a runaway slave had forfeited his life, found Paul, got converted and was now on his way back to his master as a valuable 'brother' from now on (Colossians 4:9; Philemon vs 8–20). Even John Mark, that first-term failure who caused such a rift between Paul and Barnabas, became so useful to Paul (2 Timothy 4:11) and, as Peter's assistant, wrote out one of the gospel stories. Paul spoke so highly of Tychicus, 'a beloved brother, faithful minister, and fellow servant in the Lord' (Colossians 4:7), and Apelles who was 'approved in Christ' (Romans 16:10).

To counterbalance those two at loggerheads in Philippi, there were many women who served the gospel with encouraging zeal, like Phoebe who had been such a help to so many, not least to Paul himself (Romans 16:1–2); and Tryphaena and Tryphosa—presumably two sisters—and 'the beloved Persis' who 'worked hard in the Lord' (v 12). The mother of Rufus was like a mother to Paul himself (v 13); and Nympha opened her home regularly as a meeting place for the believers (Colossians 4:15).

Then there were the husband and wife teams that gave Paul hope for the future of the church. Priscilla and Aquila appear constantly in the story of the young church; firm in their grasp of the truth they always opened their home for a church to gather, risked their lives often for the sake of Paul and, especially noteworthy since they were converted Jews, took similar risks also for 'all the churches of the Gentiles' (Romans 16:3–5; 1 Corinthians 16:19). His relatives, Andronicas and Junia were converted before Paul himself and obviously prayed him into the kingdom (Romans 16:7); their loyal support was well known among the apostles, though it clearly got them into trouble and they were at one point 'fellow prisoners' with Paul himself.

We can be so distracted by the fools and failures that we overlook the army of men and women who ensure that the church remains strong, healthy and true to the gospel. Paul knew there would be hard times ahead, but he was confident that there were sufficient wise heads and stout hearts to guide and guard the church when he had been taken into that 'Heavenly kingdom'. Even when Paul felt alone, and when he was in reality isolated in his prison cell, he could thank God for the family to which God had called him three decades before. And when he knelt friendless in the execution yard with only the buzz of the flies, the distant sounds of the city about its work, the rough scrape of steel on leather as the soldier drew his sword from its sheath, and the clink of harness as the legionary lifted his arms for a powerful thrust, Paul was not alone. Like Stephen, whom he had watched die with a face like that of an angel, Paul knew himself to be surrounded by the testimony of a great cloud of witnesses who had gone before him, and innumerable angels in their joyful gathering (Hebrews 12:1,22). And, as always, the Lord stood at his side. He was not alone even then.

To be part of this magnificent and universal family here on earth, with all the privileges of that—and to know that we shall spend eternity with such people all made perfect in Christ—is all part of God's grace to his people. The grace of the Christian community is a privilege we should never neglect.

Sufficient grace in any and every time of need is the grace of a God whose passion cares, whose promises will never be broken, whose purposes he will always fulfil and his people who will always be ours.

HOW FIRM A FOUNDATION, YOU SAINTS OF THE LORD,
is laid for your faith in his excellent word!
What more can he say than to you he has said,
to all who for refuge to Jesus have fled?

# Chapter 11

**2.** In every condition—in sickness, in health,
in poverty's grip or abounding in wealth,
at home or abroad, on the land, on the sea—
as days may demand shall your strength ever be.

**3.** Since Jesus is with you, do not be afraid;
since he is your God, you need not be dismayed:
he'll strengthen you, guard you, and help you to stand,
upheld by his righteous, omnipotent hand.

**4.** When through the deep waters he calls you to go,
you will not be drowned in the rivers of woe;
for he will be with you in trouble, to bless
and work for your good through your deepest distress.

**5.** When through fiery trials your pathway shall lie,
his grace all-sufficient shall be your supply;
the flames shall not harm you: his only design
your dross to consume and your gold to refine.

**6.** The soul that in Jesus has found its repose,
he will not, he cannot, desert to its foes;
that soul, though all hell should endeavour to shake,
he'll never, no never, no never forsake!

'K' In Rippon's Selection 1787
*Praise!* 877 © in this version Praise Trust

1. How can we show that God, who is unchanging and transcendent, can really understand our suffering?

2. Check out Paul's claim to have found sufficient grace in Romans 8:37; 1 Corinthians 15:10; 2 Corinthians 4:8–9; Philippians 4:4, 11–13. What, practically did all this mean for Paul?

3. In the light of the fact that sometimes Christians do drown and are burnt to death, how can we find comfort from Isaiah 43:1–2?

4. Can you list some of the Christians and churches that encouraged Paul so much and show just how they encouraged him?

5. Share your experiences of finding 'sufficient grace' in times of need.

# Community grace

'Grace was given to each one of us according to the measure of Christ's gift'
Ephesians 4:7

At 11.00 pm on 9 November 1989 East German border guards threw open the gates of the Berlin Wall and crowds surged through. Excited German citizens from the West tore at the wall with their bare hands and carried off pieces of the old way of life as souvenirs. This twenty-eight mile barrier—a symbol of half a century of division—was at last coming down. Those on the eastern side had been *separated* from all the benefits of the west, *alienated* from West German citizenship, and were *strangers* in their own land. Because they were members of an atheistic state they were, in theory at least, *without God* in the world, and although geographically they were in close proximity to their neighbours, they were in reality *far away*; the relationship between the two states was one of *hostility* and *alienation*, and, under the harsh boot of communism they were *without hope*. Suddenly everything changed and they were now, at long last, together with their friends and relatives. The world talked excitedly about the 'unification' of Germany. The whole world watched and rejoiced. It was as if a miracle had taken place.

Paul in his letter to the Ephesians was writing about a far greater and a real, not imagined, miracle. Ten years earlier there had been no Christians in Ephesus: only a ghetto of Jews meeting in their synagogues, pagan philosophers debating in the Hall of Tyrannus, profiteering bankers, merchants in their money changing dens, and devotees of Diana the goddess worshipping at her magnificent temple situated on the hill some one and half miles northeast of the city. To describe what these people were, in Ephesians 2 Paul used all the words I have just employed to describe the East Germans before the great barrier came down. The Ephesians were *separated* from Christ (v 12), *alienated* from citizenship in the Kingdom of God (v 12), *strangers* to God's promises (v 12), *far away* from him (v 13), *hostile* (v 14) and *strangers and aliens* from God himself (v 19). In fact they were *without God* in the world and consequently *without hope* (v 12). To shift anyone from there to somewhere else requires a miracle—and only God can do miracles. That miracle was God's undeserved saving grace towards the Ephesians which brought them into all the benefits of community grace.

Everything that was true of the Ephesians is equally true of all who have become Christians. Like them, whoever we are and whatever our background, we were separated from Christ, excluded from citizenship in the Kingdom of God, foreigners to God's promises and, as Christ rejecters, we were alienated from God and often from each other. We were hopeless, godless and far off. Then came the miracle. People from widely different interests and education, temperament and personality, religions, languages and cultures are converted to Christ; his righteousness is reckoned to their account and those who were without hope and without God become united not only to him, but to each other also. Paul was incredibly impressed by the fact that God can turn all this aggressive diversity into a remarkable unity. This is his constant theme throughout this letter to the Ephesian Christians. It was all part of the beautiful word 'grace'. Grace for community is expressed in the phrase: 'Grace was given to each one of us according to the measure of Christ's gift.' The context is gifts for sharing in the church. The apostle felt exactly the same when he wrote to the Philippians: 'You are all partakers with me of grace' (Philippians 1:7).

Let me show you what I mean by community grace by drawing attention to something you may never have noticed in this letter to the Christians at Ephesus.

## Paul's 'together' word

There is a small three letter word in Greek that means 'together' or 'with'. The Greek word *sun* often stands on its own, as it does in 3:18, '*with* all the saints'. This little word is very important and has been described as the 'aristocrat' among the prepositions. Paul had another more common word for 'with' that he could choose from, and he used that one over four hundred times. But he employed this word *sun* on its own sparingly—only around forty times in his letters. *Sun* often carries the idea of union, or what we may call 'togetherness'. In Romans 6:4–8 the word occurs three times to describe our relationship with Christ: we are 'buried *with* him by baptism' (v 4), 'united *with* him in a death and in a resurrection like his'(v 5), and we are 'crucified *with* him' (v 6).

However, more importantly for us, Paul used this little word in Ephesians as a prefix; that is, as a word bolted onto the front end of another word—either a noun or a verb—to give it the meaning of being or behaving *together*. On eleven occasions in this letter Paul chose a word with the prefix *sun* attached to it. Find them with me.

In 2:5–6 Paul used three verbs as descriptions of what Christ has done for us. He has, 'made us alive' (v 5), 'raised us up' and 'seated us with Christ' (v 6). But each verb has this prefix *sun* so that what Paul was emphasising is that we are, 'made alive together with Christ', 'raised up together with him', and 'seated together in the heavenly places in Christ Jesus'. It might be argued that the emphasis, as some translations imply, is simply upon us being made alive *with* Christ, raised up *with* him and seated *with* him—all of which is true of course. But if that was all that Paul wanted to say, he need not have chosen a verb with *sun* as the prefix; instead he could have allowed the word to stand on its own. This is especially clear in Colossians 3:1,3 and 4, where Paul wrote that we are 'raised with Christ', 'hidden with Christ', and will 'appear with him in glory'; in each case *sun* stands as a word on its own and not as a prefix. So here in Ephesians 2:5–6, by bolting it on to the front of a verb Paul wanted to emphasise the fact that Christians share together in the action. This is made more certain by the following uses of our little prefix.

In Ephesians 2:19–22 there are five nouns to describe what we are as Christians: Citizens (v 19), a household (v 19), a building (v 21), a temple (v 21), and a dwelling (v 22). Three times in those verses Paul chose a word with our prefix; so, we are, 'citizens together', 'joined together', 'built together'. And whilst the word for 'household' does not have our prefix, it hardly needs it because the word literally means 'belonging to a family'. In Ephesians 3:6 there are three more nouns to describe the local church: heirs, members, sharers. Once again each word carries our prefix, so we are, 'heirs together', 'members together' and, 'sharers together'. Unfortunately most of our translations (the NIV excepted) fail to express this clear intention of Paul. Finally in Ephesians 4:16 Paul used two verbs to describe the church in its activity and each has our prefix; we are, 'joined together', and 'held (united) together'.

So, there are eleven words in this letter with the prefix 'together', and twice it is used as a stand-alone (3:18 and 4:31). Thirteen times in all. In summary, at conversion we are made alive in Christ—together; we are raised up from death—together; we are seated with Christ in heavenly places—together. And what are the benefits of that? We are citizens together, joined together, built together, heirs together, members together, sharers together, and united together.

## Butterflies and bulldozers

The broad implications will be obvious. When we receive the undeserved grace of God for salvation, it brings us into all the privileges of the people who belong to God—the Christian community. Undeserved grace is also community grace and one application of this is that the New Testament never recognizes a Christian who is not joined to a local congregation of Christians—what we call 'a church'. It is not to say that someone cannot be a Christian unless they belong to a local church, but that the New

Testament simply does not recognize it. The letters of Paul are all written to churches or leaders of churches; Philemon was host to a church in Colossae (Philemon 1:2) and Timothy and Titus were leaders of the churches in Ephesus and Crete respectively.

There are many reasons why some Christians remain permanently on the edge, standing alone and apart from a local church. A few are like delicate flowers that have been damaged in one garden and believe their wisest course is never to put down their roots anywhere; in this way, they will not be hurt again. Occasionally they will talk darkly about having met 'too many hypocrites in the church'—as if the rest of us haven't. Their position is perhaps understandable but it is certainly not excusable. Christianity is always at risk from the world and from false Christians. Our Lord himself was betrayed by a friend and abandoned by the rest; Paul was deserted by Demas, hammered by Alexander, criticised by 'super-apostles' and offended by the quarrelling spirit of Euodia and Syntyche. But neither Jesus nor Paul abandoned the church; on the contrary, the one laid its foundation and the other built on it.

Then there are the more 'spiritual' who so enjoy good preaching that they would hate to be tied to the same man week after week. They attend all the best conferences and know all the best preachers—they have become connoisseurs of the finest rhetoric—but no one in their locality quite matches the big men on circuit. Some of these drifters may even attend a local church regularly, but they make no public commitment, no corporate promise, no declared loyalty, and best of all, they can get out easily. It is their form of ecclesiastical cohabitation. Others simply coast around from church to church, conference to conference, preacher to preacher. A more generous description is that they are spiritual butterflies: a little nectar here and there is what they are after. Butterflies often look impressive—but they have a very short lifespan.

There are also lazy Christians who stay on the fringe simply to avoid anyone expecting anything of them. They will often find some 'principle' that keeps them out of joining a local church, but in reality they prefer to stay in the comfort zone of Christianity; taking up a cross daily to follow Christ is not very appealing.

Others hold to such a narrow theology and demand agreement on so many details that there are few Christians left with whom they can have a meaningful relationship. They are like bulldozers that are quite incapable of distinguishing between a concrete slab and a Ming vase. They cannot tell the difference between the rigid phantom truths of their own preference or tradition and the beautiful and vital truths that are essential for giving or maintaining spiritual life. Consequently there is almost no one who quite fits into their constricted mould. They draw a small circle around themselves and effectively defy anyone to squeeze in beside them; they alone are 'faithful to the truth'. From their splendid isolation they can demolish everyone else.

John Newton wrote to a young man on the subject of 'On hearing sermons'. It might equally have been entitled, 'On choosing a church'. Having outlined the various kinds of preaching, and admitting that probably no one preacher embodies all the gifts of 'Christian advocacy', Newton then encouraged his reader to find the man 'where your soul may be best fed'. Having found such a preacher, the converted sea captain, who once preached no more eloquently than to harangue his insolent slave-trading crew, advised, 'You will do well to make a point of attending his ministry constantly ... the seldomer you are absent the better.' Newton offered his reasons for this advice: 'It encourages the minister, affords a good example to the congregation, and a hearer is more likely to meet with what is directly suited to his own case, from a minister who knows him, and expects to see him, than he can from one who is a stranger.' The wise pastor warned his reader: 'Especially I would not wish you to be absent for the sake of gratifying your curiosity to hear some new preacher, who you have perhaps been told is a very extraordinary man.' John had his own analogy from Scripture for those who run about after new preachers; they reminded him of Proverbs 27:8, 'As a bird that wandereth from her nest so is the man that wandereth from his place.' He then summed up these wanderers perfectly: 'Such unsettled hearers seldom thrive: they usually grow wise in their own conceits, have their heads filled with notions, acquire a dry, critical, and censorious spirit; and are more intent upon disputing who is the best preacher than upon obtaining benefit to themselves from what they hear.'

By his eleven times use of the word 'together' as a prefix, Paul was clearly insistent on the value of corporate grace. So, just what is its value? Here are three of the pictures Paul uses in 2:19–21.

## Fellow citizens (Ephesians 2:19)

Ephesus was the most important city in the Roman province of Asia and financially the most secure; to be a citizen of Ephesus was to be a citizen of Rome also, with all the *Pax Romana* security and privileges of that, including a fair trial and strong leadership. But many of these young Christians were slaves who had no rights of citizenship, and others, who would later refuse to worship the Emperor, would be stripped of theirs. Many were not Israelites before their conversion, therefore they could not even boast a great ancestry among the chosen nation of God. So, in the early dawn before they went off to their daily work, some of the recent converts who sat on the hard benches of their meeting place in Ephesus must have wondered what they had let themselves in for as they listened to one of the elders reading Paul's newly arrived letter. Just as they had not belonged to Israel so they did not belong to Rome either. They knew only too well that since following Christ they had been excluded from citizenship and treated like foreigners and aliens—often in their own home. They no longer worshipped at the temple of Diana or at the synagogue of the Jews, so where did they belong? Where was their security? They were strangers where once they felt at home. And worse, having abandoned the gods of their fathers and the state, they were ridiculed as *atheos*—atheist.

Christians should never feel comfortably at home in society. The jarring conversation and language, the crude *double entendre*, the loss of credibility because they choose not to see the most recent movie, the refusal to follow all that is 'politically correct'; these all contribute to an alienation from the very society in which they were born. One hundred years before Paul wrote this letter, Cicero, the Roman philosopher and statesman, had written of: 'The beach parties, dinner parties, drinking parties, musical parties, concert parties and boating parties' in connection with what he called, 'orgies, cohabitations and adulteries'. Nothing much had changed up to the time of the early church—and nothing much has changed since.

In the eighteenth century John Newton experienced this alienation from his society very early in his Christian life. When anchored in St Christopher's in the West Indies, the captains would spend the evenings entertaining each other on their ships. This unusual captain put up with a good deal of banter and even abuse from the other captains. They could not understand a man who prayed, read his Bible and wrote letters to his wife. 'They *think* I have not a right notion of life', John wrote in one of his letters to Mary, 'and I *am sure* they have not. They say I am melancholy; I tell them they are mad. They say, I am a slave to one woman, which I deny; but can prove that some of them are mere slaves to a hundred. They wonder at my humour; I pity theirs. They can form no idea of my happiness.' John was certain of this last point and confessed that he would have been ashamed if such men, who 'can be pleased with a drunken debauch, or the smile of a prostitute', could understand his joy.

But mere ridicule is paltry compared to the suffering of thousands of Christians across the world today. For the sake of Christ many are thrown out of their homes and employment, experience their wife and children turned against them, suffer imprisonment, torture and death.

Governments driven by the religions of atheism and Islam—of which North Korea and Saudi Arabia are only two of the more obvious examples—openly forbid anyone to convert to Christ; with the threat of torture or death, and mostly with the full support of their society.

What comfort would these young Christians find in Paul's letter before they moved off into the routine of their tedious daily work? Some of them looked across the meeting hall to where their master sat, and wondered what their new found faith had to offer them to break down this terrible social barrier where two thirds of the population owned the remaining one third and often treated them as nothing more than vocal implements? It was a miserable existence to own nothing—not even your wife and children—and to have no citizenship, no rights, no future and no hope.

Tychicus not only carried this letter from Paul to Ephesus (Ephesians 6:21) but on the same journey he carried a letter to the church at Colossae (Colossians 4:7) and one to Philemon in whose home the church at Colossae met (Philemon vs 1–2). Tychicus was accompanied by Onesimus who, some time before, had stolen from his slave master and run. Philemon was that slave master. Onesimus had found his way to the great metropolis and made contact with Paul about whom he had heard during his time in Philemon's house. The runaway slave was converted and was now on his way back to his master. The journey from Rome to Colossae would naturally stop off en route at Ephesus to deliver the letter to that church, so Onesimus listened in as the letter from Paul was read to the church.

The words 'You are fellow citizens with the saints', were calculated to jerk Onesimus awake. The elder was explaining what Paul meant here. Our true and lasting citizenship is in heaven and for now, Jews and Gentiles, philosophers and pagans, senators and schoolmasters, slaves, serfs and freemen, bankers and merchants, are all one in Christ—citizens together. The elder pointed out that just as Roman citizenship was obtained either by birth or at a cost, so both were true of the Christian's citizenship. Our great Emperor has paid the price for our peace with God at the cost of his own life, and by a new birth we became citizens of heaven. There is an immediate cessation of hostilities between us and God—and between us and each other!

When we become a Christian we are not like an illegal immigrant with all the stigma attributed to that, on the contrary we are welcomed immediately as a fellow citizen—and by the King himself. This incredible truth would register well with Onesimus. He who was stateless and perhaps did not even know who his parents or country of origin were, was assured of an eternal citizenship that no one could take away from him. It was, as Peter would write some years later: 'An inheritance that is imperishable, undefiled and unfading, kept in heaven for you' (1 Peter 1:4). This was music to the ears of Onesimus.

We are citizens of the same king—and what a king! We are under the same protection—and what a divine protector! We are heading for the same destination—and what a glorious goal that is! At the very least we must consider that if we will be with these people in heaven, however can we walk out on them here? And if we will be in perfect fellowship and harmony in eternity, how can we spend our time in petty squabbling now?

## Members of the household (Ephesians 2:19)

If Onesimus had slipped in his concentration because of his early morning church attendance, one expression would bring him back to reality: 'members of God's household'. Aristotle viewed slaves as little more than animals in value; the old and infirm were often sold off like broken beasts and the philosopher accurately concluded that, 'Three things make up the life of a slave: work, punishment and food.' Admittedly it was not all like this, and some slaves were treated well and eventually purchased their own freedom. But it was often a pure lottery which way your ownership fell. All slave revolts failed, and tens of thousands of slaves were killed in the aftermath. In the year AD 61, the very year in which Paul most likely sent this letter to Ephesus from his house arrest in Rome, the City Prefect in the capital, Lucius Pedanius Secundus, was murdered by one of his slaves. Custom required that every slave under the same roof—in this case four hundred men, women and children—should be executed. A riot to oppose such severity forced the Emperor Nero to line the route to their execution with troops to prevent disorder. News of such enormous barbarity soon found its way down to Ephesus and, as was intended, fear spread across the slave population. Others sitting around Onesimus, though serfs or freemen, had been thrown out of their homes when they became Christians. The riot over the great goddess Artemis (Diana) was still fresh in everyone's memory.

Paul was putting a new spin on these relationships: we are all 'family'. With the example of what happened to the slaves of Lucius Pedanius Secundus, we can imagine how Onesimus was feeling! So when the elder read Paul's words: 'You are members of the household of God', all eyes would turn to Onesimus. In the accompanying letter to Philemon, Paul informed Onesimus's master that he was sending his slave back: 'No longer as a slave but more than a slave, as a beloved brother—especially to me, but how much more to you, both in the flesh and in the Lord' (Philemon 15). And Paul was hoping to make a follow-up visit to Colossae to checkout that Onesimus had been treated as a brother. Onesimus felt more at ease; he was now a member of the very household in which he was a slave! This meant that his master was a brother from whom he could expect far better treatment than before and to whom he would render far more diligent service in the future.

The church as a family is a beautiful description and one of the most appealing. Today we are told that concepts like God as Father and the church as family are of little meaning in a society where so many hate a cruel father—or do not know who or where their father is—and where few know anything of the harmony and security of a good family. But that is precisely why these pictures are so relevant. The first century view of God and experience of families was even less 'Christian' than today's society. Many in the congregation at Ephesus had no idea what 'family' meant; they had lost contact with their father and mother years ago, even if they ever knew them. Their brothers and sisters were sold into slavery nations apart. Paul wants the church to live and behave as a family, so that others can come among them and learn what family is all about. If the world does not learn about family from the local church—both through its individual families and its corporate life—where else can it expect to learn about it?

Family is the great leveller. Within the context of leadership, family reminds us of the value and dignity of each member. The father is not more important than the son, nor the mother more significant than her daughter; older and younger brothers and sisters are of equal value. A good family thrives on the fact that each cares for the others; however costly this may be. Writing to the Galatians, Paul reminded them of their duty as Christians to do good to everyone, but 'especially to those who are of the household of faith' (Galatians 6:10). Onesimus would still be a slave to his master, but now the relationship would be wholly different. Philemon must model to his society what a slave owner should be like, and it would be so much easier since his returned slave was a brother. Philemon's neighbours would be scandalized by his response to a runaway slave, and even more so to hear this talk of 'brother'. This was radical in first century society. And a good family is almost as radical today. When a local church behaves like a true family it is the most beautiful society on earth.

## A holy temple (Ephesians 2:21)

Paul also wrote of the church as a 'holy temple'. With its one hundred marble columns, thirty-six of which were elaborately sculptured, the temple of Diana outside the city was one of the seven wonders of the ancient world. Ephesus was the centre for Diana worship and the city was the custodian of her religion; pilgrims travelled across the Empire to admire this magnificent structure and bring their offerings to the goddess who had entrusted her honour to the Ephesians. Some, sitting in the meeting place at Ephesus, had been converted from the worship of Diana and they no longer had an impressive building to worship in. If only the Christians had a beautiful temple.

Perhaps Paul anticipated thoughts like this and his reply would have been immediate: 'But you do have a temple. It is magnificently beautiful, far beyond that of Diana. The building has a firm foundation, a reliable cornerstone, and each part is so carefully constructed that as the blocks are fitted together the whole becomes a glorious holy temple; and, unlike the temple of Diana, this one is eternal.' The church is a dwelling place for God by the Spirit' (v 22) and forms a beautiful, spiritual temple. Our Lord himself had promised his disciples: 'If anyone loves me, he will keep my word, and my Father will love him, and we will come to him and make our home with him' (John 14:23). The Holy Spirit lives in the life of every Christian, and Paul reminded the Ephesians that the whole structure is 'joined together' and they are being 'built together' (vs 21,22) into this holy temple.

When people enter an impressive church building or cathedral there is often a hushed stillness. They talk in whispers and walk softly, but this often reflects more an attitude to a building rather than to God himself. When the community of believers worships together they are engaged in the most beautiful thing on earth; they are the holy temple worshipping the holy God. The purpose of this holy temple, and therefore the purpose of community grace is that we may be: 'filled with all the fullness of God.' That must mean that we become more and more like Christ.

## Goldfish on the lawn
The subject of community grace takes a much larger place in the New

Testament then we often realise. When Jesus talked about 'church', he meant more than the universal conglomerate of Christians, because his apostles spent much of their time and energy organising local churches. Paul established them and wrote letters to them and so did Peter. If the Gospels are about the Church, the New Testament letters are about the churches. When the apostle wrote to the Hebrew Christians, he placed this matter of church attendance high on his agenda: 'Let us consider how to stir up one another to love and good works, not neglecting to meet together, as is the habit of some, but encouraging one another, and all the more as you see the Day drawing near' (Hebrews 10: 24–25). Why was this is so important to Paul?

First because the apostle knew that meeting together encourages one another. This was obvious in the first century because courage is encouraging. Courage is contagious, as any soldier will tell you. So the opposite is true. My absence discourages the others. In that letter of John Newton back in the 1760s, he encouraged worshippers to be regular in their attendance because: 'This encourages the Minister and affords a good example to the congregation'. Every preacher knows how Isaiah felt when he complained, 'I have laboured in vain; I have spent my strength for nothing and vanity' (Isaiah 49:4)!

Another reason why we should not neglect to meet together, is that we are created for community. The whole of God's creation is designed for community. On earth there is the family and the larger community in society, and the Bible gives regulations for the good ordering of both. There is community in heaven also; we are not to imagine the saints as a host of spirits floating around in splendid isolation with light-years separating each from their neighbours! Every reference to heaven is about community and on earth the best community of all is the redeemed community.

Significantly here in Hebrews 10:25 the apostle does not use the normal New Testament word for church. That word is *ecclesia* which

William Tyndale accurately translated in 1526 as 'congregation'. But when the apostle refers here to 'meeting together' the word is drawn from the Jewish word 'synagogue' which literally means 'bring together' or 'gather together'; it is the verb 'to bring' or 'gather' with our little prefix *sun*—together. Our Creator and Saviour knew what was best for us when he planned the church. Since we are created for community we should value and take advantage of it. We need this community to help us grow and to care for us when we are weak. The first century Christians were all associated with a local church, and the New Testament letters were addressed with local churches in mind. The word 'encourage' that Paul uses here in Hebrews 10, is the same word that is used of the Holy Spirit in John 16:7—the *parakletos* or helper. No Christian can be expected to grow strong and healthy apart from the local church.

I have two ponds in my garden and they are stocked with scores of goldfish. I have discovered they thrive best in water since this is their natural environment. Very occasionally I discover one that is sick. Is it recommended that I take it out and lay it on the lawn to see if it will recover? The local church is the natural environment for the Christian, and our churches as communities must care by teaching and instruction, pastoral oversight, mutual help and sharing with one another in love.

Here in Hebrews 10 the apostle gives one more reason why we should be together in community: 'all the more as you see the Day drawing near.' This appears to be his strongest argument, and that phrase 'the Day' is found everywhere in the New Testament letters: 'the Day of God's Grace', 'the Day when God will judge men', 'the Day is almost here', 'the Day of our Lord Jesus Christ', 'the Day will bring it to light', 'the Day of redemption', 'the Day he comes', 'the Day he visits us', 'the Day of judgement', 'the Day of God'. But how is that an incentive to meet together now? It may be pleasant to imagine that Paul simply meant that since we will spend eternity with each other we had better start getting along now—but it is doubtful whether this was his point. More likely he had in mind that as the Day approaches, things will get tougher, so we need each other more.

However, I think his real thrust was to remind the readers that Christians, and not only unbelievers, are accountable to God. According to Paul in 1 Corinthians 3:13 every Christian must be careful how they build because 'the Day' will reveal it. In other words, we have a responsibility to each other in the local church, and the way we discharge that responsibility will be one of the issues for which we will be held to account before God. How much gold, silver, and precious stones will shine from the legacy of my life to the glory of God, and how much wood, hay and stubble will be burned away as rubbish? Much will depend upon how well I have related to the community of the redeemed.

The first temple of Diana was completed in 540 BC and two hundred years later it burned down. Its replacement took one hundred and twenty years to complete and was itself destroyed by the Goths in AD 263. The glory of the temple of Diana has now gone and all that remains on its site is one column in a pool of water. But where, today is the church of Jesus Christ? Across the whole world, on every continent and in every nation. It is indestructible, and when Christ returns in glory it will find its completeness in him. Until then, God has promised community grace for the community of grace. There is nothing like it on earth.

CHRIST, FROM WHOM ALL BLESSINGS FLOW
to perfect your church below,
Christ, whose nature now we share,
work in us, your body here.
Join our faithful spirits, join
each to each, with yours made one;
lead us through the paths of peace
on to greater holiness.

**2.** Move and activate and guide;
varied gifts to each divide;
gladly may we all agree,
bound by loving sympathy,
never from our calling move,
needful to each other prove,
kindly for each other care,
all our joys and sorrows share.

**3.** Placed according to your will,
let us all our work fulfill,
great and small, oppressed or free,
all in Christ shall equal be.
Love, like death, has all destroyed,
rendered all divisions void;
factions, names and parties fall,
you, O Christ, are all in all.

Charles Wesley 1707–88
*Praise!* 593 © in this version Praise Trust

1. Find the eleven words where Paul uses the preposition 'with' as a prefix. Discuss how each tells us something about our relationship in the church.

2. Discuss the reasons why some Christians never commit themselves to a local fellowship of believers. Is this ever excusable?

3. 'The church as a family is a beautiful description and one of the most appealing', Do you agree with this, and if so and how should this be seen in practice?

4. Assuming he had heard it read whilst on his way to Colossae with Tychicus, what comfort would Onesimus have drawn from Paul's letter to the Ephesians?

5. What reasons would you give for encouraging a Christian to attend church regularly?

# Sanctifying grace

'To him who is able to do far more abundantly than all we ask or think' (Ephesians 3:20)

I am certain that Paul had a sense of humour. In Ephesians 3:20 he encouraged the young Christians to believe that God is able to do 'far more abundantly than all we ask or think', and then he opened a new section of his letter in the very next sentence with the words: 'I therefore, a prisoner for the Lord'. He could expect the Ephesians to respond, 'Well Paul, if your God can do far more abundantly than all that we ask or think, what are you doing in prison?' That is exactly why he refers to himself as a prisoner at this point in his letter. Just in case these young and enthusiastic Christians at Ephesus became too extravagant in their idea of 'more abundantly', Paul put a check on any unwise excess.

The impact of his words was designed to force the conclusion that 'more abundantly' has nothing necessarily to do with getting out of prison, being freed from slavery, improving health, reducing an overdraft, passing exams, or achieving promotion. On the other hand, it has everything to do with all that Paul had been writing about beforehand and all that he is about to write; it has everything to do with his prayer that they may know the love of Christ in its fullness (3:16–19), and that that they might live lives worthy of their calling (4:1–3).

How we apply Paul's promise of 'more abundantly' reveals a great deal about our priorities. If we long to know God and the love of Christ, and if we long to live in a way that is worthy of our calling as Christians, then *that* is how we will understand 'more abundantly'. On the other hand, if the ambition of our Christian life is to find health and prosperity, excitement and a buzz, then we will apply it to that end. Therefore, one significant reason why Paul deliberately refers to himself as a prisoner is to make the Christians at Ephesus think through what he really means. He is saying, 'Does my imprisonment look ridiculous in the light of God's willingness to do more abundantly than all we ask or think? Reflect on it; perhaps your application is not what God intends it to be.'

But there is another reason why Paul refers to himself as a prisoner at this point in his letter—and we will come to that later.

## Sanctification?

The words 'sanctification' and 'holiness' translate the same Greek word which carries the idea of being separated from the service of the world to the service of God; it is derived from that word 'saint' that we considered in chapter ten. In the New Testament the word 'sanctification' is used in two distinct ways. First of all, we are sanctified by the righteousness of Christ being reckoned to our account; this, as we saw in chapter five, is known as 'imputed righteousness'. Paul reminded the Corinthians that Christ Jesus is our 'righteousness and sanctification' (1 Corinthians 1:30), and that Christians are 'sanctified in Christ Jesus, called to be saints' (1 Corinthians 1:2). It is on the basis of this imputed (reckoned) righteousness that we are justified. This is an action that is once and for all; it will never be repeated because it can never be undone.

The second use of the word 'sanctification' in the New Testament is a progressive work of the Spirit in our lives which demands our diligent activity. Paul urges the Christians at Rome to present themselves to God: 'as slaves to righteousness leading to sanctification' (Rom 6:19). Similarly we are to: 'strive ... for the holiness without which no one will see the Lord' (Hebrews 12:14). In this sense sanctification is a life-long growth into the likeness of Jesus Christ. One purpose of our salvation is that we might become steadily more like Christ (Rom 8:29). From here on in this chapter we will use the word 'sanctification' in this way.

However, the history of the Christian church has often confused more than clarified the meaning of sanctification. Besides the teaching of the Church of Rome—that sanctification is imparted to us by the ceremonies of the Church—others have their own particular views of this subject. The eighteenth century evangelist and founder of Methodism, John Wesley, taught that all the promises of God concerning holiness can be realised in this life. In a sermon on Philippians 3:12,15 called 'Christian Perfection', he claimed that a Christian can become, 'in such a sense perfect as not to commit sin, and to be freed from evil thoughts and evil tempers.' This state of complete purity is brought about by 'a simple act of faith, consequently in an instant'. He believed that there are two distinct steps of faith in the Christian life: we need regeneration and then 'entire sanctification'; this is a crisis and it was often referred to as a second blessing. From this state of purity (the quality of life) we can move on to maturity (the quantity of purity).

Wesley therefore distinguished between: justified Christians, entirely sanctified Christians, and mature Christians. Early in the nineteenth century the American evangelist, Charles G Finney, believed in 'entire sanctification, in the sense that it is the privilege of Christians to live without knowing sin.' For Finney, because we are only obliged to do what we are able to do, the standard of sanctification fluctuates with our ability; for him, there were only two classes of Christians: the spiritual and the carnal.

The 'Higher Life Movement' of William Boardman later in the nineteenth century taught that just as we can do nothing for our justification, so we cannot contribute towards our sanctification either; they are two separate acts of faith. The 'second conversion' is when sanctification is infused into us and we are free from all conscious sinning. The 'first conversion'—justification—in itself is not sufficient to save, but God will always apply the second before our death. This was very popular among many Victorian evangelicals.

A variation came from Hannah Pearsall Smith in her book *The Christian's Secret of a Happy Life* published in 1875. Rather like Finney, she taught that sanctification is relative to the Christian's ability, so that, 'purity of heart may be as complete in the early as in the later experience.' However, she taught that sanctification is not *striving* to become holy but, in a well used phrase: 'letting go and letting God'. Hannah Pearsall Smith maintained that, 'God can do nothing towards sanctifying a man until the man places himself in his hands for the purpose.' Sins of ignorance are not counted against us, and therefore we can be perfect this side of the grave. This became the foundation of what is known as the Keswick Message, though today Keswick does not follow this teaching.

More recently it has become popular to reduce the way into the Christian faith to three neat responses: I have to believe that I am a sinner. I have to believe that Jesus died for sinners. I have to believe that Jesus died for me. Providing I can affirm each of these statements I am assured that I am a Christian. It is suggested that conversion requires, 'No spiritual commitment whatsoever' and 'There is no necessary change in your life-style when you become a Christian.' We may take Christ as our saviour and subsequently we may take him as our Lord—or we may not. We have conversion without transformation. That may be good religion, but it is not Christianity.

That may be a neat and uncomplicated way of explaining the message, but that is precisely the problem. Such a simplistic approach to the massive event called conversion is not found in the Bible. In this approach, nothing more is demanded or expected than an acknowledgement of sin and the fact that Christ died for sinners. But it is hardly a major step of faith to admit to being a sinner! If sin is falling short of a standard, any standard, then no one can fail to admit to being a sinner; nobody has perfectly kept whatever standard they think they should be keeping!

All this fails to take full account of the constant theme in the New

Testament of personal warfare and struggle against sin, that God's standard for holiness is unwaveringly high, that God most certainly *does* command what is not fully attainable in this life, and that human nature even after conversion can never be entirely free from the ravages of the Fall.

Paul was adamant that the only proof of faith is a changed life; he expected that every Christian would strive to live holy for Christ and for that very reason: 'The grace of God has appeared ... training us to renounce ungodliness and worldly passions' (Titus 2:11–12). James expressed it as clearly in a verse that is often misunderstood: 'You *see* that a person is justified by what he does and not by faith alone' (James 2:24 *New International Version*). James is not saying that we are justified by our works, but that the only way justification is visible is by a changed life.

After a stormy and miserable relationship with the Christians at Corinth, Paul could at last write to them that he had heard of their complete change of mind about the sins they had before tolerated in the church. He knew that their repentance was genuine not because they said so, but because he observed all the signs of what he called 'godly sorrow'. The clearest description of repentance that we will find in the New Testament is 2 Corinthians 7:9–11. Here is a church that longed to be pure again on the issues that had so tarnished their Christian witness.

## Paul's plan for holy Christians

In Ephesians 4, Paul takes us in a different direction to understand what sanctification really means. The word 'therefore' in v 1 is significant because it forms a bridge between all that he has written before and what is to come. The one flows from the other. In fact, what Paul does here is to follow his usual pattern. In all his letters, Paul's invariable rule is to begin with theology and conclude with application. He tells the Christians what they should believe, and then how they should live.

It is a great weakness when someone becomes a Christian immediately to tell them what sort of life they should now live. We squeeze them into an evangelical mould of our church taboos and traditions and we think this will help them to grow. They have to dress as we dress, go where we go, talk as we talk, and even pray as we pray; in fact they have to enjoy what we enjoy and dislike everything we dislike. They soon learned that if they did not sing precisely from the same hymn sheet they could not maintain their relationship with us. It is little wonder many young converts fall back.

We should learn from Paul. He wanted above everything for these Ephesian Christians to go on with Christ and to live a life 'in a manner worthy of the calling to which you have been called' (4:1). That is sanctification. But it took Paul three chapters before he told the Ephesians how to live because it had taken him three chapters to tell them who they are.

A brief survey of Ephesians up to this point reveals that he had told them of God's great plan for them from eternity (1:4–5), of the incredible cost for their salvation through the blood of Christ (1:7), of God's lavish love poured out on them (1:8), of the Holy Spirit within them (1:13) and of the new life from death that they have received (2:1, 4, 5). Then Paul moved on to inform them of some of the consequences of all this. All barriers are broken down: whether they are Jews or non-Jews, pagans or philosophers, slaves or freemen, they are 'citizens together, a household together, and a temple together' (2:19–21). Each word is prefixed with that word 'together' that we considered in the previous chapter. This is a favourite theme of Paul in this letter and he returned to it in 3:6, where he told them that in Christ they are 'heirs together, members together, and sharers together'.

The weakness of too many Christians is not that they do not know how a Christian should live, but that they do not understand what being a Christian means. If we had more sermons on what Christians really are, we may need fewer sermons on how Christians should live. And perhaps also there would be fewer casualties in our churches. We can tell a Christian that he must live a clean, pure, peaceable, humble and holy life, and that he must not tell lies, commit adultery, or steal. But we can tell the unbeliever all this as well. The unbeliever is no less under an obligation to be holy. God does not have one standard for the Christian and another standard—conveniently a little lower—for the non-Christian. But what can we tell the Christian that we cannot tell the non-Christian? We can tell him what he is: why he is different and how he is different.

A man may invite me to book an expensive holiday, buy a lavish car and purchase a stately mansion—all three. I tell him he is a fool to talk to me like that since they are all far beyond my means. But he then tells me that he has sure evidence that I have inherited a considerable fortune. Now that is different. I have a new capacity, and all that he encouraged me to do is well within my power. That is exactly what Paul has been doing in this letter; he has been explaining the new capacity of the Christian so that when he gets round to the tough standards in Ephesians chapter 4 no one can opt out with: 'But I can't be like that.' When my boys were young, one of them decided that he would address me like others in the church. So be began to call me 'Pastor' instead of 'Daddy'. I let it continue for a few days and then I quietly informed him that he and his brother had a privilege that they alone shared; no one else in the whole wide world could call me 'Daddy' except him and his brother. He never called me 'Pastor' again! Suddenly his special relationship and all the privileges that were included in this were sufficient to encourage him to live as a son of his father.

God used this same approach when he gave Israel the Ten Commandments and all the laws that followed. Before he laid on them the rules to live by as outlined in Exodus 20 and following, he had told them that they were a very special people and that he was a very holy God

(Exodus 19:6,17–19 and compare Deuteronomy 7:6–11). But even before this, God had given his people the Passover—which was a clear statement of forgiveness and reconciliation to God. So, God told his people about redemption and election and only then considered them ready to learn about the detailed instructions for holiness and sanctification. Or, to put this another way, God wanted his people to learn that the reason for the Ten Commandments was not simply that it was a nice way to live, but that compared to the other nations Israel was a very special and holy people, and their God was a very special and holy God (see Deuteronomy 4:6–8).

Pascal, the seventeenth century French philosopher, mathematician and scientist, once wrote, 'To change a man into a saint, grace is necessary; and he who doubts it either does not know what man is, or what a saint is.' Pascal was right. And grace for that great work of changing a man into a saint is not only necessary, it is always available from the God of all grace.

## The sanctified Christian

In Ephesians 4:2–3 Paul lists six dignified ways we are to live as Christians: 'With all humility and gentleness, with patience, bearing with one another in love, eager to maintain the unity of the Spirit in the bond of peace.' Put all these together and they would make an enormous difference to our churches and our neighbourhoods. And because of their new capacity Paul could expect the Christians at Ephesus to live like this. He would allow no excuses. Years ago when I worked on the Council of a large multinational mission society, an awkward or insensitive member would occasionally be excused with some such comment: 'It's his Latin temperament you know.' I could never accept that kindly dismissal of what was so often a downright sinful attitude. Sanctifying grace is our new capacity to live in a manner worthy of the calling to which we have been called—which is to become more Christ-like in everything.

I find this list in Ephesians 4:2–3 very encouraging, not because I am good at keeping it, but because it is there. It was needed then and it is needed now. Here in the Ephesians 4 the standard of holiness among Christians is equally positive. What was it that distressed Paul about the church at Philippi? He made no mention of bad habits, bad thoughts, or bad interests, but he was clearly upset about bad relationships (1:15 and 4:2). Some of our churches with the most meticulous standards of right and wrong simply cannot get on together.

## Be completely humble

Humility was an attitude of mind that in the first century was uniquely Christian. The Greeks and Romans had no way of describing what Paul was thinking about here. The word he employed was never used in a good sense. In classical Greek *tapeinos* meant grovelling, low-born, slavish. A second century inscription reads, 'Do nothing *mean* or ignoble', and the word was linked to such words as: miserable, wretched, complaining, timid. The Greeks and Romans were encouraged to think big and play the man; they must be self-confident, self-reliant and macho. Personal success was everything. The alternative was to be *tapeinos*, small-minded, feeble and weak—a despicable person. In the first century, humility was a vice, not a virtue. Two German friends of mine were working among a people group in Papua New Guinea who had no word for 'thank you' or 'sorry'. Everything was always someone else's fault. A man would never say, 'I bumped into the door' but, 'The door bumped into me'. The idea of *tapeinos* held no place in the thinking of that tribe. It had little place in the first century Greek or Roman culture either.

Radically, Paul took that very word and told the Ephesians this was exactly what they were to be like. They must have a deep sense of their own littleness, a modest and self-effacing behaviour. The word is only ever used in the New Testament in a positive sense. Paul encouraged the Philippians in the same way: 'Do nothing from rivalry or conceit, but in *humility* count others more significant than yourselves' (Philippians 2:3). And then in v 8 he set before them the great pattern that the Lord of eternity and the universe '*humbled* himself'. In fact Jesus claimed this for himself when he said, 'I am gentle and *humble* in heart' (Matthew 11:29 *New International Version*). He made himself low-born and despicable.

There are Christians who complain of being overlooked, who know everything, talk incessantly about themselves, strive to build an empire, or are always pushing themselves forward. They should go back to Golgotha and look on the One who: 'Though he was in the form of God, did not count equality with God a thing to be grasped, but made himself nothing …' (Philippians 2:6). We have considered that word 'grasped' previously when looking at incarnate grace; it means to use something to our own advantage. Christ never used his power and deity for his own advantage. He is our perfect example of the meaning of humility. Paul followed his Master's example when he claimed to be the least of all the apostles and less than the least of all the saints. That was not pious waffle, it was sincerely how he saw himself. W. E. Gladstone, a British Prime Minister in the time of Queen Victoria, once claimed, 'Humility, as a sovereign grace, is the creation of Christianity'—and he was right.

## Be completely gentle

If humility is an attitude of mind—how we see ourselves, then gentleness is our behaviour—how we deal with others. Some Christians are like hammer drills. Some pastors are as well. Christians with a biting tongue, complaining spirit, or heavy-handed manner can never excuse themselves with the defence: 'That's just who I am; I can't help it.' We can help it—or else we no longer believe in the God who can do abundantly more. Harsh behaviour, cruel words and thoughtless actions are contradictions of who we are. Paul referred to himself once as a 'nursemaid', yet by nature he was a man who did not suffer fools easily.

The gentle Christian is caring and thoughtful. They give time to listen and help—like the Master himself. Because they know the love of Christ they show the love of Christ. They have a gentle tongue and a quiet manner. This does not mean that they are feeble and weak. Christ was not that. He could be angry and severe, but it was always deliberate and under control. His presence spread peace among those who listened. Any Christian can be like that! However abrasive our character, hard our nature, unyielding our personality, Christ can soften us. He did this for the vicious cruelty of both Saul of Tarsus and John of Wapping—the godless sailor and slave trader. Both became loving shepherds and gentle pastors.

## Be patient

The word used here carries the idea of not lashing out or retaliating when wronged. Do you have a quick temper? A short fuse? Are you easily stirred to irrational anger that betrays itself in over-hasty words or actions? Patience is the quality of accepting mistreatment and abuse without retaliation. Some Christians are so prickly that you can feel the needles every time you talk with them; they are programmed always to misunderstand. Are you an angry Christian? Are you angry with another Christian or with your leaders? Even when we feel that we have a just cause to be angry, we have no reason to become impatient and resentful. Calvary, as ever, is our pattern, for 'When he was reviled, he did not revile in return; when he suffered, he did not threaten, but continued entrusting himself to him who judges justly' (1 Peter 2:23).

But patience is also accepting the hand of God with quiet serenity when it seems to be against us. It is a silent spirit with God's ways. Have you a quarrel with God? Are you arguing with him because things have not worked out as you designed, or because some great disappointment has broken into your well ordered plans? Have you forgotten his great patience with you? Or as Paul so well states, 'Do you presume on the riches of his kindness and forbearance and patience?' (Romans 2:4). He asks me to have patience with his wisdom and care, whilst at the same time he shows patience with my rebellion and indifference. Someone may say, 'If only you knew my circumstances you would not write so easily about patience.' But I don't need to know about your circumstances, I only need to know about the God of more abundant grace for sanctification.

## Bearing with one another in love

The word 'patience' especially refers to enduring opposition, persecution, misunderstanding or simply the circumstances that God brings into my life; at least that is how Paul is using the word here. But the word translated 'bearing with', though similar because it means patiently enduring, is directed especially towards members of the church because Paul adds the word that is translated 'one another'.

Have you noticed how similar Paul's instructions are from one church to another? That is because all churches are, by and large, very similar; the problems and relationships in one are much like those in another. For this reason, when Paul wrote to the Colossians, he covered almost the same ground that we find here in Ephesians: 'Put on then, as God's chosen ones, holy and beloved, compassion, kindness, humility, meekness, and patience, bearing with one another and, if one has a complaint against another, forgiving each other; as the Lord has forgiven you, so you also must forgive' (Colossians 3:12–15).

In the household of faith we are all different from one another. We must learn to accept each other and bear with the mistakes and character traits and personality 'disorders' of others. There is a golden rule in the church that whilst we are never to excuse ourselves, we must always be ready to excuse others. To appreciate and respect fellow Christians as brothers and sisters in Christ—and to bear with their weaknesses—is the Christian dimension. What tears our churches apart? Or spoils our comfortableness with each other? The God of abundantly more grace can and must change these attitudes.

## Maintaining unity

This humility which is our attitude of mind, gentleness which is the way we handle others, patience in opposition and circumstances, and forbearance with one another, will all lead to Paul's next encouragement: 'Eager to maintain the unity of the Spirit in the bond of peace.' Here is Paul at his most practical. Ignore those oozy Christians who pretend that all is always well in the household of faith. We are people, and where there are people there are problems. This unity, this one-ness or together-ness in Christ is our new relationship—that is a fact. But we have to work at making the reality real. That is why some translations stiffen the phrase with 'make every effort'. The word is used variously to mean 'hurry up', 'be zealous', or 'take care'. Paul wants his readers not simply to shrug with resignation at the thought of getting on with their fellow Christians, but to do everything in their power to create family unity. He wants them to be enthusiastic about it—even excited.

The great prayer of our Lord for his disciples, that after his departure they may 'become perfectly one, so that the world may know that you sent me and loved them even as you loved me' (John 17:23), had little to do with ecumenical unity between denominations, but everything to do with the way Christians got on with each other in the family. It was the relationship between James and John, Paul and Barnabus, Euodia and Syntyche that mattered far more than how Ephesus got on with Philippi, or Asia with Macedonia. It is precisely the prayer of our Lord that Paul may have in mind here. He wants them to fulfil the Master's plan for the church by working with every effort they can muster to maintain the unity which is the very essence of their life.

Unity is not merely something to write about, sing about, talk about or even pray about; it is to be real.

A house is not made strong by any number of new coats of paint, least of all by pretty wallpaper, but when the foundation and walls are securely built together. In the church, unity is enjoyed when peace is present.

## The bond of peace

At the beginning of this chapter I said there were two reasons why Paul referred to himself as a prisoner for the Lord in the context of his encouragement in the God of immeasurably more. The first was that Paul knew it would make them think: more abundantly had nothing necessarily to do with Paul being released from prison, but everything to do with the Ephesians living as Christians ought to live. The second reason is associated with his encouragement for the Ephesians to work hard to maintain unity in the church. The word that Paul used for 'prisoner' in 3:1 and 4:1 is *desmios*, and it means one who is bound or fettered. In 4:3 he uses the word *sundesmios*, the same word with our now familiar prefix *sun* meaning 'together'; it refers to a fetter—that which binds together. This is why it is translated: 'the *bond* of peace'. Paul intended that pun and did not expect the Ephesians to miss it: 'As a prisoner, I am bound to my Roman guards—in the same way you are bound together in Christ. But make sure that your shackles are fetters of peace!' As an interesting aside, the same word can refer to the ligaments that hold the body together, and Paul uses it in just this way when he wants to describe the church under the picture of a body (Colossians 2:19).

Among the descriptions of the church in Acts is the word used when Paul wanted to 'join' the church in Jerusalem (Acts 9:26). From this verb 'to join', which is *kollao* in Greek, we gain our word 'collage'. One thesaurus I have offers as alternatives for the word collage: 'random collection, hodgepodge, clutter'. That may suit some churches perfectly, but it is not quite what Paul meant! To mix our metaphors, the church is a people bound together by the Spirit and they should form a beautiful collage. But the glue for that collage is peace; and the chemical composition of that peace is made up from five vital ingredients: humility, gentleness, patience, forbearance and unity. Paul's teaching in Colossians is the same: 'Above all these put on love, which binds everything together in perfect harmony. And let the peace of Christ rule in your hearts, to which indeed you were called in one body ...' (3:14–15).

Evangelical history is not a model of unity and peace—the liberal church has always appeared more united. We may respond, 'That's because for liberals, *nothing* matters too much', which may or may not be true; but for evangelicals the opposite failure is that *everything* matters too much. We have sadly not learned to make three vital distinctions. First, there are vital truths which give or maintain spiritual life and on which we must allow no divergence. Second, there are significant truths which are important because they are in the Bible but they are not vital to spiritual life—on these we must respectfully agree to disagree. Third, there are phantom truths which have little or nothing to do with the Bible but are a mixture of our personal preference, custom or culture; this does not make them wrong, it simply means that they do not come in the category of truth. To place this last group in the category of vital truth—and therefore to make them a condition of Christian fellowship—is schismatic and therefore sinful.

John Newton was a man of peace. He gave no quarter in the battle for the truth of the Gospel, but he never looked to skirmish with those who were his true friends in Christ. He had been pastor of his flock at Olney in Buckinghamshire for four years when he described the peace that governed the life of his church: 'We are quiet and happy at Olney. We know nothing about disputes or divisions. If you pass a flock of sheep in a pasture towards evening, you may observe them all very busy in feeding. Perhaps here and there one may just raise his head and look at you for a moment, but down he stoops again to the grass directly. He cannot fill his belly by staring at strangers. Something in this way I hope it is with us. We care not who makes the noise, if we can get the pasture. If they are *talking*, they may talk on; but we had rather *eat*.' John fed his people, not with strife and dissension, but with the word of God.

## Finally

Just in case the Ephesians had forgotten where Paul began, and may neglect to recall what sort of people they are, in vs 4–6 he rammed home their oneness with a quick fire list of the essential unity that belongs to every true Christian community:

One body—you, the local church

One Holy Spirit—living within each of you

One eternal hope—to which you are all called

One Lord Jesus Christ—by whom you were rescued from sin and its consequences

One faith—in one salvation alone

One baptism—in the name of the Father, Son and Holy Spirit

One God and Father of all—to whom we are all, ultimately accountable

We must never forget these seven essential, inevitable and unavoidable facts of our unity in Christ, and never stop working at the humility, gentleness, patience, forbearance, unity and peace that keeps the church living in a way worthy of its calling. This is the best meaning of sanctification. And it is what Peter meant when he signed off his second letter with the words: 'Grow in the grace and the knowledge of our Lord and Saviour Jesus Christ' (2 Peter 3:18). The more we know Christ, the more we will reflect his character in our lives—and that is sanctifying grace. And if we are tempted to suggest that all this is impossible, remember that our God 'is able to do far more abundantly than all that we ask or think, according to the power at work within us' because 'Grace was given to each one of us according to the measure of Christ's gift'. There is always sanctifying grace available abundantly for his people.

THE CHURCH'S ONE FOUNDATION
is Jesus Christ her Lord;
she is his new creation
by water and the word:
from heaven he came and sought her
to be his holy bride;
with his own blood he bought her
and for her life he died.

2. Elect from every nation
yet one through all the earth;
her charter of salvation—
one Lord, one faith, one birth:
one holy name she blesses,
and shares one holy food;
as to one hope she presses
with every grace endued.

3. We see her long divided
by heresy and sect;
yet she by God is guided—
one people, one elect:
her vigil she is keeping,
her cry goes up, 'How long?'
and soon the night of weeping
shall be the dawn of song.

4. In toil and tribulation
and tumult of her war,
she waits the consummation
of peace for evermore:

till with the vision glorious
her longing eyes are blessed;
at last the church victorious
shall be the church at rest!

5. Yet she on earth has union
with those whose rest is won,
and shares in sweet communion
with God the Three-in-One,
whose love has made them holy!
Lord, grant to us your grace
with them, the meek and lowly,
in heaven to see your face.

Samuel J Stone 1839–1900
*Praise!* 577

## FOR GROUP DISCUSSION

1. From 2 Corinthians 7:9–11 what do we learn about true repentance?
2. How would you summarise what it means to become a Christian?
3. How would you encourage a young Christian to live a holy life?
4. Paul's description of a holy life is summarised in the five qualities: humility, gentleness, patience, love and unity. Discuss what each of these mean in practical Christian living.
5. Discuss what issues you would place under the headings of vital, significant and phantom truth.

# The grace of prayer

'For through him we both have access in one Spirit to the Father' Ephesians 2:18

In an earlier chapter we suggested that if the stars came out only once a year, the whole world would stay up all night to see them and if the birds sang their dawn chorus only once every spring, even the most disinterested would be up at three in the morning to hear them. But what if the opportunity of praying to the God who created those stars and birds was allowed only once a year also? Imagine the count-down among Christians: the months, weeks, days and hours would be marked off to the precious moments when we could take advantage of the great annual privilege of gaining access to God and entering into the presence of the Almighty.

Books and sermons on the subject of prayer focus chiefly on the results, value, purpose or power of prayer. Certainly Scripture is full of examples to encourage us to pray, but the greatest value of prayer is the incredible privilege of access to God. That, after all, was what was lost at the Fall, and that is what is regained through the cross. For this reason, this is not a chapter on the importance of prayer, though that is indispensible; it is not a chapter on the discipline of prayer, though that is essential; nor is it a chapter on the effectiveness of prayer, though that is irrefutable; least of all is it a tirade against the churches' current lack of prayer, though that is sadly undeniable. Only one thing is in focus in this chapter: the privilege of prayer—because that is fundamental.

In the previous chapter on sanctifying grace, the point was made that rather than haranguing Christians on the way to live, it is better to tell them what they are in Christ; once they understand who they are, how they should live will be largely self evident. So, we will apply that principle to the subject of prayer. If we understand the privilege of prayer, what we should do about it will be largely self-evident.

At a particularly difficult time in our life, a dear West Indian friend sent us a card in which she added 'Cheer up. God is with you, for I have committed you in his care—and he is a very good listener. Goodnight. Wish you have a very good rest. And God bless and keep you.' I have never forgotten that delightful phrase: 'He is a very good listener'. What a beautiful privilege that Violet understood so well: the sovereign God of eternity and infinity hears my prayer—and he is a very good listener.

None of us can be relied upon to listen attentively all the time. Wives complain to husbands, parents to children, teenagers to adults and teachers to pupils: 'You're not listening to me!' We turn on the radio to get the weather forecast, but our mind is so preoccupied that we hear without listening, and are none the wiser when the pips herald the news. We come to church and hear a sermon but we draw down the blinds and drift back to the office, or to last week's holiday. Somebody reads instructions to us, but we don't understand them so we switch off, we're not listening. A thousand times in a day we are just too busy to listen. Tragically, a loved one talks to us about their fears or hopes, but we're not listening and they go away with an aching heart; a child pleads for our attention, for someone to show that they care, but their cause is trivial to us who have such important matters at hand, so we don't listen—and they wander off unloved. But God is always a good listener. No cause of ours is too trivial; there are never more important issues for him to deal with, and what is more, no one is ever ahead of us in a queue. He is never short on time or too busy. And still more encouraging in these days of recorded messages and protective secretaries is the fact that there is never a substitute for his personal attention. That is what 'access to the Father' unquestionably means.

## Prayer as access

Although the word 'access' is used sparingly in the New Testament and preached rarely from our pulpits, it is actually one of the big words of the Christian faith. In Romans 5:1–2, Paul linked it with justification, faith, peace, grace, joy, and glory, so it could hardly be in better company. Elsewhere the apostle wrote of our: 'boldness and access with confidence' (Ephesians 3:12), and here in Ephesians 2:18 he confirms our 'access in one Spirit to the Father'. In the first century, the word was commonly used of the introduction of one person to another, and in the ancient world of inaccessible despots, access into the presence of a great king was fearful. An audience was gained only by waiting and trembling.

The reality of this is illustrated in the Bible story of Esther. Esther was a Jewish Queen married to the pagan Persian King, Xerxes (Ahasuerus). The King's prime minister, Haman, hatched a cruel plan to exterminate all Jews across the Persian empire, but Esther's uncle, Mordecai, heard of the conspiracy and informed his niece. She stood alone between the King and the massacre of the Jews. But no one, not even the Queen, would dare to approach the 'Great King' without an invitation. The Bible reflects the custom of the day in the following record: 'All the king's servants and the people of the king's provinces know that if any man or woman goes to the king inside the inner court without being called, there is but one law—to be put to death.' There could be only one exception to this, and that is if the king condescended to hold out his golden sceptre: 'so that he may live' (Esther 4:11). When the beautiful Queen Esther entered the inner court of the king's palace we can hear the courtiers drawing their breath as they trembled for their queen; she was risking her life by entering, uninvited, into the presence of the Great King. And we can feel the relief and joy when the king 'held out to Esther the golden sceptre that was in his hand' (5:2). These cruel despots could act on a whim, justly or unjustly, and the whole world stood in fear and awe.

If that power was true of earthly rulers, how much more awesome is the presence and power of the eternal Creator by whose word of command stars and planets came into being, the skies were filled with birds, oceans teamed with fish, mountains rose, great and mighty beasts were created, and by whose wisdom all the laws of physics and the universe were planned? Ours is the God who puts up rulers and brings them down; who is so pure and holy that even the angels hide their faces from him, and when John the apostle saw such a vision of his glory on the island of Patmos he fell down as though dead, overwhelmed by the splendour of Christ and God (Revelation 1:17). This is the one whose presence made Mount Sinai tremble (Exodus 19:18), and whose glory filled the temple in Jerusalem (2 Chronicles 7:1); the God who will one day call everyone to account and before whom every mouth will be silent.

Yet in Romans 5:2 Paul assured us that 'we have access ...' into the presence of this high and holy God.

In the early days of plastic money, the Access card was advertised by appealing to our desire for more and more—and immediately. We were promised that it would take the 'waiting out of wanting'. What was not advertised was that we could only gain access to what ultimately we would have to pay for; the day of reckoning would certainly come. But a far greater access is that which we have into the presence of God. By turning our focus to 'things that are above' (Colossians 3:2), a prayerful spirit takes the wanting out of waiting for the things of this world. And this access is free to all, simply because none of us has the right currency to deposit against which we could draw the benefits.

At this point, all our banking illustrations fail, because none of us employs the services of a bank out of love for the manager. We bank only because of the benefits we hope to gain. But that is not the ultimate purpose of prayer. The decisive value of prayer is not what we achieve through it, but what we gain by it: an audience with the King of kings. That is of value for its own sake and is the highest value of prayer, though it is rarely thought of like this. Nothing brings more honour to God and more dignity to human nature than when a forgiven sinner approaches the Creator in prayer.

Paul loved to play with words, and one of his puns is found in Romans 5:2 where he used two very similar sounding words to punch home his point. When he wrote 'we have' obtained access, the verb form he used in the Greek is pronounced *eskaykamen*, and when in the same verse he wrote 'we stand', the verb form is *hestaykamen*. Unlike the English, there is a similar ring about these two words that would impress them on the minds of his hearers. We not only have access through the grace of prayer, but we can stand in this grace in the presence of our King; there is no grovelling here.

## Old Testament access

In Hebrews 10:19, the apostle opens for us the incredible privilege of entering what he called 'the Most Holy Place' (*New International Version*), and added that we may enter it with confidence. That word confidence originally meant 'freedom or boldness in speech', though it was often used more generally than this. It referred to a confidence that leads to boldness in approaching someone or something. Have you ever found yourself caught in the experience of being in strange and intimidating surroundings? You ask yourself, should I be here? Or, am I conspicuous as a newcomer? what do I do next? Perhaps it was a new school: what if I don't know the rules? Or a new office: what are the regulations here? Or a new club: am I following the correct etiquette?

A while back I was invited to preach in South Africa, and those who had invited me paid for me to travel on a Business Class ticket. This ticket allowed me to use some exclusive lounges, which was particularly helpful when I had six hours to lose between flights and a manuscript that I wished to read. But when I entered the Club World lounge, I was at first very hesitant. My ticket said I had a right to enter but I was unsure about the privilege, and when I first showed that ticket at the entrance I was afraid I would not be allowed in and that, to my terrible embarrassment, the lady at the reception would say: 'I'm sorry Sir, but you are not allowed in here'. But she didn't, in fact she welcomed me warmly. I had a right to be here; it was my place, and all the privileges of a Club World lounge were mine.

Where we can go with boldness Paul calls: 'the Most Holy Place'. Sadly, that may not sound exciting, but in reality it is ten thousand times more of a privilege than the Business Class lounge of British Airways. The Jews would know what the writer meant by the phrase, though not many Gentiles would, therefore back in Hebrews 9:1–10 he had explained it all.

When Israel came out of Egypt in the time of Moses, they found themselves among nations all of whom already had priests and sacrifices. But Israel was to be different; they were not to worship in the way of the nations, and were not even to enquire how the nations worshipped (Deuteronomy 12:4, 31). God himself would provide them with every aspect of their way of worship, even to the finest detail: the material to be used in the curtains, the clothes to be worn by the priests, the oil for lamps, construction of the altars and equipment—nothing was left to imagination or guesswork. The Israelites were not to worship anyhow, anywhere, anyway, but 'as I command you'. So, in Exodus and Leviticus we find the details of the Tabernacle and six hundred years later the magnificent temple of Solomon followed the same general pattern.

There was only one entrance to the Tabernacle and immediately two objects confronted the priest on duty: a great bronze altar for sacrifice and a large bronze basin which was a bowl of water for ceremonial washing. The message was at once clear: the priest could proceed no further in his worship of God without a sacrifice by shedding the blood of an animal, and a ritual washing away of sin.

At the far end of this outer court was the Holy Place, or literally in the

Hebrew just one word meaning 'the holy'. Within this Holy Place there were two rooms; in the first room the priests went about their daily business replenishing the oil in the lampstand and replacing fresh bread on the table; only the priests were allowed here. Dividing this room from the second room was a large, thick curtain of blue, purple and scarlet linen richly decorated. And behind this curtain was the 'Most Holy Place' or literally in the Hebrew 'the holy, holy'. The word holy was simply doubled in order to emphasise how holy. This holy, holy room represented the presence of God, and into this room only the High Priest was allowed, and only once a year on the great Day of Atonement (*yom kippur*). Here was the Ark—a box covered with gold and with two golden cherubim on the lid, which was called 'the atonement cover'. This Ark of the Covenant represented the immediate presence of God who had promised Moses: 'There I will meet with you … and I will speak with you' (Exodus 25:22). The only other article in this room was the altar of incense.

We can imagine the awe and fear of that Holy Place. No one came lightly into the presence of God; and if they did, they bore a terrible consequence, as Nadab and Abihu and later Hophni and Phinehas discovered. The first carelessly offered what the Bible calls 'unauthorised fire' on the altar of incense, and the second treated the Ark of the Covenant like a box of magic (Leviticus 10:1–2 and 1 Samuel 4:1–11)). If these records appear to be drastic responses to minimal oversights, we have missed the whole point. God intended to set a serious example to his people from the outset—one that they would never forget: 'Among those who are near me I will be sanctified, and before all the people I will be glorified' (Leviticus 10:3). God had told his people that they must worship only in the way he instructed so that they would always approach him with reverence and awe; to come any other way would spell disaster.

Sadly, lessons forgotten must be repeated. When, half a millennium after Moses, King David brought the Ark of the Covenant from Kiriath-jearim to Jerusalem, it was placed on a new ox cart for the journey. The instructions had always been clear that the Ark was never to be handled and should only be carried between two poles on the shoulders of four priests; somebody, somewhere at sometime had overlooked this vital directive and had removed the poles; but there were no excuses, because the large rings in each corner of the Ark should have served as a reminder (Exodus 25:12). On its journey east to Jerusalem, the oxen stumbled, the cart wobbled and, fearful that the precious cargo might topple off, Uzzah the priest put out his hand to steady it. Suddenly Uzzah dropped to the ground beside the Ark of God and the whole procession came to a terrified halt. David complained to the Lord, but he knew the rules, and when, three months later, the journey was resumed it was being carried on the shoulders of the priests.

Why all these stories? On the principle that, 'Whatever was written in former days was written for our instruction' (Romans 15:4), they are there to teach us how holy God is, and how carefully we must come to him in worship. Through Christ we may come boldly and with confidence to God, but the trembling and fearfulness of the Old Testament worshippers are there to remind and warn us, and we should never lose that sense of awe and wonder expressed in so many of our hymns and by so few of our congregations. The questioning of God through Jeremiah has lost none of its power today: 'Do you not fear me? declares the LORD; do you not tremble before me?' (Jeremiah 5:22). Whilst something wonderful has happened to change the way we come, nothing has happened to change the awesome holiness of God and therefore the care with which we should approach him.

I like the word 'celebration' that has been minted in the past few decades to describe Christian worship, but there is a danger: too often we are encouraged to approach God as if we were one big happy family celebrating mum and dad's golden wedding. Of course there is joy and gladness in worship, but when did we last tremble in his presence? The results of trivial worship may not always be precisely what they were three millennia ago, but tragic results there certainly will be. When Isaiah saw the Lord Jesus Christ in the temple he heard angels crying, 'Holy, holy, holy' (Isaiah 6). It is rare for Hebrew to add to the doubling for emphasis, but if the Tabernacle was 'holy' and the inner sanctuary 'holy, holy', then the presence of God is 'holy, holy, holy'. That should speak for itself.

## Access through the blood

There is something more for us to consider in this great privilege of prayer. The apostle tells us that we come 'by the blood of Jesus, by the new and living way that he opened for us through the curtain, that is, through his flesh' (see Hebrews 10:19–20). This strange language will be clear if we keep in mind that earlier picture of the Tabernacle. With one eye on Hebrews 10:20–22 I want to take you on a short but significant journey. Remember, there is only one entrance to the Tabernacle and the first thing we meet is a great bronze altar. Over the centuries thousands of animals have been killed there, to show how serious sin is and what is the cost of forgiveness.

It is now the annual Day of Atonement. The High Priest enters the outer court of the Tabernacle and walks slowly to the bronze altar where he sacrifices a bullock, takes some blood in a bowl and live coals from the altar, pauses to wash at the great bronze basin, and moves on to the Tabernacle itself. Through the entrance and into the first room, he passes the lampstand and the table of bread and then, cautiously and with fear, through the blue, purple and scarlet curtain. No one has been here for a whole year. There has been no dusting, sweeping, or polishing of the gold, and the stain of the sprinkled blood from last year is still visible. The High Priest places some of the coals on the altar of incense and sprinkles the blood once on the Ark of the Covenant, and seven times in front of it. All the time the incense is rising towards heaven. And this is just for his own sins.

The High Priest now returns to the great altar of Burnt Offering and sacrifices a goat—then he repeats all that he has done before, though this time for the sins of the nation. But he has not quite finished. A second goat is waiting beside the altar; on this one he lays his hands, confesses the sins of the whole nation over it, and sends it off into the desert. This animal is known as the 'scapegoat'. The Hebrew word is *azazel*, which even today Hebrew scholars are at a loss to know its true translation and so we have settled for the word William Tyndale introduced in 1530.

How could one goat die for the sins of a whole nation, and how could another carry the nation's sins far away into the desert? Neither is possible. But they both present for us a picture of the Son of God who can and did. As Paul expressed it: 'This is an illustration for the present time' (Hebrews 9:9 *New International Version*). We can now understand what lies behind the picture of the 'hearts sprinkled clean' and the 'bodies washed with pure water' in Hebrews 10:22. These are all references to the great altar, the basin of water, and the blood sprinkled on the Ark in the Most Holy Place. And this is how we are to understand the death of Christ on Calvary. He was a sacrifice in our place and our High Priest to present that sacrifice to God: 'He himself bore our sins in his body on the tree' (1 Peter 2:24). That single word 'himself' is intended and is emphatic; there is no substitute for him because he was a substitute for us.

This is offensive, tens of thousands of animals sacrificed over hundreds of years—the noise and blood, the stench, flies and dirt. Animal lovers recoil and theologians retreat. It is all so primitive that it has no place in the thinking of Christianity. Something more civilised would be more acceptable. But that is precisely the point. If this offends us, how much more offensive was it that God's holy, pure, blameless Son should die in such a cruel, mocking death and in full gaze of a jeering crowd? In his letter to the Hebrews, the apostle deliberately referred to the blood of the sacrifices a dozen times and to the blood of Christ seven times—which is only one less than in all his other letters combined.

The reality is that he died that way to show how vile our sin really is, how terrible in the sight of a holy God, and how perfectly God will forgive when his Son has paid the price. How else will God get across to us the seriousness of sin? According to Paul in Romans 3:25 Christ died this way to turn away the just anger of God against our sin, that is the meaning of 'propitiation'.

Nothing but the blood of Jesus will make amends for our sin. The guilty conscience that we hope no one will uncover, a distant past that we are afraid one day will return to hound us, a long covered secret that inescapably haunts us, all these can be entirely forgiven and for ever. Christ can cleanse our conscience from dead works like these (Hebrews 9:14). Because he is our scapegoat.

Just as the scapegoat disappeared over the horizon and Israel knew that their sin was taken away for ever, so forgiveness is full and complete when we trust only in Christ. The pictures God uses to express what he does with our forgiven sin are impressive: he will plunge them into the ocean, remove them as far as the east is from the west, grind them into the dust, dissolve them like the morning mist on a summer day, wipe them from his memory, remove them as far as the infinity of space, turn his back on them, and erase them from the record of our life.

## Access to the Father

We have now arrived back at our starting point: 'Through him we both have access in one Spirit to the Father' (Ephesians 2:18). Similarly Hebrews 10:22 encourages us to 'draw near to God'. The God of power who created the universe, the God of purity who is utterly holy, invites us to come to him in prayer confidently and with full assurance of faith. But here we are encouraged to address him not as eternal creator, sovereign Lord or omnipotent God—but as our Father!

Many prayers are exclusively Christ centred, but when the apostle referred to Christ always making intercession for us through his resurrection, he did not have in mind our Lord perpetually on his knees ferrying the requests of his people and uploading them to the Father. It is his very presence in heaven that is our intercession; the fact that he died and rose from the dead and is now seated with the Father is the guarantee that all for whom he died are eternally secure. In that sense 'he always lives to make intercession for them' (Hebrews 7:25). Our Lord himself made the pattern very clear to his disciples: 'In that day you will ask in my name, and I do not say to you that I will ask the Father on your behalf; for the Father himself loves you ...' (John 16:26–27).

The 'throne of grace' (Hebrews 4:16) is a picture of both the Father and the Son seated in glory, surrounded by the adoring angels and saints, and ready to respond to the prayers of those still battling on earth. Because of this it is quite true that our prayers do come to Christ just as they come to the Father, but there would be no access to the Father apart from the Son—and we must forget no part of that statement. It is not that we cannot pray to Christ or that we should not pray to Christ, only that we need not pray to him, and that in the New Testament we are not encouraged to pray to him. Christ is not our prayer carrying mediator, but our heaven opening mediator. Christ died so that we could gain access to the Father.

And what a privilege to call God 'Father'! In an age when as many families fall apart as stay together, when leadership in the home is despised or ignored and when countless children sob themselves to sleep at night wondering when and how the burning row downstairs will ever end, the idea of God as Father has lost much of its lustre. But it need not. This is the time to reassert its magnificent meaning.

There is something so reassuring in the word 'Father'. Properly understood it carries all the associations of leadership and love, protection and provision, warmth and affection. A good father cares and takes an interest, listens to the anxieties and concerns of his children, and encourages and rebukes them. He gives advice and warns of danger, and he picks up the weak when they fall. A good father commands respect but dispels fear. Ours is a world of fear: the fear of war, of terrorism, of poverty, of heartbreak and death, of the unseen and the unknown. Nothing has changed since the century in which Paul was writing when he encouraged the Christians in Rome: 'All who are led by the Spirit of God are sons of God. For you did not receive the spirit of slavery to fall back into fear, but you have received the Spirit of adoption as sons, by whom we cry, "Abba! Father!"' (Romans 8:14–15). What a fantastic statement that is!

Genealogies may not matter much today, but in Bible times they were essential. Your parentage, and particularly your father, was your passport into society and into the future. To be able to trace your line of descent back to a great man was more important than the fortune you left when you died. So, when Paul wrote to a mixed congregation of converted bankers and lawyers, soldiers and slaves, Gentiles and Jews, he encouraged them with a reminder of their true parentage. The theme of adoption runs like a silver thread through the New Testament. John informs his readers: 'To all who did receive him, who believed in his name, he gave the right to become children of God' (John 1:12). Paul, writing to the Ephesians, encouraged them that this was something God wants for us, plans for us, and finds great pleasure in: 'He predestined us for adoption through Jesus Christ, according to the purpose of his will' (Ephesians 1:5). And to the Galatians we were redeemed: 'So that we might receive adoption as sons' (Galatians 4:5). Paul gladly uses the common legal term for adoption and typically hijacks it for his own use. All who have been chosen by God to become part of his family may confidently count themselves as friends and brothers and sisters of Jesus and sons and daughters of the Father. Jesus is not ashamed to call them brothers (Hebrews 2:11).

Paul even runs ahead and looks forward to the time when it will be more *evident* that we are the children of God than it is now. He is clearly excited as he thinks of that day when: 'The creation itself will be set free from its bondage to decay and obtain the freedom of the glory of the children of God.' Meanwhile: 'We ourselves ... groan inwardly as we wait eagerly for adoption as sons, the redemption of our bodies' (Romans 8:23). As children, we will inherit everything that the father has planned and prepared for us (Romans 8:17).

Why does Paul preserve that little Aramaic word *abba* in Romans 8:15? Why did he not use the common Greek word for 'father' which is *pater*? Ever since Christ himself used the word 'abba' to address his Father in the garden of Gethsemane, it had become a very precious word for Christians; never could they forget the intimacy of that occasion when their Lord, in his emotional and spiritual agony before the cross, prayed 'Abba, Father, all things are possible for you' (Mark 14:36). When we use this same word to approach God in prayer, we are humbly asserting our right of access no less than that of his only Son, and our privilege of access with the status of his children.

Whether or not the word abba carries the child-like familiarity that has often been ascribed to it—and this has been more recently questioned—it is certainly a word of high status and firm relationship. There are no half measures with God: all who are born again by the Holy Spirit are children of God—with all the privileges that implies. Therefore, as Martin Luther once commented, the word 'abba' is more eloquent than 'the most eloquent rhetoricians that ever were in the world.'

We must live securely in this relationship. Paul encourages us to come to God: 'Praying at all times in the Spirit with all prayer and supplication' (Ephesians 6:18). If 'all prayer' means 'all kinds of prayer', then we may come with adoration and praise, with thanksgiving and gratitude, with intercession and petition; we may come when our heart is bursting with love and devotion, and when it is clouded with fear and anxiety; we may come in the odd moments of peace and through the long hours of pain; we may come in frustration and failure, as well as in anticipation and achievement; we may come when we feel like prayer and when we do not. But our right and privilege is to pray: not in grovelling fear or awesome dread, but in bold assurance and joyful confidence. Why then is it as hard to bring saints to prayer as it is to bring sinners to the cross?

Every prayer is an expression of our consciousness that we are living in the light of the great privilege of being God's children and therefore have not simply a duty but a delight to approach him; and it is an expression of the certainty that he who is a good listener will hear us. Our God is awesomely powerful, holy, and just, but he is also a loving, caring Father to all his people, and he invites them to talk with him—that is the magnificent grace of prayer.

THERE IS AN EYE THAT NEVER SLEEPS
beneath the wing of night;
there is an ear that never shuts
when sink the beams of light.

2. There is an arm that never tires
when human strength gives way;
there is a love which never fails
when earthly loves decay.

3. That eye is fixed on angel throngs,
that arm upholds the sky,
that ear is filled with heavenly songs,
that love is throned on high.

**4.** But there's a power which we can wield
when mortal aid is vain,
that eye, that arm, that love to reach,
that listening ear to gain.

**5.** That power is prayer, which soars on high
through Jesus to the throne,
and moves the hand which moves the world,
to bring salvation down.

John A Wallace 1802–70
*Praise!* 613

## FOR GROUP DISCUSSION

**1.** 'God is a very good listener'. How would you illustrate this from the Bible?

**2.** What is the relevance of the Tabernacle and Temple to our subject of prayer?

**3.** 'It is not that we cannot pray to Christ or that we should not pray to Christ, only that we need not pray to him, and that in the New Testament we are not encouraged to pray to him. Christ is not our prayer carrying mediator, but our heaven opening mediator. He died so that we could gain access to the Father.' How far do you agree with this and what are its implications?

**4.** What do you consider are the greatest incentives for prayer?

**5.** 'Praying at all times in the Spirit with all prayer and supplication' (Ephesians 6:18). What does this mean?

# Grace for giving

'You know the grace of our Lord Jesus Christ, that though he was rich, yet for your sake he became poor, so that you by his poverty might become rich' 2 Corinthians 8:9

A few years ago, the British Government produced a report on the nation's charitable giving under the title *A Generous Society*. The results showed that giving, as a proportion of national wealth, actually dropped by 25% between 1992 and 2002. As we grew more wealthy, we gave proportionally less! Evidence of that is that the poorest 20% of the population gave proportionally four times as much as the richest 20%. The report also revealed that one third of the population do not give anything to charity in a month, and that when they do give, it amounts to a mere 1.3% of household expenditure—whereas 4% is spent on alcohol.

By contrast, the results of a survey by the Christian 'Macedonian Trust' showed that 30% of Christians who give, actually give ten percent or more of their income to their church. Just over half of Christian married couples gave ten percent to charity.

The Bible has a lot to say about giving. God, all through its pages, encourages his people to give:

'If there is a poor man among your brothers in any of the towns of the land that the LORD your God is giving you, do not be hard-hearted or tight-fisted towards your poor brother. Rather be open-handed and freely lend him whatever he needs … Give generously to him and do so without a grudging heart; then because of this the LORD your God will bless you in all your work and in everything you put your hand to. There will always be poor people in the land. Therefore I command you to be open-handed towards your brothers and towards the poor and needy in your land' (Deut. 15:7–10).

'Religion that God our Father accepts as pure and faultless is this: to look after orphans and widows in their distress and to keep oneself from being polluted by the world' (James 1:27).

Paul dealt with the subject of money often, and he did so without embarrassment. But he was never more down-to-earth and practical than when he was writing to the Christians at Corinth; he has much to write about giving at the end of his first letter to them (16:1–2), but in 2 Corinthians 8 Paul has a particular reason for writing to them on this subject. There had been a famine across Palestine and the Christians there were generally poor. By contrast the Corinthians—and many other Christians across Asia—were rich, and God had given them a desire to help their brothers and sisters in Judea, even though they had never met them. That was a massive cultural shift, since famine relief in the first century was largely unknown.

It all began in Antioch, when the prophet Agabus predicted that a severe famine would spread over the entire Roman world. Consequently, 'the disciples, each according to his ability, decided to provide help for the brothers living in Judea. This they did, sending their gift to the elders by Barnabas and Saul' (Acts 11:27–30). Apparently this caused a ripple effect throughout the churches, and as Paul travelled around the young churches in Asia, he gathered together funds for the Christians in Judea. Being a wise man, and not wanting anyone to accuse him of embezzling the churches' gifts, he would not handle the money himself, but instead each church was encouraged to send two men with Paul to accompany their gift; their return home would be the guarantee of the safe delivery of that church's gift. It must have been quite a party by the time they reached Judea. The whole event provides an important lesson for Christian churches and organizations to ensure that their financial dealings are always totally open and honest.

However, Paul also believed that there is a spiritual obligation to give to the support of those who bring spiritual blessing to the church. Here he is writing to the church at Rome: 'For if the Gentiles have come to share in their spiritual blessings, they ought also to be of service to them in material blessings' (15:27). And to the Galatians: 'One who is taught the word must share all good things with the one who teaches'(6:6). Paul made the same points to the Thessalonians and Timothy (2 Thessalonians.3:8–9 and 1 Tim.5:17–18).

In an intriguing passage in 1 Corinthians, Paul applied an Old Testament passage that most of us would never think of appealing to for the support of those who preach and teach. In 1 Corinthians 9:9 he draws on the instruction in Deuteronomy (25:4) that the oxen grinding the corn should be allowed to eat some of it. This, incidentally, is an excellent example of how valuable principles for today can be drawn from the Mosaic law. Paul's conclusion is simply: 'If we have sown spiritual seed among you, is it too much if we reap a material harvest from you?' (1 Corinthians 9:11). In these references Paul is particularly referring to the support of gospel preachers, however the same principle must cover all those in need and especially among the family of believers (Galatians 6:10).

## The Spirit and giving

Whenever the Spirit of God has come in power into the life of the church in a time of spiritual revival, there has always been a spontaneous upsurge in giving. In his *Lectures on Revival* in the 19th century, William Sprague commented 'It is amidst the outpourings of the spirit of God that men are trained to engage actively and efficiently in the great enterprise of Christian benevolence. Here they have their hearts and their hands opened on behalf of those who are sitting in the regions and the shadow of death.'

When God was at work on the Isle of Lewis between 1824–35 the minister, Andrew McLeod, wrote of the collection to help the poor: 'Considering the circumstances of the people, I bear testimony, that their liberality and zeal in this case have caused to provoke very many to similar duties. It was most delightful to see the old head and the young scholar of eight or nine years, joining in this contribution. The will preponderates over the purse, so that we cannot do exactly what we would [like to].'

The same was true in North Korea between 1906 and 1910. During that time the church doubled its membership and three years later almost doubled again. The Christians were giving half their earnings to the work of the Gospel. Among the Wallamo Christians in Ethiopia the following is reported: 'At a conference in 1949, the churches gave to support 40 evangelists and promised that in future half of all local church offerings would go to support evangelists. The enthusiasm spread and the Christians made "faith promises"'. Out of their meagre resources this is what they gave: 'A sheep, a donkey, a horse, a blanket ... the produce of ten coffee trees. These promises were not made lightly, but as a serious obligation between the individual and the Lord ... During the following year, each one worked hard to pay the promise in full, often in small instalments. By the next conference, a careful check showed that every promise had been paid.'

The story is told of one old woman with very little that she could give. She rushed into the ladies' Bible Class just as they were about to make their offerings. Out of breath and gasping, she cried: 'Oh thank you Lord. Thank you for bringing me here in time.' Then she explained that she longed to give to the work but had only a few pennies. With these she bought some cotton and sat up late each night spinning it into thread. Finally she walked five hours into the market, sold her thread and returned just in time to make her offering. The widow's mite.

Exactly the same happened during the spiritual revival in the time of King Hezekiah of Judah. The people gave so generously that great heaps of produce and money mounted up in Jerusalem and became almost an embarrassment. Here is a report on that occasion: 'The Israelites gave generously … They brought a great amount of tithes of everything … They piled them in heaps … The chief priest answered the King "Since the people began to bring their contributions to the temple of the LORD, we have had enough to eat and plenty to spare, because the LORD has blessed his people, and this great amount is left over."' (2 Chronicles 31:1–10, *New International Version*).

Why should it take a time of spiritual revival to loose our hands on the world and enlarge our hearts for Lord?

## God's pattern for giving

Paul had been encouraging the Corinthians to complete the giving they had promised sometime earlier. In order to goad them into action he has quoted the example of the Macedonian churches. They gave at a time of severe trial and yet 'their abundance of joy and their extreme poverty have overflowed in a wealth of generosity on their part'. In fact they gave more than they could really afford to give, and willingly, 'begging us earnestly for the favour of taking part in the relief of the saints' (2 Corinthians 8:1–5).

It must have been galling for the Corinthians, a wealthy and conceited church, to have the Macedonians quoted at them so continually. It is in this context that Paul suddenly caught them by surprise. Whilst apparently referring back to the Macedonians by continuing, 'I say this … to prove by the earnestness of others that your love also is genuine' (v 8), he unexpectedly introduces the highest example of giving that it is possible for them, or us, to imagine: 'You know the grace of our Lord Jesus Christ, that though he was rich, yet for your sake he became poor, so that you by his poverty might become rich' (2 Corinthians 8:9). This verse must have been the text for a thousand sermons expounding the incarnation of Christ. However, that is not its context. It is here as an example of giving. It is the pattern of God's giving and he is the one who gives the grace of giving.

### First, God's giving reflects his priorities

This verse is mirrored in Romans 8:32 'He who did not spare his own Son, but gave him up for us all, how will he not also, with him graciously give us all things?' God gave his Son, whom he loved with an unbroken harmony, into the hands of sinful men. Why? because his priority was not his unbroken fellowship with his Son, but 'giving him up' to rescue sinful men and women. Our rescue was more important than the welfare of his Son! And according to 2 Corinthians 8:9 this was precisely reflected in the willingness of the Son himself to leave that perfect harmony with his Father in order to accomplish our salvation.

There is our pattern. Our giving reflects our thinking and our thinking controls our priorities.

A wealthy young man approached Christ with an excellent question: 'Teacher what good deed must I do to have eternal life?' Our Lord's response concluded with the challenge to 'Sell what you possess and give to the poor'. That challenge found him out and 'he went away sorrowful for he had great possessions' (Matthew 19:16–22). When some Christians die, they leave their treasure behind—others go to receive it. Our giving betrays which one we are. If there is one thing that finds out our true character and priorities it is our attitude to our property and our money.

### 2. God's giving is liberal

When Paul drew attention to God's gift in sending his Son, no one in the church at Corinth could object to the example. Perhaps they were tired of the wonderful generosity of the Macedonians held before them, but they could never argue with the example of Jesus Christ who gave up everything for our sake. The little anyone would give for the famine relief in Judea or for the gospel preaching of the apostles was meagre by comparison. When James reminded the churches that 'God … gives generously' (James 1:5), everyone would have to agree. Paul's final thrust comes at the end of the next chapter when he closed off this section of his letter with the exclamation: 'Thanks be to God for his inexpressible gift'. Paul continued the same theme of the extravagant giving of God in 1 Timothy 6:17 'Command those who are rich in this present world not to be arrogant nor to put their hope in wealth, which is so uncertain, but to put their hope in God, who richly provides us with everything for our enjoyment' (*New International Version*). God's generosity should be answered by ours.

### 3. God's giving is joyful

The Macedonians gave not only generously but joyfully, however there seems to have been some reluctance on the part of the Corinthians. It is all too common to give out of a sense of Christian duty or even legalism without a delight and joy. Once again, Christ is a pattern: 'Let us run with endurance the race that is set before us, looking to Jesus, the founder and perfecter of our faith, who for the joy that was set before him endured the cross, despising the shame and is seated at the right hand of the throne of God' (Hebrews 12:2). Our Lord did not leave heaven reluctantly or grudgingly, and nor did the Father send him unwillingly; his incarnation was with the joyful anticipation of the value of his life and death for a myriad of rebels against his Father's rule.

### Our response to God's giving

With these three great principles of God's giving as our pattern, we can discover how Paul encourages the Corinthians to give. It will be valuable to have 1 Corinthians 16:1–2 and 2 Corinthians 9:6–12 in front of you for this next section.

'Now about the collection for God's people: Do what I told the Galatian churches to do. [2] On the first day of every week, each one of you should set aside a sum of money in keeping with his income, saving it up, so that when I come no collections will have to be made' (*New International Version*).

'Remember this: Whoever sows sparingly will also reap sparingly, and whoever sows generously will also reap generously. [7] Each man should give what he has decided in his heart to give, not reluctantly or under compulsion, for God loves a cheerful giver. [8] And God is able to make all grace abound to you, so that in all things at all times, having all that you need, you will abound in every good work. [9] As it is written: "He has scattered abroad his gifts to the poor; his righteousness endures for ever." [10] Now he who supplies seed to the sower and bread for food will also supply and increase your store of seed and will enlarge the harvest of your righteousness. [11] You will be made rich in every way so that you can be generous on every occasion, and through us your generosity will result in thanksgiving to God. [12] This service that you perform is not only supplying the needs of God's people but is also overflowing in many expressions of thanks to God' (*New International Version*).

## 1. Thoughtfully

'Each one must give as he has made up his mind' (2 Corinthians 9:7). Our giving should not be casual or careless but a clear response to careful planning. Not only in our overall giving, but in our particular giving. We must ask, 'Is this a genuine need? How much is needed? Is it wise to give anything?' Gregory of Rome in the sixth century wrote: 'Do not give little where much is needed, or much were little is enough.' Or as Paul encouraged the Thessalonians: 'Even when we were with you, we would give you this command: if anyone is not willing to work, let him not eat' (2 Thessalonians 3:10). That may appear harsh, but it was wise. The same principle will make us cautious before we give to a beggar in the street or at the door. It will stiffen our resolve not to be intimidated by those pleading letters that are designed to make us feel guilty if we bin them. If our giving is thoughtful and discerning, we will already have apportioned our money as God wants us to. We will vigilantly check whether our giving will be carefully targeted by the recipient organisation or how much may be wasted.

## 2. Proportionately

Paul encouraged the Corinthians to give as we may prosper (1 Cor.16:2) or as the translation above has it, 'In keeping with [our] income'. The principle of proportionate giving is so embedded in the Bible that the Christian cannot avoid it. The Old Testament principle of tithing is well-established and whilst some suggest that they are not obligated to the covenant commitments of Israel, it is hard to see how the grace of giving would lead us to be any less generous. In fact, there were two clear thermometers of spiritual life in Israel: observing the Sabbath and giving the tithe. It is perhaps significant that those two are avoided by many Christians today!

According to Numbers 18:21–24, one tenth of people's income was used for the support of the priests and Levites who worked full-time in the tabernacle/temple service. In addition there were the 'firstfruits', which was the first portion of their harvest and then came the 'freewill' offerings. The subject is scattered all through Old Testament. The first reference is in Genesis 14:20 and four hundred years later the principle was reaffirmed to Moses. A thousand years beyond Moses, the prophet Malachi also had something to say on the subject. The people of Israel held back from giving to God and they were accused of robbing him: 'Will man rob God? Yet you are robbing me. But you say, "how long have we robbed you?" In your tithes and contributions. Bring the whole tithe into the storehouse, that there may be food in my house. And thereby put me to the test, says the LORD of hosts, if I will not open the windows of heaven for you and pour down for you a blessing until there is no more need' (Malachi 3:8–10).

Clearly our Lord encouraged the same principle of giving: 'You tithe mint and dill and cumin and have neglected the weightier matters of the law: justice and mercy and faithfulness. These you ought to have done without neglecting the others.' (Matthew 23:23).

When Paul added 'storing up as he may prosper' ('In keeping with his income' *New International Version*) he was assuming that many of the Christians at Corinth would prosper. Most of us do. Even in times of recession and falling values we are still among the rich in this world. Most of us have a better standard of living than ten years ago, five or even two. We have more of what we need and we need less of more. The danger is that 'expenditure increases to take up our income'—but that is how the world plays the game.

The Christian belongs to another world. Should we not consider pegging our standard of living at a certain level and then stay there. Why should our standard keep rising whilst that of our brothers and sisters in many parts of the world continues to fall. We can make a difference. Today, all over the world, the work of God is hindered because of a lack of funds. The principle is 'proportionately', and it is better to focus on what that means rather than haggle over the detail.

### 3. Cheerfully

'Not reluctantly or under compulsion, for God loves a cheerful giver' (2 Corinthians 9:7). Christians can spend a disproportionate amount of time and words discussing whether the tenth is required or not, and whether it should be from gross or net income. Sometimes we are only discussing this to persuade ourselves towards the minimum and settle our conscience. 'Cheerfully' means not how little can I get away with, but how much can I prudently give? The Macedonian church, the next door neighbours to Corinth, was a model of Christian giving: 'And now, brothers, we want you to know about the grace that God has given the Macedonian churches. Out of the most severe trial, their overflowing joy and their extreme poverty welled up in *rich generosity*. For I testify that *they gave as much as they were able*, and even *beyond their ability*. Entirely on their own, they *urgently pleaded with us for the privilege of sharing* in this service to the saints. And they did not do as we expected, but *they gave themselves first to the Lord* and then to us in keeping with God's will' ( 2 Corinthians 8:1–5).

Look at those italicised phrases! They were poor themselves, but pleaded for the privilege of giving. They gave as much as they were able—then some. But can you see why? 'They gave themselves first to the Lord'. That was the reason. Total commitment to the Saviour. Their eyes were on far better treasure.

## 4. Regularly

'On the first day of *every* week …' 1 Corinthians 16:2. For us that may be monthly or quarterly. No matter, it is the principle that does matter. Not, when I can spare it or when I remember it, but regularly.

This is something we should teach our youngest children. As soon as they are old enough for pocket money/allowance we must teach them to give proportionately. Christian parents should never pass out a small coin as the children go off to Sunday School. That teaches them nothing. They should be encouraged to take a proportion of their own money and if they get in the habit of giving proportionately and regularly now, think what that will mean for Gospel work over the next seventy years and more.

I am aware that for young workers on a low income, young marrieds with a high mortgage, and young families with growing responsibilities, this is not always easy. Nor is it easy when teenagers go off to university and expect a blank cheque, or when retirement places us on a fixed income. The problem is, this includes us all!

But cheerful and regular giving that is proportional to my income and discerningly decided, is what God looks for. That will be a fragrant offering to God. Paul could write to the Philippians: 'It was kind of you to share my trouble. And you Philippians yourselves know that in the beginning of the gospel, when I left Macedonia, no church entered into partnership with me in giving and receiving, except you only ... The gifts you sent, [are] a fragrant offering, a sacrifice acceptable and pleasing to God. And my God will supply every need of yours ...'(4:14–19).

## 5. Generously

'Remember this: Whoever sows sparingly will also reap sparingly, and whoever sows generously will also reap generously' (2 Corinthians 9:6 *New International Version*).

This is exactly the principle that Paul encouraged Timothy to pass on to the church at Ephesus: 'As for the rich in this present age, charge them not to be haughty, nor to set their hopes on the uncertainty of riches, but on God, who richly provides us with everything to enjoy. They are to do good, to be rich in good works, to be generous and ready to share ...' (1 Timothy 6:18–19). And John followed the same pattern: 'If anyone has the world's goods and sees his brother in need, yet closes his heart against him, how does God's love abide in him?' (1 John 3:17). We are those rich. We may not own a Jacuzzi or a Jaguar, but that hardly means we are poor. Most of us here could down-market our life-style with little hurt to ourselves or our family. Some more, some less. But all some.

An important principle is a principle found in Proverbs 11:24–25, 'One gives freely, yet grows all the richer; another withholds what he should give, and only suffers want. Whoever brings blessing will be enriched, and one who waters will himself be watered.' Whilst we may correctly apply this to the spiritual blessings of those who share God's word, it undoubtedly refers also to the down-to-earth reality that 'It is more blessed to give than to receive' (Acts 20:35). Countless Christians have discovered that God is no man's debtor and those who give generously will be richly blessed, if not in material blessing, certainly in spiritual benefit. It is never possible to out-give God.

In addition, the more we give, the more God will enable us to give 'He who supplies seed to the sower and bread for food will supply and multiply your seed for sowing and increase the harvest of your righteousness. You will be in enriched in every way for all your generosity ...' (2 Corinthians 9:10–11).

A most important principle is quality not quantity. God is our example here as ever. Some may find it impossible to believe that the death of one man 2,000 years ago can atone for the sins of millions all through human history. One man in place of millions! But look who that one Man was. Quality not quantity!

When our Lord watched the Pharisees flamboyantly dropping their gifts into the public offertory, he paid far more attention to a poor widow who put in two very small copper coins. In his estimation 'This poor widow has put in more than all the others'. They gave from their wealth, but she gave all she had to live on' (Luke 21:2). If we long to give, and give what we are able then what we give is acceptable 'according to what one has, not according to what he does not have.' (2 Corinthians 8:12).

What is it that opens the hands of God's people to give like God himself gives? It is nothing other than grace.

THE GIFTS WE BRING EXPRESS OUR LOVE
to you who left the heavens above
and showed through poverty and pain
a God who gives and gives again.

*Freely, freely, freely we have received;*
*gladly, gladly, gladly we love to give.*
*Our gifts we bring to you, our praise we sing to you,*
*giving and giving and giving again.*

2. Though earthly wealth you never knew,
our greatest riches come from you.
Our needs are all by you supplied
and no good thing are we denied.

3. From love of money, save us, Lord;
make us obedient to your word;
seek first your righteousness and will,
and all our stewardship fulfil.

4. Lord, you've entrusted to us all
the wealth we have; some great, some small.
As you have prospered us, we give;
and yet in giving we receive.

5. The truth is clear within your word:
you love a cheerful giver, Lord.
So make us joyful as we bring
our gifts, our lives- an offering.

Brian Hoare
© Author / Jubilate Hymns
Praise! No. 599

# Chapter 15

1. How does the example of God's giving leave us a pattern to follow?

2. Spend time with 1 Corinthians 16:1–2; 2 Corinthians 8:1–7 and 2 Corinthians 9:6–12 to discover all that Paul has to say about Christian giving. There is more than we have discovered in this chapter. How will this affect your own giving in the future?

3. Discuss how you think the Christian should respond to the Old Testament principle of the tithe.

4. How would you respond to the Christian who claimed they could not afford to give anything to God's work?

5. Would it ever be right to borrow money to give to God?

# Rejected grace

'We appeal to you not to receive the grace of God in vain' 2 Corinthians 6:1

In the opening chapter of this book we said that grace is the most beautiful word in the Bible and a hallmark of Christianity. No world religion has an equivalent word so rich in meaning and so profound in its value. Grace is God's kindness and care over the whole of creation and his control over all the events of this world. Grace is God's law that teaches us the best way to live, and it is his undeserved love by which he reckons the righteousness of Jesus Christ to our account, covers over all our sin, and never again counts our transgressions against us. Grace is the willingness of his Son to lay aside his glory and become a man, and it is his persistent authority that wins the affection and response of our heart and then pardons us. His grace assures us that we are secure for ever, and that he has a perfect plan for our lives whoever we are. When we are weak, he provides sufficient grace and at the moment of our conversion he brings us into the church which is community grace. His sanctifying grace supplies all that we need to conform us more to the likeness of Christ, his prayerful grace assures us of the glorious privilege of access to the Father, and his ultimate grace will finally bring us safely into his heavenly kingdom.

In fact, we have claimed that every approach of God to us, and every word of God to this world, is grace. Whatever God says to humanity is grace. Not just his promises but his warnings also. When God warned Adam and Eve: 'In the day you eat of that fruit you will die', and when he cautioned Israel in the wilderness that those who did not obey his laws must be 'cut off' from the nation, and when our Lord alerted Judas: 'Woe to that man by whom the Son of Man is betrayed', and when the writer to the Hebrews counsels, 'How shall we escape if we neglect such a great salvation'—that is all grace. God does not *have* to speak to us. The fact that he says anything at all is his undeserved kindness.

Every challenge of the gospel, every plea to the sinner to repent, every presentation of the message of Jesus Christ is grace. Every moving of the Holy Spirit in the conscience, every quickening of the pulse under the hammer of the word of God, this too is grace.

But not all who receive God's grace benefit from it. Some hear and reject, others simply turn away and neglect it. There are tragically millions who can marvel at the grandeur of magnificent scenery, the immensity of the universe around us, or the incredible mechanism of our world, and walk away mumbling about 'blind chance'. Nothing can be more terrible than to hear and then reject or neglect God's grace in whatever form it comes to us—and nothing is more certain than that this happens regularly in our churches.

There are others across the world who have only an outline of God's grace: they can see love and beauty in the world around them—what Paul refers to in Romans 1:20 as 'his eternal power and divine nature'—but it leads them nowhere. Millions more, from their perspective in a Calcutta slum or a Filipino squatter camp perched on a rubbish tip, can see far less of God's grace. But among a congregation of those transformed by this very grace are those who, though involved in the worship of the Creator and listening to what this God has revealed in his word, are nevertheless deaf to the meaning of grace. Simply to be among such a community is grace; and yet many despise it and neglect it, or inwardly scoff at it and finally reject it. Yet still, in his grace, God allows time to repent. In a million pictures, through a thousand circumstances and a hundred voices he points to himself.

However, it is a fearful thing to provoke grace by assuming that it will always be available. When Paul wrote to the church at Corinth he knew by their lifestyle that there were some who had never responded positively to the grace of God and he urged them: 'We appeal to you not to receive the grace of God in vain' (2 Corinthians 6:1). Over those in Galatia who had returned to a salvation by works, Paul lamented, 'You have fallen away from grace' (Galatians 5:4). Simply by being connected with the Christian congregations at Corinth or in Galatia they had all received a measure of grace, but some had turned it into a wasted benefit. Grace is not always available. It is only too possible to fall away from a grace that is so close; to allow the hope of peace with God to slip from our hand at the very moment when we almost have it within our grasp.

Our national poet William Cowper, whom we met in chapter nine, was never certain of his personal salvation; even though he had no doubt that Christ died to save, it seemed to be beyond his own reach. In what is considered to be one of his most moving short poems *The Castaway*, Cowper pictured a sailor swept overboard in a storm. His shipmates threw casks, ropes and even the hen coop into the sea in a vain attempt to keep him afloat; sometimes with hope but mostly in despair he struggled in the water. To save herself in such a storm, the ship could not turn or stop, and the drowning mariner watched as the crew sailed on:

'Yet bitter felt it still to die
Deserted, and his friends so nigh.'

In a pitiful expression of his own spiritual state, the poet compared the sailor's plight with his own, in which he felt overwhelmed by the loss of a salvation he could not grasp:

'No voice divine the storm allay'd.
No light propitious shone;
When, snatch'd from all effectual aid,
We perish'd, each alone:
But I beneath a rougher sea,
And whelm'd in deeper gulphs than he.'

With friends so close who are secure in Christ, many will die alone and overwhelmed by their unbelief.

Nothing could be more urgent than that we are careful not to lose what is so clearly within our grasp. This is why the New Testament is full of challenges to check out where we stand with God; we may be fooling others, even ourselves, but never can we deceive God. Deep inside, privately, silently, many know that they are rejecting God's grace that has come to them in all its varied forms.

## Some hear and reject

Peter wrote about scoffers who mocked the Christian confidence in the second coming of Christ. They deliberately rejected the word of God, ridiculed the very idea of eternal grace and laughed at the warning of the Flood in the time of Noah. 'Forsaking the right way, they have gone astray', is how Peter described them in 2 Peter 2:15. They must have known the truth at one time, because they were forsaking a path they once walked. They made a conscious decision to reject the word of God and the message of his grace. In 2 Peter 2:20–22, the apostle wrote of those who rejected the grace they once benefitted from. They had been changed by their contact with the gospel of Christ. They presumably listened to the message, came to a knowledge of 'our Lord and Saviour Jesus Christ' and had been impressed by the purity of his life and the moral standards of Christianity—which contrasted so beautifully with those of the world. They made a decision to follow this 'way of righteousness', and consequently tidied up their life. In the words of Peter they even: 'escaped the defilements of the world.' But it was all short-lived. They had followed a code and to some extent the historical Jesus, but there was clearly no true repentance or new birth; the entanglement of the world was too great and, in Peter's vivid description borrowed from the biblical proverb, like a dog they returned to their own vomit.

Too many in our churches have learned the word of God from infancy and all through Sunday School and the youth group. Perhaps they responded positively at an early age, and to a degree it preserved them from many snares and temptations. They did not get into the wrong set and they never joined a gang; clubbing and the drug scene was not for them. All around them was the example of those who followed 'the way of righteousness', and they could see that it was a better way than that of their peer group in the world. They enjoyed—though not always consciously—the grace of Christian parents and grandparents, youth leaders and friends, all of whom prayed and were saying, 'Come this way and we will do you good.' But tragically, at the end it did them no good. They rejected a young life surrounded by grace and, to use Peter's own analogy, like a washed pig they return to wallow in the mud.

Often when I travel the country and find myself sharing a meal with Christian parents whose children have long left home, it is only natural to enquire about the family. Once we have passed the preliminaries about universities and degrees, successful professions or trades, happy (or unhappy) families, and the pleasure of grandchildren, sadly I can too often anticipate the response when I enquire about their spiritual state. Voices become lower and more serious, faces tighten and eyes moisten. I learn that they once made a profession of faith, some were even baptised and worked in the Sunday School or youth group, or on the audio desk, perhaps even in evangelism. But now? They go nowhere to worship God; their parents are prayerful, of course, and hopeful, and some of the children are friendly towards the gospel, whilst others are firmly opposed. It may seem unkind and extreme to compare them to Peter's dog or pig, but in reality that is just what they are: they have returned to a world without Christ and have abandoned the 'way of righteousness'.

To reject such an early life of grace is terrifying in its consequences.

## Others hear but neglect

Not all make a conscious decision to reject God's grace. They may attend church regularly, or occasionally, and are perpetually 'interested' and 'thinking about it'. The one thing they have certainly not done is to consciously reject the message. When asked what they are doing with it, they answer, 'Not a lot at present; but I probably will.' That is their great self-deceit, they feel sure they will respond positively one day. But they probably wont. I have known people leave church in tears having been so challenged by what they have heard, but they have left church in tears before—over many years.

One of the saddest complaints of Paul in his letters concerns a man called Demas. Somewhere around the year AD 62 Paul wrote from house arrest in Rome to the church at Colossae. The final greetings came from Luke, the beloved physician, and Demas, both of whom Paul described as 'my fellow workers' (Colossians 4:14 and Philemon 24). Two years later, when Paul expected his execution at any time, he wrote sadly to Timothy that 'Demas, in love with this present world, has deserted me and gone to Thessalonica' (2 Timothy 4:10). Demas must have neglected all the signs of backsliding in his own life. He did not wake up one morning and decide to reject the gospel—it rarely happens that way. But little by little he neglected all that he knew of the grace of God until he slipped away to Thessalonica to live without the pressure of being known as a Christian. Perhaps Demas still called himself a Christian. But all the evidence had gone. And without the evidence there can be no assurance. This is exactly what Paul warned the Corinthians against: 'Working together with him, then, we appeal to you not to receive the grace of God in vain' (2 Corinthians 6:1).

'If I am not one of the elect, there is no hope for me.' I have known people spend half their life worrying over this, to which I can only reply, 'Yes, you are quite right; and all the time you excuse yourself from commitment to Christ with that sort of reasoning, you never will be one of the elect!' Some may not like the theology of that, but the reality is only too apparent.

## Some hear and confuse

Grace and numeracy have a lot in common! There are always some who add, subtract or multiply—with grace as the only constant.

Paul wrote to the church at Galatia because he was concerned for their *addition* to the message of grace. When he warned them that they had 'fallen away from grace' (Galatians 5:4), it was because they were adding to the message of unearned and undeserved grace by demanding obedience to some aspects of the Jewish ceremonial law. They were attempting to be justified by observing the law—admittedly not very much of the law, but law nevertheless. There is still a vast swathe of so called Christendom that believes the only way to heaven is by the death of Christ plus good works. They may be our own good works, like charity and kindness, or they may be the good works of the 'super saints' that we can trade to make up our deficiencies; those works of 'supererogation' that we considered in chapter ten. Either way, if we think we can add anything by way of our works then we have spoiled grace.

Imagine that you present me with a valuable painting. You suggest that I hang it in a prominent place in my lounge, and you explain its value because it was painted by Harmens Van Rijn Rembrandt, the Dutch Renaissance master. I duly follow your instructions, but when you visit me next you discover me in front of the picture busy with my palette and paints. In response to your none-too-polite enquiry what I think I am doing, I comment that I considered the bottom right hand corner to be a little too dark so I thought I would lighten it—but only a little. Your reply will be immediate and urgent: 'Leave it alone. Don't touch it. That is the work of the master and if you try to improve on it, you will only devalue it.' The lesson is plain: to add to the work of the Master, that he perfectly completed on the cross, will completely ruin it. However little you may add by way of your own effort, it can only devalue all that he has done for you.

On the other hand, when Paul warned Timothy of false teachers in the church at Ephesus, his concern was not addition but *subtraction*. Hymenaeus and Philetus were representative of those who were claiming that the resurrection was already past (2 Timothy 2:17–18). Exactly what they were trying to say Paul did not make clear, but unsurprisingly he commented that they were 'upsetting the faith of some'. They were denying a fundamental truth of the Christian message and robbing the young converts of their great expectation of the resurrection to come. Whether these two men could rightly be called Christians Paul did not say, but they were clearly weak in grace because Paul urged Timothy to be 'strengthened by the grace that is in Christ Jesus' (2:1). The apostle went on to point out that they have been ensnared by Satan and that if Timothy boldly and faithfully instructs them: 'God may perhaps grant them repentance leading to a knowledge of the truth' (2:25–26).

There are many today who whittle down the truth of Christianity by denying what they find hard to believe, or what does not sit comfortably with a pseudo-scientific fraternity that maintains science has all truth locked in place. The virgin conception of Christ, the supernatural combining of human and divine natures in one person, the miracles of his ministry, his death as a substitute on behalf of sinners, the literal, physical resurrection of Christ, his ascension back into heaven and his promise to return one day in glory—all these are beyond a full explanation. But to deny any one of them is to destroy grace by subtraction.

However, as great a danger is that of *multiplication*. Jude wrote of those who: 'Pervert the grace of our God into sensuality and deny our only Master and Lord, Jesus Christ' (Jude 4). These people were not denying the word of God, so in that sense they were not subtracting from the truth, instead they were 'perverting' the truth, and that word means to change or transpose. They did this by twisting the truth to make it say what they wanted, in order to give authority for their immoral conduct. Many today are eager to justify their behaviour from Scripture, but in order to do so they have to distort the truth to provide an excuse for them to satisfy their own preferences. The Bible can be used to prove anything we wish—providing we ignore its plain teaching, its consistent message, and the context of the passage we are exploiting.

It is tragic to hear of Christians today trying to justify from Scripture their gross materialism, their immoral conduct in cohabitation (or worse), their adultery to escape a sad marriage, their homosexual relationships, and their eagerness to marry an unbeliever. Even shady business dealings, dishonest tax returns, and unlicensed software on a computer can be easily justified once we choose to separate one part of Scripture from another and stir its clarity into the muddy swirl of our own inclinations. It is possible to provide a long list of issues over which Bible Christians had no quarrel for centuries, but all of a sudden some discovered a new way of interpreting texts—coincidentally just after the world of pseudo science or political correctness had come to those same conclusions.

Multiplying grace is what Paul had in mind in Romans 6:1. He anticipated that some might claim that once we have received free and unlimited grace we can go on sinning so that more and more grace will be needed to forgive! It may seem incredible that anyone should argue like this, but Paul thought they might, and his response was to conclude that such a line of thought betrays that they have never really found new life and forgiveness in Christ.

A young man once sat in my study and quoted my own theology to me. He had been disciplined over immoral conduct for which he was totally unrepentant, and had no interest in abandoning. He had been an active member of the church and yet I told him that right now I doubted his salvation, and so should he. Immediately he reminded me that I had often preached that we can never lose our salvation—once a Christian, always a Christian. I agreed, but pointed out that he had not been listening to something else I repeatedly preached: the single clear evidence we have that we are Christians is the consistency of our lives; as James reminded his readers, the only way that you can see that a person is justified is 'by works, and not by faith alone' (James 2:24). No one can see another person's faith, they can only see its result in action. I told my young friend that at this precise moment there was no evidence of his salvation, and that should make him very afraid. In reality he was using the grace of eternal salvation as an excuse to multiply sin.

## The result of rejected grace

There are at least two passages in the New Testament that cause a great deal of debate among some Christians and a lot of anxiety among others. In Hebrews 6:4–6 the apostle wrote, 'It is impossible to restore again to repentance those who have once been enlightened, who have tasted the heavenly gift, and have shared in the Holy Spirit, and have tasted the goodness of the word of God and the powers of the age to come, if they then fall away, since they are crucifying once again the Son of God to their own harm, and holding him up to contempt'.

Who are these? They are the very people we have been describing. Those who one way or another, and for one reason or another, have abandoned the grace they once knew and even professed to experience. They are often people who sit around us in church every Sunday. These people are inside, not outside; or at least they were inside and some are now outside; and if there are any still on the inside they are heading for outside! They have experienced so much. They knew what it was to have an understanding of the message of Christ, they experienced times when the Spirit of God was real and present, and convicting them of sin. They perhaps even went through a time of repentance and they loved to listen to the word of God. But then, all that once was so dear to them they trod under foot and rejected the Christ whom they claimed had died for them. They never really found salvation, though it looked very much like it, and in fact for a time they believed that they had received forgiveness. That is frightening.

Some years ago a man showed me around a church that had once been the scene of a great spiritual revival. In fact, he had been present at the time and could talk animatedly about the large crowds, with people gathering outside and looking in at the windows, and about the powerful preaching; he knew that the whole village had been affected by the work of the Spirit and many lives had been radically changed. Sadly, as he talked, it was clear that he knew nothing personally of the experience of new birth and conversion. He had 'shared in the Holy Spirit', had 'tasted the goodness of the word of God', and had even experienced something of the 'powers of the age to come', but it had left no life-changing mark on his life. That is what the apostle described in Hebrews 6:4–5.

There is another statement, in Hebrews 10:26–29 that warns us of this same danger: 'If we go on sinning deliberately after receiving the knowledge of the truth, there no longer remains a sacrifice for sins, but a fearful expectation of judgement, and a fury of fire that will consume the adversaries … How much worse punishment, do you think, will be deserved by the one who has spurned the Son of God, and has profaned the blood of the covenant by which he was sanctified, and has outraged the Spirit of grace?'

Some say that this shows you can lose your salvation if you backslide. But that flies in the face of all the Scriptures that promise us that nothing in all creation can separate us from the love of God (Romans 8:31–39 and John 10:28 for example). Others think it is a hypothetical case with Paul saying, 'Of course this cannot really happen, but what if it could …' But that flies in the face of logic. Paul is not so stupid as to give us a warning of a danger that was entirely imagined. This is for real. It refers to those who, having received a knowledge of the truth trample on all the privileges that they have received.

But the apostle referred to 'the blood of the covenant by which he was sanctified'. What is that if it is not conversion? Perhaps it is similar to the encouragement of Paul in 1 Corinthians 7:14 that unconverted partners in a marriage are 'made holy'( some translations have 'sanctified') by the believing partner. In other words a life can be made more clean or holy as a result of contact with Christians—or in this case, 'the blood of the covenant'. Unquestionably those who listen regularly to the message of Christ dying for sinners, will be affected by such an example of grace and will often wish to live in a better way. Both John Bunyan and John Newton record times before their true conversion when they prayed regularly, fasted for long periods and read their Bible daily; in fact they gave everyone the impression that they were serious-minded Christians. In reality they were nothing of the kind. This self-deceit is repeated all too often among those who are deeply moved by the example of Christ or the ceremonies of the church.

However, a better translation of this phrase could be: 'by which [there is] sanctification'. In other words, if you abandon Christ there is no other sacrifice for sin. Where else will you go? I once spent years trying to help a young man come to faith in Christ. He read everything I gave him and met with me often to talk about the Christian faith, but somehow he just could not trust. One day I took a chance. I hoped I had judged my man accurately, so I suggested that perhaps Christianity was not for him and that he might do well to try another religion. His immediate reply was what I had hoped for: 'Oh I could never do that, because I know there is no other way of salvation but through Jesus Christ'. He came to faith soon afterwards. Had he at that point turned his back on Christ and looked elsewhere, where else would he have found salvation?

The terrifying prospect is that for anyone who rejects Christ there is nothing to look forward to except what Paul calls, 'a fury of fire that will consume the adversaries'. Whatever else that terrible phrase means, it must refer to the hot anger of God. It is so much harder to win someone back to Christ once they have known the truth and rejected it, and that should be an awful warning not to let go the grace that we have.

John Newton learnt this lesson in a frighteningly tragic way during his final voyage as a captain. On Sunday 21 October 1753 in a light breeze, Newton's crew of twenty-seven weighed anchor and steered their little ship called the *African* across the Atlantic. On this journey John took with him a young man named Job Lewis. He had met him seemingly by chance on the quayside at Liverpool, and when the owner of Lewis's ship went bankrupt, John offered to take him on board. An entry on the ship's muster roll refers to 'Captain Job Lewis, Volunteer and Captain's Commander.' Explaining his apparent care to Mary, Newton wrote simply: 'There are other reasons for my concern, which I need not mention to you.' Those reasons could be found on board *H.M.S. Harwich*, nine years earlier, where Newton, newly converted to unbelief and free living, perverted the mind of the impressionable young midshipman to the same ugly trend. Lewis had been discharged from the *Harwich* a few days before Newton, but now he was as careless as Newton had once been. With a sense of grief the older and wiser Newton hoped to lead Job Lewis to a better way of life. His intention was more commendable than his judgement.

Job Lewis was the greatest trial to Newton. His blasphemy and loose morality was a mirror of John's early life, and constantly he felt an accusing finger pointing in his own direction. Job ridiculed the services Newton held for his crew on Sunday, worked hard to undo the captain's influence, frequently reminded John that it was he who had first infected his mind with ideas of personal freedom, and was generally a pain to Newton all through the voyage. At last, on the African coast, Newton purchased a small boat called the *Racehorse*, fitted it for trade, set up Lewis as captain and provided him with a crew. Job Lewis went on board on 18 January and a month later he was dead. He died of his excessively immoral life of wine and women and, according to those around him, left this world in rage and despair: 'Pronouncing his own fatal doom before he expired, without any appearance that he either hoped or asked for mercy.' It is a man like this that Peter compares to a dog returning to eat its own vomit.

# Chapter 16

## A fearful expectation of judgement

I do not wish to appear dramatic or extravagant, but there will be something more terrible about the judgement of God for those who once sat so close to the truth. This is very clear in Scripture.

We cannot escape if we turn away from the one who has spoken to us by his Spirit through the word (Hebrews 12:25). There is no escape. In Revelation 6:15–16 we have a vivid picture of world leaders calling on the mountains to hide them from the anger of Christ who comes as their judge. But there will be no hiding place for anyone—least of all for those who treated the cross as a thing of contempt. In a plain and unambiguous statement the apostle warned, 'It is appointed for man to die once, and after that comes judgement' (Hebrews 9:27). Nothing could be clearer: both death and judgement are inevitable. But more than this, our Lord himself warned that those who come closest to the truth will be judged more strictly. To those who rejected his message and miracles Jesus warned that it would be more bearable on the day of judgement for the citizens of Sodom and Gomorrah, than for those who, having heard his word and seen his work then reject him (Matthew 10:15; 11:23–24)). Just how more unbearable it will be, he does not tell us, but we have his word for it.

All such people will be utterly without excuse. God will say, as he said to Israel nearly three millennia ago: 'What more was there to do … that I have not done?' (Isaiah 5:4. See also Romans 1:20). We may think, 'Well, judgement is a long way off, I can leave it for now.' But we do not know how far off it is. Not one of us has a guarantee of seeing tomorrow's sunrise. And punishment deferred may be all the more severe. Imagine seeing so clearly what you know you could have grasped, and loved ones—a husband or wife, a mother or father, a child or friends with whom you enjoyed so much here—entering heaven without you and you are locked out for ever. So near, yet so far. If I may turn just a little the agonised prayer of Christ recorded in Matthew 23:37, it will be a terrible thing for many who experienced so much of his grace to hear him say: 'O friend, O sinner, you who ignore my word, reject my cross and neglect my grace! how often I would have gathered you as a hen gathers her brood under her wings, and you would not!'.

In his classic *Pilgrim's Progress* written in the seventeenth century, John Bunyan described Christian entering heaven to a great welcome and fanfare of the angels. Christian and Hopeful were safely over the river of death and securely in the Celestial City. At this point Bunyan draws attention to another man coming up to the riverside, his name was Ignorance. However, he got over the river without half the difficulty the other two men met with because he took advantage of the offer of a ferryman by the name of Vain-Hope. Ignorance came alone to the gate of the celestial city and began to knock for entrance; he was fully confident that he would gain admittance immediately. However, he was asked where he came from and what his business was, and Ignorance replied, 'I ate and drank in the presence of the King, and he has taught in our streets.' When asked for his certificate, that they might go in and show it to the King, Ignorance fumbled for a moment, but found none. Let Bunyan himself conclude the story: 'So they told the King, but he would not come down to see him, but commanded the two shining ones, that conducted Christian and Hopeful to the City, to go out, and take Ignorance, and bind him hand and foot, and have him away. Then they took him up, and carried him through the air, to the door that I saw in the side of the hill, and put him in there.' Finally Bunyan adds these terrible words: 'Then I saw that there was a way to hell, even from the gates of heaven, as well as from the City of Destruction.'

No one will then say, 'It's unfair'. God is a righteous Judge. It will be a terrifying thing to fall into the hands of God on the wrong side of grace. We may now follow our pleasure, but we will have a fearful eternity to regret allowing God's glorious grace to slip from our experience. If we trade with sin we will bank judgement; but if we receive grace freely we will enjoy all eternity with our Friend and Saviour—and with the community of God's redeemed. So many are so close to grace, but are rejecting it and they know they are. Yet Christ is only a word away and we can call on him at any time and receive his free, undeserved and unlimited grace. For now is the day of salvation. Tomorrow may be an eternity too late. No one scores goals after the final whistle is blown.

WHEN YOU, MY RIGHTEOUS JUDGE, SHALL COME
to fetch your ransomed people home,
shall I among them stand?
Shall such a sinful child as I,
who sometimes am afraid to die,
be found at your right hand?

2. I love to meet among them now,
before your gracious feet to bow,
though vilest of them all;
but can I bear this piercing thought:
what if my name should be left out,
when you for them shall call?

3. Prevent, prevent it by your grace;
and be, dear Lord, my hiding-place
in this, the gospel day!
Your pardoning voice, O let me hear,
to still my unbelieving fear,
nor let me fall, I pray!

4. Let me among your saints be found
when all shall hear the trumpet sound,
to see your smiling face;

then loudest of the throng I'll sing,
and all the courts of heaven will ring
with shouts of sovereign grace.

Lady Huntingdon's Hymn Book 1774
*Praise!* 963 © in this version Praise Trust

## FOR GROUP DISCUSSION

1. How can we explain that God's warnings of judgement and punishment are also grace?
2. How would you counsel a friend who, like the poet Cowper, believed that Christ did not die for them and that they have no hope of being saved?
3. Discuss how some people miss salvation by adding, subtracting or multiplying the good news.
4. In the light of the fact that we cannot lose our salvation, how would you explain Hebrews 6:4–6 and 10:26–27?
5. Read the following passages and gather together the fearful facts we learn about the final judgement: Matthew 10:15, 11:23–24; Hebrews 12:25; 2 Thessalonians 1:5–9; Revelation 6:15–16. Can you recall any parables of Jesus that also cover this subject?

# Ultimate grace

'An eternal weight of glory beyond all comparison' 2 Corinthians 4:17

In preparing this final chapter, I felt like someone writing a travel guide for a city he has never visited, of which he has read only sketchy records from previous travellers—only one of whom had ever been there—and has little more to guide him than rumours of its magnificent splendour that defies human imagination and language! I searched Paul's letters and could not find a better definition of the ultimate grace of God than his simple statement: 'An eternal weight of glory beyond all comparison'. In the space of just four words in Paul's Greek he offers us a definition of his final destination and his supreme hope. As his outward body wasted away, Paul's inner spirit was growing stronger and stronger. He had learnt to see his anxiety and suffering as a 'slight, momentary affliction' (v 17). However gruelling the march, however disappointing the news, however painful the suffering, he will remind himself that it is just for a moment by comparison with what lies ahead. It is preparing him for: 'An eternal weight of glory beyond all comparison.' Paul lived constantly in the light of the future, and declared the same thing to the Christians at Rome: 'I consider that the sufferings of this present time are not worth comparing with the glory that is to be revealed in us' (Romans 8:18).

## 'An eternal weight of glory'

Whatever the 'weight of glory' is, it is 'eternal'. A recent scientific theory suggests a never ending universe—without beginning or end. Apparently, the universe is a continuous cycle of total self destruction out of which a new universe is born ready to destroy itself in order to make way for the next—that really is something to look forward to! In reality, we know nothing here that is eternal. Growing old, wasting away and death are all irresistible ingredients of this life. In Romans 8:23 Paul describes the whole of creation 'groaning' under the burden of disease, decay, violence and death, and longing for the day that Paul refers to here in 2 Corinthians 4:17. In terms of this life on earth, and our investment in it, we are all ultimate and inevitable losers. This is why Paul, wise man that he was, kept his eyes on eternity and encouraged the young Christians to do the same: 'Set your minds on things that are above, not on things that are on the earth' (Colossians 3:2).

The end of our short phrase in 2 Corinthians 4:17 is also easy to grasp. This eternal weight of glory is 'beyond all comparison'. The word that Paul uses gives us our word 'hyperbole'—something that is greatly exaggerated. It is beyond explanation because there is nothing to compare to it. No words can describe it and no imagination can excel it. Human language will inevitably fall short because our finest poetry, our strongest comparisons and our most dramatic pictures will fail to explain heaven to us completely. It is beyond hyperbole. We are about to describe the indescribable, explain the inexplicable and keep a steady eye on the invisible—that doesn't look too hopeful as a final chapter in a book.

What is this 'weight of glory' that Paul places between 'eternal' and 'beyond all comparison'?

Glory is a common word in the New Testament, used 167 times in all. Paul uses it about eighty-five times if we include the letter to the Hebrews among Paul's letters. Originally the word meant the worth or value of something and eventually an opinion or estimate, and hence an assessment of someone's character. It referred to all that a person is. The Greek word is *doxa*, and we use it in our word 'doxology' to refer to a short song of praise to God. However, the word glory is mainly used in the New Testament to refer to God the Father or the Son, and here are some examples of its use:

Jesus Christ is the glory of God—2 Corinthians 4:4,6

We see the glory of Christ and are being transformed from one degree of glory to another—2 Corinthians 3:18

When Christ appears we will be with him in glory—Colossians 3:4

Hell means to be excluded from God's glory—2 Thessalonians 1:9

Christ's purpose was to bring many sons to glory—Hebrews 2:10

Peter tells us that, 'glory will be revealed', we will 'receive a crown of glory' and we are 'called to his eternal glory'—1 Peter 5:1,4,10

Jude encourages us that we will be presented, 'blameless before the presence of his glory with great joy'—Jude 24

It will be no surprise to find that the word appears often in the last book of the Bible, and it occurs in all the songs of heaven—Revelation 4:9,11; 5:12, 13; 7:12; 19:1,7

Finally heaven is made bright with the glory of God—Revelation 21:23

Apparently, understanding the word 'glory' will take us a long way into heaven.

## The hyperbole of heaven

If the word 'glory' is the single word that best defines heaven, it seems a little odd that Paul writes of the *weight* of glory; and the more so when we discover that the word 'weight' (*baros*) refers to a heaviness, burden or trouble; it was used of something oppressive—a heavy load. In the first century it is found in the context of taxation! Surely a word like that is best suited to the suffering Paul has described in vs 8–10. But perhaps that is just why he uses it here. We would think of all his suffering as *baros*, a heavy weight; but Paul called it a temporary lightweight—'slight momentary'—by comparison with something that is substantial. For Paul, glory is the heavyweight of reality.

If our definition of 'glory' is correct, then 'an eternal weight of glory' is a summary of all that God is. We can therefore best describe heaven as the one place where the full character of God is eternally revealed and enjoyed. All that God is, heaven is. This would make Paul's conclusion that heaven is 'beyond comparison' an understatement, but still he is determined to keep his eyes on that which is unseen (2 Corinthians 4:18). Paul wants to maintain twenty-twenty vision of the invisible.

Heaven, therefore, is not to be described by what we are like, still less by what we like, but by what God himself is like. All that God is will be enjoyed by all that we become. How far we can grasp this will reveal how fully our minds are set on 'things above' (Colossians 3:2). Heaven is filled with the glory of God (Revelation 15:8), and it is this glory that gives heaven its light (21:23). Struggling to find some words that will describe the perfect splendour of heaven, the apostle John claims that the glory of God, which is the radiance of heaven, is 'like a most rare jewel, like a jasper, clear as crystal' (21:11). God is pure and perfect, he is all knowing and all wise, he is the all powerful Creator and Sustainer, and he is loving and compassionate. The glory of God is all that we could ever describe him to be—and infinitely more besides.

To attempt a portrayal of the character of God will be doomed to failure. John Blanchard, in his book, *Does God Believe in Atheists?* declares 'in a nutshell' fourteen descriptions of God, but John would never pretend that he has made the first—let alone the last—comment on the subject. The fullness of God will always defy man's imagination, understanding and language. However, for our subject, what we may look for are those aspects of God that are reflected in his creation—including us. The fact that he is unique, self existing and eternal, must, by definition, belong to him alone and will never be ours—not even in heaven; God *is* eternal whereas we *receive* eternal life. However, since the human race was created 'in the image and likeness of God' (Genesis 1:26), we should look for those characteristics of God that are reflected in his creation; and according to Paul, his 'eternal power and divine nature' are clearly seen in the world around us (Romans 1:20). It will be the re-creating of these qualities in us—in all their eternal beauty—that will be the true 'glory' of heaven. Perhaps this is what C S Lewis meant when he described us as being 'more human than human' in heaven.

Heaven is never portrayed in the Bible as a full stop on all that we are here, but a continuation. Eternal life is not something that begins when we die, it is the possession of all true believers now. Even though she claimed to believe it, I doubt whether Martha fully understood our Lord when he promised, 'Whoever believes in me, though he die, yet shall he live, and everyone who lives and believes in me shall never die' (John 11:25–26). According to the apostle John, when we see Christ in the full glory of his heavenly character, we will be transformed to be like him; this is our ultimate destiny (1 John 3:2). Paul glories in the same fact: 'We shall all be changed' (1 Corinthians 15:51–52). However, the continuation is only on the basis of an unimaginable transformation.

## Heaven by negatives

Listen to any sermon or read any book on heaven and it is almost certain that you will learn as much about what heaven is *not* as what it *is*. Heaven is described by negatives: there is no sin, no pain, no death, no tears and so on. The Bible itself speaks in this way, though briefly: there will never be need for the sun to shine there, and nothing unclean, detestable or false will enter there; never again will there be hunger, thirst, darkness, scorching heat, pain, tears or death (Revelation 7:16–17; 21:4, 23, 27; 22:5). It is easy to talk about what heaven is not because there are so many things that some would like to offload in the next world. However, the true glory of heaven is not what it is not, but what it is. What do we know about God that will help us to understand what it will be like for us to be changed into his glory? From here on, it is my purpose to explain the inexplicable without once stating what heaven is not.

## Heaven is purity and holiness, goodness and love

That is what God is. Here on earth we are never to think of God as like us—though pure; on the contrary we are like him—though polluted. Every thought, every word, every intention, every action and reaction from God is only, and can only ever be, wholesome and holy. In heaven, all relationships will be transparent and honest; they will be pure and lasting.

When Paul encouraged the Colossians with the reminder that the Father has 'qualified you to share in the inheritance of the saints in light' (Colossians 1:12) he was referring to the completeness and purity of everything: holiness, joy, the knowledge of God, the love of God and the worship of God. All relationships will be God-centred and pure. The call of the seraphim that Isaiah heard in the temple: 'Holy, holy, holy is the LORD of hosts.' (Isaiah 6:3) was a summary of everything about heaven. There is nowhere more pure, clean and full of the presence of God.

To help us grasp this, for a moment forget the picture of heaven in terms of crystal rivers, a rainbow covered throne, jewel-studed walls and the tree of life. We need to understand it in the light of Paul's remarkable statement in Ephesians 1:14 in which he tells us that the Holy Spirit: 'is the guarantee of our inheritance until we acquire possession of it, to the praise of his glory.' The Holy Spirit in the life of the Christian is a deposit which guarantees the final possession of our future inheritance. I plan to buy a house and arrange with the lending company that I will repay by instalments until the house is finally mine. They will require a deposit as evidence that I will be able to keep up the payments; but the deposit has to be in the same currency as the final payment. They will not be impressed if I plead that I do not have five thousand pounds but that the children's guinea pigs have recently produced a fine litter—and the promise of more to follow—and will they do instead? The Holy Spirit is the same currency now that we will enjoy when heaven becomes ours. He is the one who creates in us a passion for God and for holiness—he makes God real to us; he creates in us not only an awareness of eternity but an eager longing for it. In other words the Spirit begins to equip us now for what we will receive then. This is precisely what Paul meant when he prayed for the Ephesians: 'Having the eyes of your hearts enlightened that you may know the hope to which he has called you, [and] what are the riches of his glorious inheritance in the saints.'

Every longing desire we have now for purity and holiness, goodness and love will be fulfilled totally and eternally in heaven, because these are all part of the character of God into whose likeness we will be transformed. All our activity and relationships in heaven will be open, honest, rich and full—and as pure as God himself is pure; everything that we do and say and think will please him—and us—perfectly, because we will be changed into the likeness of Christ (1 John 3:2). To be like Christ in every respect except only his deity, is part of this unimaginable transformation.

## Heaven is communication and appreciation

When we refer to God as a person, we are not applying to him an attribute that we recognise in the human race. On the contrary, *our* personhood is derived from and is a reflection of our Creator. When the Triune God declared, 'Let us make man in our image, after our likeness'

(Genesis 1:26), this was not God talking to himself but it was a revelation of the God he is, and at the same time a revelation of what we are like *because* of what he is like. He is not like us, but we are like him.

God is a God of communication. There is communication in heaven between the three persons of the Godhead, revealed in that little phrase 'Let us make man in our image' (Genesis 1:26). There is also constant communication between God and the angels who are his agents (Hebrews 1:7,14) and whose focus is upon the Son (1:6). The last book of the Bible is filled with activity and communication between the inhabitants of heaven. The best of all relationships in Heaven will be centred around the Lord who died for us. When John saw into Heaven itself, he saw 'a Lamb standing, as though it had been slain' (Revelation 5:6); that mysterious and puzzling picture helps us to understand that these are accounts not of something that we will *literally* see in heaven, but they are explanations of all that the Lamb will mean to us when we see him as he is. We will appreciate him so perfectly in heaven. When the Bible tells us that we will 'see him' as he is (1 John 3:2), we will do much more than gaze at his splendour—a splendour as bright as the sun itself (Revelation 1:16)—we will enjoy the fullness of friendship with him. Heaven is not merely staring but sharing. And we will be transformed into the same pure holiness (Matthew 13:43).

Perhaps it is significant that when Paul spent the last remaining days of his earthly life in a Roman prison and penned his final instructions to his own faithful legionaries for the gospel, he introduced a word that he had rarely used before in his letters. It was the word that we call 'epiphany', and it means an unveiling; it was a common word used in the first century of the gods when they supposedly came to help men on earth, and Paul knew that many of the kings of the Seleucid (Syrian) dynasty had added *Theos Epiphanes* (God made manifest) to their titles. As he often did, Paul turned a common word to his own use. Four times to Timothy and once to Titus he used the word 'epiphany', because the glorious expectation of seeing Christ in all his unveiled beauty captured his soul in those closing days before the executioner's blade fell. Paul wrote of 'the appearing of our Lord Jesus Christ' (1 Timothy 6:14), and those who 'have loved his appearing' (2 Timothy 4:8), and those who are 'waiting for … the appearing of the glory of our great God and Saviour Jesus Christ' (Titus 2:13). To see Christ in all his unveiled glory, excited Paul's imagination more than anything else could.

What makes the human race uniquely human is that we are a reflection of our Creator. When he declared that all he had made was 'very good', it must mean that God took a great delight in what he had made. It is not the dispassionate comment of the teacher at the end of the student's essay, it is the enthusiastic commitment of the parents admiring their newborn baby. And God passed this ability to communicate and appreciate to the human race. Our capacity to talk and value far surpasses anything in the animal kingdom.

We may marvel at the bee that returns to the hive loaded with nectar and does a little dance to show his buddies how far and in what direction they need to fly to pick up their next load, but the human race has far more sophisticated ways of providing directions. A dog wolfs down his dog nuts day after day and seems perfectly satisfied, but few people would be content with cornflakes for every meal, day in, day out. The richness of communication and appreciation are unique to the human race.

The complexity of human language and our enjoyment of a vast array of beauty through the senses of sight, sound, smell, touch and taste must surely reflect something of God himself. It is not without reason that heaven is described in terms of all that is most dazzling and beautiful here. It is a place of music and song and of sweet smelling incense (Revelation 5:8), where the gentle hand of the Father brings joy to the face of his children (Revelation 7:17) and where a banquet is laid for all his friends (Revelation 19:9).

When God created a world with intriguing and colourful fish deep in the oceans, and insects, flowers, birds and animals that would still enthral the human race thousands of years on from Eden, this was surely because he is a God who appreciates and communicates beauty and order. He wrote these two characteristics into the genetic coding of all men and women, and in the new heaven and new earth he will allow that reflection of himself full reign. We will have an eternity to communicate and appreciate. The best here will be surpassed in heaven by a thousand hyperboles. The restored beauty of our present creation that is liberated and obtains 'the freedom of the glory of the children of God' (Romans 8:21) is part of the unimaginable wonder of the new earth.

## Heaven is relationships renewed

From all eternity the relationship between the Father, Son and Spirit was one of constant and secure harmony. The only thing that ever came between the Father and Son was our sin. And the purpose of that breach, reflected by the cry from the cross 'My God, My God, why have you forsaken me?', was to bring about the reconciliation of our broken relationship with the Father.

When Adam and Eve were created, their own relationship together as compatible companions and the calm and peace of God 'walking with them' in the cool of the day, was a beautiful reflection of the perfect harmony in heaven. The human race was created for community and every reference to heaven is about community: a banquet, a people, a great choir, a city. One of the greatest enjoyments of life is simply to be with those whom we love and trust. Constant babble is not always the best way for communication; silent company can be invigorating. It must surely be this human enjoyment of true relationships that led Paul to encourage the Thessalonians with the promise that when Christ comes again, he will 'bring with him those who have fallen asleep' and that those who are alive will be caught up 'together with them' to 'meet the

Lord' (1 Thessalonians 4:14–17). This passage is full of deliberate references to relationships—even the word 'meet' was used of the official welcome given on the arrival of an important public figure. Paul wanted to reassure the Christians who had recently experienced death among their members, that there would be a glorious and welcome reunion. Heaven is a re-creation of relationships to what they were always intended to be.

Around the year AD 30, a proud young lawyer, Saul of Tarsus, gave his word for the stoning of Stephen to begin. He watched dispassionately until the lifeless body of the first Christian martyr lay soaked in blood on the desert floor. Thirty four years later that same Saul from Tarsus, but now a recipient of grace, knelt in the prison yard as the Roman sword severed his own neck. Now picture Stephen and Paul enjoying friendship together in that Kingdom where peace and joy, love and trust reign for ever. That is ultimate grace.

Somewhere in the year 1748 John Newton was trading for slaves along the coast of New Guinea. We can correctly imagine a man, separated from his wife and child, herded below into the stinking hold of a 120 foot vessel; he never saw his family again. This man survived the cruel journey to the West Indies, was sold onto a plantation, and ended his life a few years later under the barbaric conditions of a pitiless estate manager. However, before his death our man responded to the message of Christ from a Moravian. What he did not know was that the man who tore him away from his family had also become a Christian. Imagine the reunion of these two men in heaven! That too is ultimate grace.

Not long ago someone handed me an article culled from a magazine. Around the picture of two smiling men, one with his hand on the shoulder of the other, was their story. Tom Kelly had been a sniper with the Irish Republican Army and James Tate had been an Ulster Volunteer Force commander. Two men on opposite sides of a bitter and bloody divide—sworn enemies. Both wound up in the Long Kesh prison, and were there in 1974 when trouble broke out in the jail; given an opportunity each would gladly have killed the other. Their story coincides when, on release from prison they eventually came to faith in Christ. Tom Kelly and James Tate work side by side for peace and reconciliation. What reunions will ultimate grace reveal!

I believe in the apostolic succession! Someone, a legionary or merchant, brought the message of Christian hope to this wild part of the Roman Empire and shared it with a native inhabitant. It was passed on through the fall of Rome and into the Anglo-Saxon kingdom under Alfred: neighbour to neighbour, friend to friend, merchant to merchant, parent to child; in the hovel, in the forest, in the field, in the university. It was still there in the hearts of my spiritual forefathers through the dark ages of ignorance following the Norman conquest; someone passed it on to a friend. All through the Reformation, the Commonwealth, the Tudors and Stuarts and Hanovers and into the time of Victoria and through two terrible world wars, my spiritual ancestors were passing on the same message—until someone shared the gospel with me more than nineteen hundred years after it all began. That is the real apostolic succession, and that is my true 'family tree'. I cannot research it here, but I will have eternity to meet them all and to hear their stories.

I used to think that the most God-honouring way to explain heaven was that we would spend all our time adoring the person of Christ. I do not think like this any more. What a glorious privilege to know the saints from every tribe and culture and language, and to hear their personal stories of grace. Will that not be among the most Christ-honouring things we can do with eternity?

## Heaven is wisdom and knowledge

That God is all-knowing and all-wise should be uncontested among true Christians. Knowledge does not guarantee wisdom, but wisdom guarantees the right use of knowledge. God knows the past, present and the future—and all perfectly. His knowledge is unbounded and his perfect wisdom ensures that his knowledge is applied for our ultimate benefit. He always acts and behaves in such a way that no other action or behaviour could have been better.

Human enquiry and the thirst for knowledge is a reflection of God. The animal world never explores much beyond its own immediate environment. Lions from Africa do not trek into the arctic, nor do polar bears show a passion to swim to India. Even the birds that migrate long distances are not intrepid explorers; they each keep to a clearly defined route. Animals may stumble across answers, but they never ask questions. Mankind, on the other hand, has a passion to know and to explore. He will climb the highest mountain simply because it is there. Mariners circumnavigated the world and we now send men into space and reach for Mars. Always and relentlessly the human race is pushing frontiers. This is the result of creation in the likeness of God.

In this life there will always be 'secrets that belong to the Lord' but in heaven all those secrets are in the open. There are so many questions that we cannot answer now, but on the door of heaven hangs a notice which reads, 'Enquire within', for that is where all the answers will be found: full, satisfying, perfect and complete answers. Here we accept by faith that the infinitely powerful and caring God is, as the hymn writer Samuel Medley expressed it: 'too wise to err, too good to be unkind', but Heaven will provide an understanding why all things were as they were. 'The earth will be filled with the knowledge of the glory of the LORD as the waters cover the sea' (Habakkuk 2:14 and Isaiah 11:9).

Perhaps also heaven will fill in the gaps of the gospel story? John assured us that there were 'many other things that Jesus did' and that if they were to be written down 'the world itself could not contain the books that would be written' (John 21:25). It must therefore have been desperately hard for John to keep his short Gospel record to a manageable length. But with eternity stretching before us, there will be 'time' enough to tell every story Jesus told, and review every body that he healed and every life that was transformed. And that will bring honour to Christ. I have always wished that I could listen in to the Bible study that Jesus gave on the road to Emmaus (Luke 24:27)—perhaps in heaven I will.

## Heaven is discovery and construction

We need not imagine heaven as a place of static inaction where all that can ever be done is instantly achieved. On the contrary, heaven will be a place of vibrant life and action, of discovery and—perhaps—of creating power. Like our Creator himself, we are not only capable of appreciating beauty, but we have the outstanding ability to create it. Will that Creator-like gift really come to an end in heaven, or will it be re-created as an exact reflection of the one who made us?

This world with its kaleidoscope of colours, sounds, sights, scent, taste and touch, is not only a reflection of the character of God but it would all be unimaginable if we did not actually experience it here. If we had only ever lived on the moon we could never imagine this earth. The evidence of this is seen in the fact that the planets we know of are dull and uninteresting by comparison. They may be vast and mysterious, but they are boringly bland. Thank God they are not our final odyssey.

Our God has imagination, together with creative power and enjoyment of it. He is an infallible engineer and a wise architect; he is the most perfect artist and the most exquisite musician. This is all part of the glory of his character. And if we are to be like him, will we not share in this glory and therefore go on creating beauty and order? What if there is still a universe of amazement to discover? Or universes beyond universes? What if the creating glory of God did not stop at this little ball in space that we call earth? What if we have not yet tiptoed into the outskirts of his infinity or hardly begun to understand 'what God has prepared for those who trust in him' (Isaiah 64:4; 1 Corinthians 2:9)? Will the inventiveness and imagination of mankind cease when we no longer see through a glass darkly? Will we be less than human in heaven—or more human than human? In every imaginable and unimaginable way, heaven is *plus ultra* for the Christian—more beyond.

When Peter tantalisingly referred to the day that this present world and universe will be 'burned up and dissolved' (2 Peter 3:10), he wrote of 'new heavens and a new earth in which righteousness dwells' (v 13). That may not look much of a description, but a little thought reveals far more than we first imagined. Peter might have left his promise at the dissolution of our heavens and earth, but he deliberately wrote of a replacement of what we already have. In other words there will be some form of continuity that will enable us to recognise an earth and heavens. Who really knows what this earth was like before sin ravaged what was originally 'very good'? And who knows whether the vast universe, which is now so coldly inhospitable, may not have been a beautiful place of inviting wonders?

## Ultimate ultimacy!

Heaven is a new everything of which there can be nothing better. Time will be measured into eternity; we will have a new body, new relationships, a new appreciation of the Father and the Son, a new experience of joy, a new life, new values—and the list is as endless and as unimaginable as God himself.

The word 'heavens', relating to the skies and space above us, occurs on just over twenty occasions in the New Testament, whereas 'heaven' as the kingdom belonging to God appears more than three hundred times. The picture that follows the 'new heaven and the new earth' in Revelation 21 is that of 'The holy city, new Jerusalem, coming down out of heaven from God, prepared as a bride adorned for her husband' (Revelation 21:2). As with so much in the final book of the Bible, we are wise to take it as a picture of something that could never be wholly described in human language or concepts. Jerusalem was the place of God's earthly dwelling and where he especially met with his own people. Here then is an assurance that when the new heavens and new earth are created, heaven and earth will become one and God will be among his people. There will be no commuting from the new earth to heaven!

Everything that we have discovered about heaven, we discovered by reference to the character of God himself: purity, holiness, goodness, love, communication and appreciation, relationship, wisdom and knowledge, discovery and construction.

Perhaps, after all, John provides the best *description* of heaven when he heard a loud voice from heaven anticipating the end of all things with the claim: 'God himself will be with them' (Revelation 21:3). Heaven will be the dwelling place of God among his people.

What is deliciously attractive for those who will arrive in heaven from a weary life of hard labour, cruel persecution or painful suffering is the promise that 'there remains a Sabbath rest for the people of God'. A long break is all the more pleasurable after a period of hard work. C S Lewis referred to heaven in the simple expression: 'Term is over, the holidays have begun'. Even more delightful was the comment of the three year old grandchild of a friend of mine. After church one Sunday she declared in a toddler's loud whisper: 'Now, the plan is to go home'. How magnificently profound—after the service, the plan is to go home.

AWAY WITH OUR SORROW AND FEAR!
We soon shall recover our home,
the city of saints shall appear,
the day of eternity come.
From earth we shall quickly remove,
and mount to our native abode,
the house of our Father above,
the palace of angels and God.

2. Our mourning is come to its end,
when, raised by the life-giving word,
we see the new city descend,
adorned as a bride for her Lord;
the city so holy and clean,
no sorrow can breathe in the air;
no gloom of affliction or sin,
no shadow of evil is there.

3. By faith we already behold
that lovely Jerusalem here;
her walls are of jasper and gold,
her buildings as crystal are clear.
Immovably founded in grace,
she stands as she ever has stood,
her builder she brightly displays,
and flames with the glory of God.

4. No need of the sun in that day,
which never is followed by night,
the splendours of Jesus display
a pure and a permanent light:
the Lamb is their light and their sun,
and with his reflection they shine,
with Jesus inseparably one,
and bright in his radiance divine.

5. The saints in his presence receive
their great and eternal reward;
in Jesus, in heaven they live,
they reign in the smile of their Lord:

the flame of the holiest love
is kindled on seeing his face;
this all their enjoyment above:
on Jesus's beauty to gaze.

Charles Wesley 1707–88
*Praise!* 966

## FOR GROUP DISCUSSION

1. Paul uses the word 'epiphany' to refer to the return of Christ (1 Timothy 6:14; 2 Timothy 4:8; Titus 2:13). What is the significance of this?

2. Range in order your most longed-for privileges of the new heavens and new earth and discuss why you have chosen them.

3. Habakkuk 2:14 and Isaiah 11:9 refer to the earth 'filled with the knowledge of the glory of the Lord as the waters cover the sea.' In the light of this chapter, what do you think that means?

4. How does Ephesians 1:14 assist our understanding of what heaven is like?

5. Why do we not long for the return of Christ and for heaven?

# About Day One:

## Day One's threefold commitment:

- To be faithful to the Bible, God's inerrant, infallible Word;
- To be relevant to our modern generation;
- To be excellent in our publication standards.

*I continue to be thankful for the publications of Day One. They are biblical; they have sound theology; and they are relevant to the issues at hand. The material is condensed and manageable while, at the same time, being complete—a challenging balance to find. We are happy in our ministry to make use of these excellent publications.*

**JOHN MACARTHUR, PASTOR-TEACHER, GRACE COMMUNITY CHURCH, CALIFORNIA**

*It is a great encouragement to see Day One making such excellent progress. Their publications are always biblical, accessible and attractively produced, with no compromise on quality. Long may their progress continue and increase!*

**JOHN BLANCHARD, AUTHOR, EVANGELIST AND APOLOGIST**

Visit our website for more information and to request a free catalogue of our books.

**www.dayone.co.uk**

## The Bible—an auhentic book

BRIAN H EDWARDS

192PP PAPERBACK, 978–1–84625–465–9

In the face of its critics, the author rigorously examines the narratives, letters, genealogies, geography, prophecies and even the silences of the Bible. Its authenticity persistently comes out robust and reliable.

Along the way, fresh light is thrown on familiar accounts and, unexpectedly, lists of names come alive with interest!

Also included are a unique aid to develop our daily time with God and a reading programme to help us read the Bible right through in nineteen months.

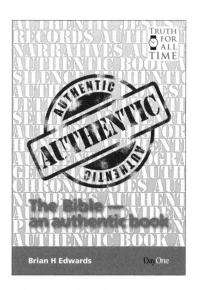

BRIAN H EDWARDS

288PP PAPERBACK, 978–1–90308–733–6

This book is a superbly written modern commentary on God's changeless laws in today's changing and godless society. It unpacks the crammed meaning of these terse commands, and applies them pointedly to life in a deregulated age.

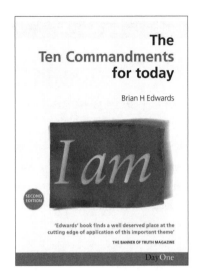

The
Ten Commandments
for today

Brian H Edwards

*I am*

'Edwards' book finds a well deserved place at the cutting edge of application of this important theme'

THE BANNER OF TRUTH MAGAZINE

Day One

'Edwards' book finds a well deserved place at the cutting edge of application of this important theme.'
—*THE BANNER OF TRUTH MAGAZINE*

'Seldom have I appreciated a book more than this one...'
—*THE GOSPEL MAGAZINE*

'This is a highly readable treatment of a vital subject and can be gratefully recommended.'
—*EVANGELICAL TIMES*

'... Unpacks the crammed meaning of these terse commands and applies them pointedly to life in a deregulated age, and directs us to Christ who gives pardon and righteousness to those who turn to him from their habitual law-breaking.'
—*ANDREW ANDERSON, INTERNATIONAL BAPTIST CHURCH OF BRUSSELS, BELGIUM*

BRIAN H EDWARDS

160PP PAPERBACK, 978–1–84625–226–6

Israel's first king began with great promise and ended in tragedy. The author traces Saul's head start into the monarchy and the accelerating spiral into possibly the most lamentable biography in the Bible. Along the way there is much to learn from a king whose story is told in Scripture so that we might learn the ways of a man who fell out with God and fell in with the powers of darkness. And there are surprises along the way, not least in the story of his son who, but for the purposes of God, would surely have made an excellent king. However, on the blood-spattered walls of Beth Shan, the story does not quite end. There is another member of Saul's line who shines with bright hope and reflects the character of his godly father in contrast to that of his tragic grandfather.

An accessible book for every reader which, as well as bringing the three characters of Saul, Jonathan and Mephibosheth to life and clarifying difficulties in the text, concludes every chapter with questions for thoughtful discussion suitable for group or personal study.

**Saul and sons**
Decline and fallout in the family
of Israel's first king

Brian H Edwards

CLIVE ANDERSON AND BRIAN H EDWARDS

256PP LARGE FORMAT HARDBACK,
978–1–84625–416–1

Fully illustrated in colour throughout

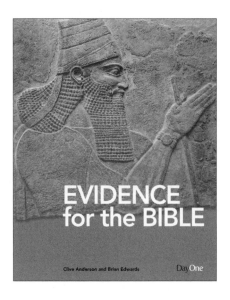

*Evidence* will surprise and inform you as you turn over the soil of history with the pages of your Bible. The witness of the trowel authenticates and illuminates the people and events, lifting them from the pages of the Book and setting them in the context of time and place. Join us on an exciting journey with this evidence from the past.

'This is a marvellous introduction to the finds of archaeology that illumine our understanding of the Bible. It helps the reader to see that the biblical events and writings took place within history. When the reader studies the Bible, this book will serve as a wonderful tool to help get at its depth and richness. I highly recommend it.'
—DR JOHN D CURRID, CARL MCMURRAY PROFESSOR OF OLD TESTAMENT AT THE REFORMED THEOLOGICAL SEMINARY, CHARLOTTE, USA

'Clive Anderson and Brian Edwards have captured the essence of generations of middle-eastern archaeology, historical context and biblical landscape in a quite remarkable way. Their book is accessible, informative and enjoyable. The pictures beautifully complement the text. The Bible comes alive. I warmly and wholeheartedly commend it to everyone who wishes to be a little wiser and better informed about the Book which has formed our culture and is the source of the Chrisian Faith.'
—THE VERY REVD JAMES ATWELL, DEAN OF WINCHESTER

CLIVE ANDERSON AND BRIAN H EDWARDS

44PP BOOKLET, 978–1–84625–502–1

This pocket-sized booklet, which highlights just a few of the many discoveries that show the Bible to be reliable, is a 'taster' of the much larger and fully referenced book *Evidence for the Bible*.

Like the larger book, it is fully illustrated in colour throughout.

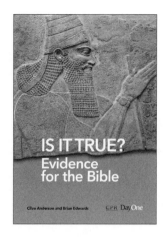

**IS IT TRUE?**
Evidence
for the Bible

Clive Anderson and Brian Edwards    CPR Day One